THE BEST VIEWS
— OF —
BRITAIN

THE BEST VIEWS
OF
BRITAIN
Geoffrey Young

PARTRIDGE PRESS

LONDON · NEW YORK · TORONTO · SYDNEY · AUCKLAND

For my family

TRANSWORLD PUBLISHERS LTD
61–63 Uxbridge Road, London W5 5SA

TRANSWORLD PUBLISHERS (AUSTRALIA) PTY LTD
15–23 Helles Avenue, Moorebank, NSW 2170

TRANSWORLD PUBLISHERS (NZ) LTD
Cnr Moselle and Waipareira Aves,
Henderson, Auckland

Published 1989 by Partridge Press
a division of Transworld Publishers Ltd
Copyright © Geoffrey Young

British Library Cataloguing in Publication Data
Young, Geoffrey, *1936–*
   The best views of Britain.
   1. Great Britain. Description & travel
   I. Title
   914.1′04858

ISBN 1-85225-037-2

Photoset by Rowland Phototypesetting Ltd
Bury St Edmunds, Suffolk
Printed in Great Britain by
Hazell, Watson and Viney Ltd, Member of BPCC, Aylesbury, Bucks.

CONTENTS

INTRODUCTION

This book is an exploration of the BEST VIEWS in Britain.

In the past many people, some quaint, others of heroic stature, have written about these views or drawn or painted them. Through their words and pictures we can discover the different ways that views have been seen in the past. It is an entertaining detective story because it does uncover shifts in our thinking. Attitudes about views and countryside that we take for granted today are sometimes of very recent hatching.

But we wouldn't think the way we do today if they hadn't thought the way they did then.

In this book we present our 30 BEST VIEWS as photographs. We could have chosen sketches, or paintings – that is how views were shown in the past. But photographs are part of our modern life.

It is said that a good news photograph is worth a thousand words. As you can see, the same is true here.

ritain has an outstanding range of views to admire. In spite of the fact that our mountains are modest, and our rivers are not very long, the British countryside offers some of the most varied scenery in the world. And viewpoints giving distant views lie within easy reach of all of us.

The widest British view is from the top of the Wrekin in Shropshire. It is not high by any standards (406 metres [1334 feet], hence the word top instead of summit) or even the highest hill in Shropshire. Accidents of geology and the shape of the land yield a glimpse of Snowdon 110 kilometres (70 miles) away to the north-west and Kinder Scout 95 kilometres (60 miles) to the north-east, and sight of 15 different counties below. But is the best view always the widest, or furthest? Part of the magic quality of a view lies in the stamp of the countryside and county that lies below the hill – which is why the view we have chosen for VIEW 1 is not from the Wrekin.

They lie like a painted patchwork, our coloured counties, each one as distinct as its name. Some of this variety can be read straight from any map. Straight roads would spell flat plains, while kinks (and natural lakes) are tokens of hilly scenery. Large-scale Ordnance Survey maps are printed with contours which show varied slopes and hill forms, but the fine-grained detail, the clothing of field, wood and hedge cannot be judged in advance. Every view can yield a surprise or two.

An Eye For A Map

BOX ONE

Old maps possess charisma. Up on the wall, they look as pretty as a picture.

Which is what they are, in a way; an odd view of the view.

Although there had been early plans showing estate boundaries and the like, amongst the earliest larger-area maps are those made by Christopher Saxton who in 1575 was sent around the country by the Privy Council. The county maps of his contemporary John Speed are also notable.

Reflecting the needs of travellers of the time, these maps named settlements, sometimes showing them symbolized by a church or row of houses. Rivers and their bridges, vital information, were shown. However, hills are childishly drawn hummocks giving little idea of the nature of their terrain, and for good reason – no traveller would go out of his way to climb them. In the following century John Ogilby carried the traveller's map a step further with strip road maps.

Such maps could be reworked and reprinted for many years. Early in the eighteenth century they were being rushed out for the ever growing number of people who were travelling (some of them to visit viewpoints), but they usually remained drawn in the old customary style. The Society of Arts put the issue out to competition, and by the 1750s the winner Thomas Jefferys was making maps showing the higher ground shaded with hachures.

The first Ordnance Survey maps appeared in the mid-nineteenth century, commissioned as their name suggests for military as much as public benefit.

Although they seem to look very different, today's large scale Ordnance Survey maps need maintain some ancient traditions in the way of using symbols. However, their printed contours can be read to tell us the lie of the land easily enough.

Regional, county-wide and even parish-wide variety in the view is related to the rock which underlies the green. Native stone which has been quarried nearby gives a local cosiness to the churches, farms and cottages. They suit their scenery. In such areas as the Dales, the Cotswolds and the Lake District, this match is obvious. Elsewhere, stone is hard won from the ground, lying too deep below looser deposits such as beds of gravel and clay. In such areas the cottages are of timber and brick.

The Rock Below The View

BOX TWO

Although white chalk is about the only rock that everyone can be guaranteed to recognize, rocks are easy enough to understand.

They are of three main kinds. IGNEOUS or 'fire formed' rocks derive from molten magma squeezed from below the earth's crust. If this cooled slowly deep below the surface it yielded granite with large mineral crystals, such as is seen on Dartmoor. If it cooled quickly where it spewed up from a volcano either on the ocean floor or on dry land, it created finely crystalline basalt. Volcanoes also cough up vast amounts of dust and ash which become compacted into tough rock. Such ash rock has been sculpted to create the craggy scenery of the central Lake District.

SEDIMENTARY rocks were deposited in layered beds, often as sediments under water – rather like the mud, sand, and gravels we see today. Such rocks often contain shells or other fossils. Shells both large and microscopic are usually created from the limy mineral calcium carbonate which the organisms extract from the water around them. Rocks with large measures of this mineral are known as limestones. They can be greyish in colour, or stained yellow or red by iron minerals. White chalk is a very pure kind of limestone.

Apart from limestones, the sandy millstone grit which creates much of the smooth Pennine scenery, shales, and pebbly 'puddingstones' are also sedimentary rocks.

In the earth's long history, there have been many series of crustal disturbances. Existing rocks have been changed by heat, or by the pressure of the weight of rock above. Welsh slates which were quarried to roof much of Britain in Victorian times are an example. These METAMORPHIC rocks also include marble, which is transformed limestone, but we do not have this in Britain. The white 'marbled' veins containing sparkles of metal ores which are seen in some rocks are usually of quartz, one of the minerals of granite, the mineral of sand. Heat and pressure have caused it to permeate the cracks and irregularities of the rock roundabout.

The rock story holds many surprises. The millstone grit of the Pennines was laid down perhaps as long ago as 300 million years in a rivermouth delta when Britain lay on the steamy equator. Continental land masses do not stay still. The red sandstones of the Midlands and places in the North were laid down some 240 million years ago when Britain was desert. Equally bizarre in the British view are coral reef limestones, found in many places.

The slow movements of the land masses crinkled the rock layers as easily as we can crumple a tablecloth. Sometimes the folding is dramatic. But no sooner was higher ground being lifted in this way than erosion began to bite. Wind, rain, tumbling streams and frost and ice weather any slope; the debris is carried by the rivers towards the sea to create in their turn new layers of sedimentary rock.

In Britain, 'Strata' Smith (an engineer working on the canals) discovered that by and large, the rock layers are slightly aslant, so that the older rocks lie to the west and north, the more recently formed to the east. However outcrops of ancient rock can appear even in 'new rock' country.

The view is created from and by rock, but in a way a view is often a negative. When we stand at the top of the Malverns at VIEW 1, or on the Cotswold ridge at VIEW 3, or on Box Hill in Surrey at VIEW 3, or atop Helvellyn in the Lake District we gaze across land which has disappeared; it has been eaten away, eroded away, hundreds of feet of it.

A view can give a tremendous impression of the vastness of geological processes.

Everywhere, rock and the processes of geological change, however shown, lie below and behind the view we see.

In Britain, we can find rocks made up of the dust and ashes shot out by past volcanoes (though not so often frozen lava itself) and stream-cut gorges to match in intricacy if not size those of Europe and further afield. We have placid valleys, hill slopes of every kind. They can all be read geologically as we see in some of the VIEWS in this book.

We ourselves are fresh in the view. The series of Ice Ages which sculpted and moulded much of today's scenery was coming to an end about 12,000 years ago. Some 6,000 years ago our first farmers settled here – a wink ago in geological terms. At this time Britain was barely separated from Europe by the rising sea in what is now the English Channel. But now for the first time man could start to challenge nature, and himself begin to change the patchwork of the view.

As far as we can tell, a liking for a good view came later still. Obviously, people have always climbed hills, but the first person on record to do so just to admire the view from the top was Petrarch, a Florentine by birth, in about 1340. He is often called 'the first Renaissance man', the first modern man with medieval times behind him. Perhaps he was. In any case, in climbing to see a view, he acted in a way which is familiar today.

Certainly, it is difficult for us metaphorically to stand ourselves in medieval man's rather nasty leather bootees; attitudes were so very different then. Views provide examples of this. High hills and mountains, to us in our own century quite admirable places, were to medieval man as bad as deserts, abandoned by God, suitable only for testing the willpower of hermits. For the prophet Isaiah, they'd all be brought low in due time anyway (and the valleys exalted). Or, as a medieval man might have reasoned: 'high spots can have their uses, for castles and other defences, but mountains are a different matter. Though they bear all the hallmarks of our Creator, if He meant them to be climbed He would (surely) have made them flatter!' We must not laugh at our own ancestors, for we ourselves would have thought the same at that time.

VIEWS BREED DREAMS

Some of the wall paintings seen in houses excavated in the Roman city of Pompeii near Naples show scenery depicted in rather a modern-looking way, with hills in profile dotted with trees, and with birds singing. Perhaps such paintings could also have been found on the walls of the best British villas.

Whether or not this was so, by the Middle Ages this now ancient art had been forgotten. Scenery was now being drawn childishly, or so it seems at first glance. Apparent lack of skill is only part of it: this drawing also echoes a different way of seeing the world.

Although medieval people could of course recognize a hazelnut or a turtle dove and eat both of them if hungry, there seems to have been little to make them want to wonder about what they saw and try to understand it. This was partly because they were brought up to see the natural world in terms of religion and allegory. Mountains, forests, animals – these were all merely symbols of saintliness, temptation or whatever, awaiting them on their journey through life.

Indeed, although most people in Medieval times had their hands in the soil in one way or another, and although king and nobility clearly enjoyed hunting and spent much of the week at it, there seems to be no direct evidence that people enjoyed the countryside for itself in the way we take for granted today. Perhaps they did – there is no way of knowing. However, for the medieval church, the second power in the land, nature itself was suspect. Flowers, the song of birds, the country things that it is part of our modern culture to value could be evil. As a twelfth-century cleric put it 'the delight of the senses is rarely good, mostly bad'.

So, when translated from its original dense dialect, it is haunting, at the end of medieval times, to read of someone walking with pleasure in the day-to-day countryside which may be little altered for our own eyes 600 years later.

Below the Malverns, VIEW 1, lies the country described in *The Vision of Piers Plowman* by William Langland. A contemporary of Geoffrey Chaucer, Langland was born around 1330 at the foot of these Malvern Hills.

The narrative describes how 'In a Summer season when soft was the sun' he dressed shepherd poor and set out to roam the world, seeking marvels. On a May morning below these Malvern Hills, tired, he lay to rest under a bank by a stream and as he lay and leaned and looked upon the water, he slumbered in a sleep, so pleasantly it sounded. And he dreamed. We do the same kind of thing on holiday, and the warmth of May is still as gentle after the long winter.

The snatch of evocative phrases at the start of *Piers Plowman* leads into a preacherly plot about the Christian need to win salvation, rather less genial than the gusty tales of Chaucer, but with some nice satire nonetheless.

The dreamy geography evoked by *Piers Plowman* still lies within the view from the Malverns. The tale's hill capped by a tower is surely British Camp, the prehistoric earth-banked stronghold which broods over slopes which plunge dungeon-steep. Here the spreading prospect is surely the plain which Langland peopled with the world's folk, all maniacally pursuing life, regardless of tower or dungeon. Streams still make their way alongside the ancient fields.

Hills do conjure dreams of many different kinds. Sir Edward Elgar, who died in 1934, also loved this countryside as a lad. At the age of seven he was found sitting on a river bank clutching pencil and paper and 'trying to write down what the reeds were saying'. These swaying rhythms seem to re-echo in some of his music.

Later Elgar returned to the area and delighted in walking these Malvern Hills. Once he stood with his mother watching the evening sunlight catch the British Camp. 'Look at that lovely old hill,' she exclaimed, 'can't we write some tale about it? It's full of interest.'

In less than a month, Elgar began to write *Caractacus*.

Later came the *Enigma Variations*, inspired in part by the close friends he made while living here – Troyte Griffith for example, a Malvern architect who shared his long country walks. While living below these Malvern Hills, Elgar also wrote *The Dream of Gerontius* which brought him international fame.

It says much that 'the Malvern Hills', the most evocative of all hill names, positively breathing sweet music in the ear, means simply (moel-bryn) 'bare hills'! And rock bare the Malverns can seem, in some lights.

TRACKING DOWN POINTS OF VIEW

o we climb hills just for the view? Or is it partly for the sheer physical pleasure of wading up through wet, heady-smelling bracken to reach, panting, the grasses delerious in the wind at the top? It's a bit of fun to better a hill, even in the car. Does the breeze at the top waft invigorating ozone, like the sea? A touch of vertigo to add tang to the sweet-and-sour sauce of feelings? We can catalogue many things, as did one Archdeacon Coxe atop the Brecon Beacons in South Wales; 'I felt a mixed sensation of animation and lassitude, horror and delight. My spirits almost failed, even curiosity was suspended and I threw myself exhausted on the ground. . . .' He was writing at a time when the well-read liked to stretch their emotions as well as their legs.

It is easy to scoff, yet silly to do so, for ideas cannot be polished except by trying them out. Coxe writing 150 years ago can be matched to modern writers. For Ronald Blythe, views 'offer a kind of sensual or moral challenge – they open arms, offer an emotional challenge, one dallies with the feeling one should do something, cross them, enter them'.

Today's right answer is often a blend of what has already long ago been said. Our system of common law is a case in point; matter of fact and sensible as it seems today, it is largely based on innumerable now forgotten precedents and legal battles. It has 'just growed'. And today's enjoyment of views has also grown and changed from one generation to another. The views held on views in the past seem sometimes quite startling today.

Words crystallize feelings. Through notes and diaries, journals and books we can trace the way thoughts and opinions changed and evolved in the past. Poetry too can yield milestones, and here we can start with James Thomson, who died in 1748, aged 48. He was to become a favourite of every explorer of the countryside in search of scenery or views to paint. He was also popular in his lifetime, staying in the grandest houses.

He was once seen eating a peach straight from the branch – and with both hands in his pockets. The eighteenth century was a great age of gusto and enthusiasm, as we shall discover.

Amongst other things Thomson gained the post of Surveyor General of the Leeward Islands, which (having paid a deputy to do the job) left him £300 a year – a classic perk of the time and proving his importance.

His poetry published as 'The Seasons' was often pirated, another sign of success. It explored the effect of the four seasons on nature and on man, celebrating open air delights and sensations. Both grand vistas and details were captured, including such quaint pleasures as swains gathering nuts or admiring a rainbow, or shepherds shearing sheep.

Here from 'Spring':

Meantime you gain the Height, from whose fair Brow
The bursting prospect spreads immense around;
And snatch'd o'er Hill and Dale, and Wood and Lawn,
And verdant Field, and darkening Heath between,
And villages embosom'd soft in Trees,
And spiry Towns by dusky Columns mark'd. . . .

Endearingly simple it seems, yet 'embosom'd soft in Trees' is how we like our villages today – in part because this notion was so popularly read, two centuries ago.

The Seasons was possibly the first full poem with the countryside as its theme, taking the countryside in its own right as a main subject, but poetry had by then begun to make use of countryside – and views. In fact writing and reflecting on life as seen from a favourite viewpoint had already produced a special breed of hill poem, which played its part in helping to make climbing a hill 'just for the view' seem so natural a thing to do.

Words From The Hill

BOX THREE

Britain evolved a breed of *hill* poem, in which as well as description, *virtues* could be woven into the view from the top.

The first was *Cooper's Hill*, penned in 1642 by Sir John Denham. A man with his feet on the ground, he became Surveyor-General over Christopher Wren, the architect of St Paul's Cathedral. An Air Forces Memorial now stands at his viewpoint overlooking Runnymede, Surrey, where the Magna Carta was signed, alongside the River Thames:

O, could I flow like thee, and make thy stream
My great example as it is my theme,
Though deep, yet clear, though gentle, yet not dull,
Strong without rage, without o'erflowing full.

There was to be more to be read into the view:

> *Though with those streams he no resemblance hold*
> *Whose foam is Amber, and their gravel Gold,*
> *His genuine, and less guilty wealth t'explore,*
> *Search not his bottom but survey his shore.*

. . . for old Father Thames brought not only beauty to the scene but wealth through trade. As we see in VIEW 2, the hill poet could also become quite splenetic at what he saw below.

Some hill poems painted the view in words. Well known in its day was *Grongar Hill*, written by John Dyer in 1726, celebrating the view from a summit in the Vale of Towy Dyfed:

> *Old castles on the cliffs arise,*
> *Proudly towering in the skies!*
> *Rushing from the woods, the spires*
> *Seem from hence ascending fires!*
> *Half his beams Apollo sheds*
> *On the yellow mountain-heads!*
> *Gilds the fleeces of the flocks;*
> *And glitters on the broken rocks!*

In more recent times, Robert Bridges, Poet Laureate, published The Testament of Beauty in 1929. It was notable for selling better than any poetry in the previous 100 years:

> *I was late in my long journey, when I had clomb to where*
> *the path was narrowing and the company few,*
> *a glow of childlike wonder enthralled me, as if my sense*
> *had com to a new birth purified, my mind enwrapt*
> *re-awakening to a fresh initiation of life;*
> *with like surprise of joy as any man may know*
> *who rambling wide hath turn'd, resting on some hill-top*
> *to view the plain he has left, and see'th it now out-spredd*
> *mapp'd at his feet, a landscape by beauty estranged*
> *he scarce wil ken familiar haunts, nor his own home,*
> *maybe, where it far lieth, small as faded thought.*

In these early hill poems, the land below was viewed not simply as an essay in distance and in the enchantment it can lend. The flowing landscape below could also be seen as the embodiment of liberty, generous ideas, and the good life.

In those days people preferred to look out across vales golden with corn, with cattle contentedly grazing in the meads. Today we find views across wilderness equally enticing, and this would have puzzled those hill poets.

Many of the best Vale views are gained from the ancient, prehistoric tracks that keep to the high ground, well above what was in their heyday a tangle of forest and marsh in the valleys below. . The original routes were not roads, nor even the green tracks that many are today, but wide ways braiding themselves across what was ground open to the sky without a fence in sight. But on today's tracks which follow their line you can truly walk in the steps of time, an invitation difficult to refuse.

Below, the line of the ancient Ridgeway is followed by today's footpath. The Ridgeway runs atop the high chalk ground, from the Salisbury Plain to the Chilterns and beyond.

FROM A PROSPECT TOWER

Following in the steps of the poets, ordinary travellers too could wax enthusiastic about the view of the vale. There can be no doubt that in time the vale view was recognized as prime.

The sudden variation from the hill country of Gloucestershire to the Vale of Severn is strikingly sublime. You travel for twenty or five-and-twenty miles over one of the most unfortunate desolate counties under heaven, divided by stone walls, and abandoned to the screaming kites and larcenous crows; after travelling really twenty and to appearance ninety miles over this region of stone and sorrow, life begins to be a burden, and you wish to perish. At the very moment when you are taking this melancholy view of human affairs, and hating the postilion and blaming the horses, there bursts upon your view, with all its towers, forests and streams, the deep and shaded Vale of Severn. . . .

Below, a view of the Cotswolds in support of Sydney Smith! To the stone walls we nowadays add wire fencing.

So wrote Sydney Smith around the start of last century, and writing moreover of the Cotswolds, today one of England's favourite tourist areas with its charming villages, green fields – and stone walls.

A word or two strikes an odd chord today. Although 'sublime' has now become a kind of version of our word 'nice', it had once been a word of deeper meaning, as we'll see. Kites, slow-gliding, carrion birds which gave their name to the children's toy, have been persecuted down to a few pairs in remote Welsh fastnesses.

Was Smith, a professional essayist with a reputation as a wit, laying it on? His harsh appraisal of countryside grazed by the famous Cotswold sheep (the wealth from which created the fine churches, manor houses and farmsteads we see today) seems odd indeed.

He was, however, still echoing the outlook of the earlier hill poets. Landscape, to be enjoyed, had to be the richest lands of the plump cornfields, the lush riverside meadows and the swelling orchards which lay only in the vales.

The Diary View

BOX FOUR

Glimpses into the ways people reacted to the view in the past appear in letters and especially in the diaries of the time, for they could record journeys across the land, comparing place with place. Fresh and entertaining they often are.

Celia Fiennes journeyed in the years 1682 to 1712, a time when routes were so bad that travellers could lose their way on the Great North Road itself. This well-connected lady (never short of a relation to stay with) visited Stonehenge and Somerset, Cornwall and Penrith, Oxford, Cambridge, Tunbridge Wells and York and many places else. She had crossed the Cotswolds a century before Sydney Smith (quoted opposite): but recorded nothing more than '30 mile done by 12 of the clock'. If she comes over rather primly, her sheer appetite for new facts of all kinds makes her a good read. This eye for details includes at times kitchen sense for the making of clap bread and other regional recipes. She is less ambitious about scenery (her favourite term of praise is 'neat') but she can charmingly describe a view as 'very delicate and diverting', or a river as 'lovely'.

For Daniel Defoe, better known as author of *Robinson Crusoe* than for his *Tour through the Whole Island of Great Britain* (1724–7), land and scenery also take second place to man's ingenuity and industry. In the Lake District he found that 'nor were these hills high and formidable only, but they had a kind of unhospitable terror in them. Here were no rich pleasant valleys between them, as among the Alps; no lead mines and veins of rich ore, as in the Peak, no coal pits . . . but all barren and wild, of no use or advantage either to man or beast. . .'.

Preferring business to the empty areas we now prize, Defoe, like most of his age, welcomed the sight of the then young industries in the view. Even those who created the fashion for views which burgeoned in the eighteenth century could also admire industry. In those days, of course, industry rarely thundered hard on eyes and hearing.

Half a century later, Arthur Young was equally impressed by the sheer energy of industry; 'horribly sublime' he found Coalbrookdale, the shrine of the Industrial Revolution where iron was first smelted with coke. Young was however a notable improving farmer, moving ahead with novelty and change. He was appalled by some ancient (we would call them quaint) practices he found surviving in places like the Lake District. Here an ox-drawn plough much the same as that described in the Bible was still used.

To travel, Young left his home in the splendidly named village of Bradfield Combust in Suffolk. Fanny Burney, a relative, describes how his life was made wretched by his wife, a woman of violent language and such a red face that she looked like a fiend. More than a lust for novelty forces people to take to the high road.

The open road summoned another practical agriculturalist, William Cobbett. His *'Rural Rides'* of 1830 detail land but also people. He himself was reared at the plough-tail, he couldn't remember a time when he was not busy with bird scaring, weeding or harrowing. Almost a caricature of Merrie England, he lauds the productive field, and makes a splendidly biting read on the subject of barren ground and other wastes: Windsor Forest for example, then largely open ground, was 'as bleak, as barren and as villainous a heath as ever man set eyes on'.

But Cobbett reads deeper. He sees that the richer the soil, 'the more destitute of woods, the more purely corn country the more miserable the labourers'. Once he could not buy corn for his horse or even a scrap of bacon for himself – and that 'in a village with barns 200 feet long and ricks of enormous size'.

This state of affairs was largely brought about by the

enclosure of the countryside into new fields by the land-owners and the pushier and richer farmers – the fields that fill many of today's views (see VIEW 22). As part of the process, many of the country folk were robbed of their rights to land, even to the old common grazings. The entire produce of the countryside now went into the (often newly built) barns of the new farmers.

Another early traveller of note in our story is Thomas Gray, poet. On his Lake District tour of 1769, he is on record for having drawn the curtain in his coach to shut out the sight of the steep crags!

In diaries such as these, some entries may have been long thought over by candlelight in the quiet of the evening after the day's journey, others instantly penned on paper. Although the authors might have been surprised to discover us creating a whole thesis of viewmanship on a chance remark of theirs, they do reveal attitudes very different from those counted normal today.

AND THE TOURIST GUIDE

Thomas Gray's guide to the Lake District was published in 1775, bringing an influx of tourists to the area. And that brings us to an interesting conundrum – what makes a tourist?

One definition would be that people such as Gray in his century or in our own day such as Hunter Davis (author of entertaining books on the Lake District and the Roman Wall) are true *travellers*. They describe the area afresh as if visiting a new land – Gray because of the novelty of his journey in his own period, Davis because of the novelty of his approach in our own time.

The *tourist* buys the guide books written by those first two. But that is really only part of it – the tourist buys not just a guide book, but the whole idea of the area expressed within its pages. Tourists do not really want to explore the real life of the area – they are shy, they don't have the time. Instead they accept only the 'quaintness', 'character', 'wildlife' or whatever chosen by the author as his pitch.

There is nothing to be ashamed of in this. We are all tourists – somewhere else.

And by now, many were enjoying it. By Smith's time, travelling to see views was commonplace.

Across the countryside a whole new system of improved roads, the turnpike or toll roads, had not only eased travel but also reflected a growing demand for it. Not the wealth alone but also the aspirations of the new middle classes of society were swelling. For many with the cash and time to spare, scenery became a succession of 'prospects' to be visited in turn like pictures in a gallery.

This also led to the building of places to see the view *from*. Belvederes became popular. These were look-outs, either a kiosk on top of the roof of a mansion or a happily situated small terrace or summer house in the mansion grounds.

Meanwhile, out in the open countryside, many viewpoints were crowned with prospect towers, spreading as someone put it 'like beacons of good taste'. Our VIEW 3 is from a fine example on the Cotswold edge slightly to the north of where Sydney Smith waxed apoplectic.

These towers were matched by a good many eyecatchers, to be looked at, not from. How these were spawned on the view is an entertaining story to be told later.

BLUE REMEMBERED HILLS

'Tis distance lends enchantment to the view,
And robes the mountain in its azure hue

So penned Thomas Campbell in 1799, a poet of short fame but enduring lines ('Let us do or die' was another).

Distant views from prospect towers and other high spots are blue'd by the dust in the air. Vice versa, artists use blue tones to suggest distance in their paintings. At one time there was even a market for Claude glasses, named after the noted landscape painter Claude Lorrain. These pocket mirrors, hollowed and tinted, allowed the views to be seen not only blue'd but also in miniature – a real life picture as it were, for the days before cameras. True, the laws of optical reflection meant that the view had to be seen backwards with the glass held up in front of you.

Colour In The View

BOX FIVE

The nostalgic blue colour of distant hills is simply an optical phenomenon.

The 'white' light of sunlight is an amalgam of light of various wavelengths (colours). These when seen together appear white. These colours are separated by fine rain, when they are seen as a natural spectrum, a rainbow:

Red – the longest wavelength, Orange, Yellow, Green, Blue, Indigo, Violet

(Richard Of York Gave Battle In Vain).

Falling on a young beech leaf, all but the green and yellow wavelengths are absorbed by the plant tissues, hence the light that bounces back and that we see is yellowish green. With more blue reflected, the result would be a darker green. If some red is also reflected, the leaf appears browner.

Dust, and there is plenty of it in the air above us, scatters the short blue wavelengths most, red the least. The sky above appears blue. There is quite a bit more dust nearer the ground, hence the overall colour reaching us from distant darkish objects such as ranges of hills becomes blue'd. (It is interesting that the colour of deep, *clear* water is also slightly blue, as can be seen in some of the rocky pools in the Lake District and other hills, an effect found also in chlorinated swimming pools.)

The red sunset is created when the western sky refracts or bends the light of the setting sun. When the air is dry, the red part of the spectrum predominates here. At dawn, if there is damp air on high, it reflects back the red rays of the rising sun to give a rosy horizon. Hence

Red sky at night, shepherd's delight;
Red sky in the morning, shepherd's warning

Leonardo da Vinci was among the first artists to adopt a kind of colour-perspective in addition to the perspective of drawn lines. With this 'aerial perspective' as he called it, colours were used (and often still are) to help create an impression of depth in a picture. Blue is for distance, the middle ground is yellow-green, the foreground brownish.

In matters of seeing the mind has a will of its own; it interprets what the eyes notice. If someone points towards us, it is *very* difficult to see what we are in fact looking at – a short stumpy object. Our mind insists that it is long and slender, because that is what an 'arm' is.

The world around us is a mosaic of shapes and colours which our mind interprets for us. In everyday life, we perhaps do not think about colours or even remember the colours of things we have just seen. They are just one of several useful clues to help us to recognize, that is to *name*, things. The actual colour of a country tarmac road may be strongly violet, and a photograph may (depending on the developing) also show it as violet; it is, however, 'seen' as grey. Only when putting it into a painting, or analysing one, will its real colour be realized.

And that is not the end of it. Some claim that colours can possess other properties in painting. Orange and red, both 'warm' colours, come to the fore, they seem to advance. Blue-green, a 'cool' colour, retreats.

One point at issue here is that a painting need not capture a real landscape as our eyes see it: our minds read the painting for us. We are, each generation, brought up rather differently from our parents in this respect. The art we see has moved on a step in the meantime. For this reason, the furore and even outrage caused by some paintings in the past seems quite incomprehensible today.

Something perplexing follows, however. If we have to rely on our minds to tell us what we notice and recognize when

Right, water meadows near Salisbury, by John Constable. He submitted it to the Royal Academy in 1830. It was rejected. 'Take away that nasty, green thing,' cried the selectors.

we look at the view in front of us, perhaps what we see is together with what we feel an invention of our education, our national culture? How real a view is it?

And there were dangers in this – one enthusiast visiting the Lake District tumbled into a waterfall in the process. Nonetheless the Claude glass became a must for fashionable tourists of two centuries ago.

However, when distance blues, it becomes something more besides. It seems to take on an extra dimension: it becomes tranquil, rather melancholic perhaps, touched with nostalgia. The far blue distance is out of reach, another land (and until quite recent times, of course, it was often a day's travel away).

Nostalgia is a melancholy created by loss or absence from home or country, something out of reach. Nostalgia and melancholy can certainly be identified with landscape, although the exact feelings are difficult to pin down perhaps. Here are A. E. Housman's lines, written earlier this century:

> *Into my heart an air that kills*
> *From yon far country blows*
> *What are those blue remembered hills,*
> *What spires, what farms are those?*

That is the land of lost content,
I see it shining plain,
The happy highways where I went
And cannot come again.

For Margaret Drabble, in her excellent book *A Writer's Britain, Landscape into Literature*, Housman here fuses things seen in a view with intense inner, deadly personal longing. We recognize it, although we may not be quite sure what it is we recognize.

We all suffer nostalgia; it is part of the human condition. For some it is often directly linked with childhood happiness, with scenes and events barely remembered. Holidays can be great breeders of nostalgia.

But this nostalgia for place, countryside and views need not only be a very private emotion. It can be national in scale and can even be invented.

Here in Britain we have perhaps the prime example in the writings of Sir Walter Scott. He superimposed a symbolic landscape on the one we actually see. Single-handed, he created for those who were not themselves Scots a nostalgia for Scotland and its mountains which is still so strong today and is taken for granted by those (most of us) who have never read a line of Scott.

'There is,' he once admitted, perhaps guiltily, 'nothing so easy as to make a tradition.'

Above, two Claude glasses; these slightly curved mirrors gave a bluish tint to distance, as seen in Claude's paintings.

Scott himself lived in the Scottish Borders. He delighted in the view of the blue Eildon Hills seen from a favourite spot on Bemersyde Hill. And from the tops of the Eildons, he claimed to be able to point out 43 places famous in war and verse. It was this strong feeling of historical nostalgia which gained him his reputation and went a long way to restoring Scotland's prestige lost after the redcoat victories of the mid-eighteenth century.

Like that other popularizing giant, Wordsworth, Scott was branded by his early memories, spending days with the Border shepherds, running free, watching the kestrels. Once he was found lying on his back, clapping his hands at the lightning, crying 'Bonny' at every flash.

A rich seed bed lay in the Border tales he heard:

> *Of lovers' slights, of ladies' charms,*
> *Of witches' spells, of warriors' arms;*
> *Of patriot battles, won of old*
> *By Wallace wight and Bruce the bold;*
> *Of later fields of feud and fight,*
> *When, pouring from their Highland height,*
> *The Scottish clans, in headlong sway,*
> *Had swept the scarlet ranks away.*
> . . . ('Wight' means valiant)

Although his strongly written tales are rarely read today, they are national institutions all the same – who has not heard of the Lady of the Lake? In his lifetime his tales were sensational successes.

Scott's nostalgic Highlands, the lands of the mountain and the flood, lay to the north of his beloved Eildons. In one respect, Scott had fertile ground, for (as we see in VIEW 5) in few other areas of Britain is the view we see today so closely linked with actual dated history as it is in the Highlands.

Through his writing, Scott did a great deal to ease their bruisings. With their bare rocky aspect they already had immense natural dignity. The heroes and the escapades he described might have seemed an obvious fiction to those who actually lived in the glens, or who could remember from a grandparent what life had really been like. But they were not the people who bought the historical novels and narrative poems in such spectacular numbers (and who borrowed them from the ever more popular subscription libraries).

Walter Scott in this way created a new kind of market for views. With his *Lady of the Lake*, 1810, he popularized the Trossachs and brought visitors flocking to them.

But the old haunted spirit of the Highlands is best captured at Glencoe as we see in VIEW 5, where this link between history and scenery is so very clear.

Although unique as a popularizer, Scott was however not the first literary giant to be awed by the Scottish Highlands. Samuel Johnson had passed through the Highlands on his tour in 1773 and considered that they could do with more trees. But he did admit that thoughts 'excited by a view of an unknown and untravelled wilderness are not such as arise in the artificial solitude of parks and gardens . . . man is made unwillingly aware of his own weakness, and meditation shows how little he can perform'. He also regretted that Scottish roads offered little diversion; there were so few people to meet or overtake – hardly today's complaint.

Johnson and his companion James Boswell were in a way already hot-foot after fashion, though they would perhaps have been loath to admit it. Other well-known names had begun to winkle themselves from the cosiness of London, Oxford and Cambridge, and travel.

Thomas Gray, poet, author of the most famous elegy in the English language ('Elegy in a Country Churchyard' of 1751) was enthusiastic about this remote scenery. 'The (Scottish) lowlands are worth visiting once,' he wrote, 'but the mountains are ecstatic. None but these monstrous creatures of God know how to join so much beauty with so much horror. A fig for your poets, painters, gardeners and clergymen, that have not been among them, their imagination can be made up of nothing but bowling greens, flowering shrubs, horse ponds, shell grottoes.'

Gray was one of those who, by satisfying a growing public thirst for new feelings, helped establish the fashion for views from the mid-eighteenth century on. He never, by the way, travelled without a Claude glass in his pocket, the better to see a view.

Roving Lord Byron, who had been schooled at Aberdeen at the start of the nineteenth century, also chipped in:

> *England! thy beauties are tame and domestic*
> *To one who has roved o'er mountains afar;*
> *Oh! for the crags that are wild and majestic!*
> *The steep frowning glories of dark Loch na Garr*

(Lochnagar is a cluster of summits near Balmoral)

THE NOBLE MOUNTAIN

t doesn't need to be said that artists as well as writers can popularize views of mountains or any other kind of countryside. The great J. M. W. Turner had also visited the Highlands on a journey through Britain, sketching as he went. He thought 'Scotland a more picturesque country to study than Wales – the lines of the mountains are finer, the rocks of larger mass.'

It was in Wales, however, that we see a painter (rather than a poet) being brought in to aid national identity. How this came about is described in VIEW 6, a view of Snowdon.

The artist in question, Paul Sandby, was praised by other artists. Thomas Gainsborough thought him a man who painted 'real views from nature' rather than just picturesque compositions. And that is a good enough prompt to investigate what a 'real view' can be.

In the 1760s, Snowdon was painted from its portals at Llyn Nantlle by Richard Wilson. It is interesting to compare this picture with what the camera sees today. When we also compare it with a typical landscape by the artist Gaspard Dughet (also known as Poussin) we can see that it is somewhat more than just a view of Snowdon.

Past Masters In The View

BOX SIX

When Snowdonia's majestic scenery was becoming widely popular 200 years ago, three different kinds of masterpiece of landscape painting were recognized. They were European, although much admired and collected by the English.

Those of Claude Lorrain and his contemporary in the seventeenth century, Gaspard Dughet (also known as Poussin) showed scenes invented and peopled to echo a melancholic nostalgia for the lost Classical world of ancient Greece and Rome. The poems of Virgil were a favourite quarry of topics for these paintings.

Equally gripping, but atmospheric in quite a different fashion were the wild and savage mountain scenes of Salvator Rosa, who also lived in the seventeenth century. Here was a Romantic artist's depiction of landscape.

Left top, ideal landscape by Gaspard Dughet, 1640's. Left below, rugged landscape and cascade, by Salvator Rosa.

Horace Walpole made an entertaining comment on the Alps; '. . . precipices, mountains, torrents, wolves, rumblings, Salvator Rosa . . .'

Third were meticulous landscapes from Holland, also dating from the same century. Topographical, the pictures showed an interest in day-to-day details of the view – even trees were for the first time being painted as noble creations in their own right.

Above, Snowdon from Llyn Nantlle by Richard Wilson painted in the 1760's. He has added drama to the scene by raising the slopes (compare this with the photograph from the same viewpoint, page 122).

Wilson was in fact born in Wales, though he studied in London and worked in Italy for a time. It was while abroad that he fell under the spell of earlier painters such as Gaspard and Claude Lorrain (see page 65). They had established themselves as masters of a kind of landscape which reeked of nostalgia for the lost worlds of Rome and Greece. Here at Snowdon, we can see just how much Wilson's picture is in debt to them. It is more than a view of the mountain with a few figures; the view is interpreted in a rather formal way.

To give the view a greater sense of distance, Wilson used the simple visual trick of raising the viewpoint somewhat – rather as if we saw it from a balcony. And the picture is planned in a kind of code, rather like a stage set.

Between theatre curtains (here trees) the eye is led down a central vista where distance is created by colour – earthy colours for foreground, then touches of green, and bluish tones for the distant mountain. Water helps to focus the light. Compositions like this are often still used today. Gaspard and Wilson place figures in the view, posing them theatrically. 'Classical' painters such as Gaspard and Claude often took the cue for their pictures from the Latin poetry of Virgil; heroes as well as quaint shepherds could people their paintings.

Richard Wilson, the 'father of English landscape painting' was perhaps the first Briton to make real views the subject of *oil* paintings. Indeed the acerbic Sir Joshua Reynolds, the first President of the Royal Academy (of which Wilson was also a founding member) said that his landscapes were 'near common nature'. This was praise indeed. In the 18th century, even day-to-day home landscapes were fast becoming fashionable. Here in Britain this interest created a brand new tradition – the *watercolour* painting of the view.

Its roots lay in washes, using brown sepia from cuttle-fishes to add shadow to ink drawings and so to create effects of light. At first the landscape drawings of the time tended to be topographical, showing clear and exact details of what was to be seen in the view. Sometimes views were literally copied directly from nature by using a *camera lucida* (a glass prism splitting the light so that eye can see and hand draw at the same time) or a *camera obscura* (a small darkroom like a pinhole camera in which the view was focussed onto a sheet of paper to be traced).

By the eighteenth century, however, colour was also being used. In time artists such as Paul Sandby went beyond just colouring their drawings and began to draw with a paint-loaded brush. They also began to use colour to enhance the view they saw, making it seem more melancholy, or stormy, or whatever.

So, by the turn of the eighteenth-century these artists were not just extending their skills to record nature, they were also using them to *interpret* what they saw. By doing so they changed not only the kind of picture of the scenery that we like, but also the way we ourselves look at views today.

Thomas Girtin and J. M. W. Turner 'acquired for watercolours the title of paintings'; something we now take for granted. Girtin created atmospheric views. He delighted in the play of light on rough country with cloud shadows sweeping across. Turner, although his better-known masterpieces are in oils, was also a dab hand at atmospheric watercolour.

Above, The falls of Clyde, a watercolour by J. M. W. Turner, painted in 1801.

Hard detail was not necessarily lost in these new watercolours, but it often became secondary to the wish to communicate more of the atmosphere and spirit of nature.

In addition to this, new audiences were being moulded. For some time pictures had been copied as engravings, and so printed into books. These prints could also be coloured, by hand or by overprinting with colour blocks.

Now societies and academies (The Royal Academy was founded in 1768; the first watercolour society in 1808) began to hold regular public exhibitions of paintings. (Hitherto these could only be viewed in the studio of the artist or on the walls of patron or buyer.) Art could now quickly both mirror and mould public taste for a view.

And as watercolours could be tackled by amateurs with much less effort than oils, they too could try to capture what they saw in the countryside. Feelings for a view could only intensify.

As with all developments, there are some delightful sidetracks. One Alexander Cozens, in attempting to arrive at 'universal' landscape – pure landscape and nowt else if you like – tried beginning his pictures not from what he saw in the view but from irregular blots he made on the paper. He once wrote. 'Composing landscapes by invention is not the art of imitating nature: it is more; it is forming artificial representations of landscape on the general principles of nature, [choosing] beauties dispersed in nature.'

Below, blot drawing in the Cozens' manner, by Joseph Wright, 1786.

BEAUTIFUL AND SUBLIME VIEWS

hen the ice-cut, craggy scenery of Snowdon and other mountains was first gripping imagination, the in-word to use to describe it was *sublime*. It was a word that cropped up in writing of many kinds, and was used with eagerness. Certain key sites became recognized as a necessary visit for the first scenic tourists. Here *atmosphere* of a kind which might appeal to a poet or a painter, and *geology* which could truly appal anyone, combined together to create a sublime view. There is nothing so dead as dead enthusiasms, but at these places, Gordale Scar is one, (VIEW 7), geology massively creates mood. We know just how they felt!

The eighteenth century was a time when science was becoming familiar and reason becoming a creative force. If the secrets of the air, invisible and intangible, could be discovered and its ingre-dients measured, why could not such things as beauty also be defined and measured?

'Though all sorts of waving lines are ornamental, there is but one . . . to be called the line of beauty – number 4' wrote William Hogarth.

Many attempted the task. The artist William Hogarth, best-known for depicting outrageous and uproarious humanity in the round in such sequences as *The Rake's Progress*, tried his hand. In his *'Analysis of Beauty'* of 1753, he proposed a perfect Line of Beauty, a shallow *S* curve which keeps the eye in continuous but not too strenuous motion. With it he claimed that beautiful pictures could be made, whether of landscape or anything else.

Hogarth, however, was not the leader in the chase; nor in fact was the leader an artist. A key figure in the safari of ideas was Edmund Burke, yes, the author of the immortal line 'the price of liberty is eternal vigilance', a linchpin of today's democracies. Attempting to define and assess emotions, he decided that anything, any object or collection of objects, possessed properties. Some gave weight or colour for example, but others could make it beautiful, while others could make it sublime.

Believing also that everybody was born with senses as good as the next, such things as beauty could be appreciated by all who chose to do so.

In his *'Philosophical Enquiry into the Origin of Our Ideas of the Sublime and Beautiful'*, 1758, the *beautiful* he thought, had smoothness, smallness, gradual changes, delicate colours – for example, the gentle slopes and streams of a lush valley view (or a lovely woman's body) gave pleasure. The beautiful could inspire love, cheerfulness even.

The *sublime* was something else. It possessed such qualities as vast dimensions, of which depth or height were particularly potent; a sense of infinity which encouraged the imagination to extend itself; and difficulty. (This we can take to mean that the sublime was not easy to achieve, and certainly couldn't be taken for granted.) The recipe could also include (maybe jointly as contrasts) such things as light and darkness, suddenness, loudness and silence.

The sublime gave little chance of emotional indigestion, as perhaps beauty might. It was frightening. 'Indeed terror is in all cases whatsoever, either more openly or latently, the ruling principle of the sublime'; so wrote Burke.

VIEW 7 – of Gordale Scar – is a supreme example of the sublime!

Ambitious artists, by attempting to capture the sublime on their easels, helped to underline its meaning as a compliment, an accolade.

In Burke's time, the recognized master artist of the sublime was Salvator Rosa, who matched Gaspard and Claude in popularity with many collectors. What he showed was wittily summed up by

Horace Walpole's comment on the Alps: 'precipices, mountains, torrents, wolves, rumblings, Salvator Rosa.'

And in his own time, Snowdon as painted by Richard Wilson was also counted sublime.

Fit match for these is a picture of our VIEW 7, the painting of Gordale Scar, completed by James Ward in 1814. Perhaps its size alone would guarantee that; it is almost 4.2 metres long by 3.3 metres high (14 feet by 11 feet), one of the larger pictures in London's Tate Gallery!

As comparison with VIEW 7 shows, Ward was not so much interested in showing exactly what was there, but in creating impact. He stressed such features as the sheerness of the cliffs to exaggerate the feeling of terror.

That the sublime could be pictured in this way meant that it could

Below, Gordale Scar by James Ward, 1814. The bull and fighting stags are added symbols of potency in this scene.

40

be understood; and in time the language of viewmanship and guide books rose to the challenge. Yes, we accept today that cliffs *frown*, rocky gulfs *yawn* open to revealing cathedral-like vistas. . . .

But cliffs do not frown nor rock faces yawn. In ways such as this our mind's eye has been bred to the view.

THE PICTURESQUE VIEW

eaping down from their coach (horse-drawn) to nod hello to the view, the first tourists of two centuries ago did not want to agonize over the definition of the beautiful and the sublime. They wanted to be told where to look to see it. In other words, like all tourists today, they wanted guide books, and guide books had to be created.

One quaint fellow did aid the process. His name, the Reverend William Gilpin (1724–1804). His profession, school-master parson. And with long holidays that he put to good use.

He helped put forward the idea of looking at landscapes as if they were pictures, and he did a lot to underline the idea of picturesque beauty.

'Picturesque' meant paintable – something that would make a good picture. It could, like that word 'nice', mean anything or nothing, depending on whether granny, the greengrocer or the grandee is using it, and when. However, in Gilpin's day the picturesque was held to be a quality distinct from the beautiful and the sublime; rather a hybrid, more akin to beauty, but with something of the ruggedness of a sublime view. Or, as one wit put it, 'the vicar's horse is beautiful, the curate's is picturesque'.

Words In The View

BOX SEVEN

Philosophers, of course, argue that a feeling is only valid if there is a word to describe it. Dated by their first appearance written in a diary or letter, or on a printed page, many of the words used of and about views have quite a recent origin.

That word *landscape*, for example. In its earlier form it was 'landskip', a Dutch word. Milton uses it in this form:

> *Streit mine eye hath caught new pleasures*
> *Whilst the Lantskip round it measures*

A word used for a picture of inland scenery (as distinct from a sea painting or a portrait), by 1630 it was also being used for the prospect from a viewpoint. More than a century later *scenery* came on the scene as stage decoration in 1770; by 1784 the word was being used for the general appearance of a place viewed with a picturesque eye. Scenery became the features which made a view 'picturesque'; that is, a fit subject for a picture, or paintable as we would say today.

That most useful-useless of view words 'nice', first appeared in its present sense of . . . well, nice . . . of dainty appetizing food in 1712; colloquially as agreeable in 1769; and of agreeable, attractive, pretty appearance in 1793. 'View' was first used to mean an area covered by the eye from one point in 1606; it was applied to a drawing, print or painting of a prospect in 1700.

'Countryside' is very much a word of our own century, although 'country' (as opposite to town) appeared written in 1526. 'Pastoral' was originally linked with herdsmen (pasture); then at the end of the 18th century it came to embody simple goodness, which (it was becoming fashionable to assume) lurked in the countryside.

As interesting as these dictionary raids, are words which link attitudes of mind to what is seen. Use then and now is sometimes rather different.

Here is Celia Fiennes in the Lake District in 1698: 'I was walled on both sides by those inaccessible high rocky barren hills which hangs over ones head in some places and appear very terrible . . .'.

'Terrible' for her meant exciting terror; frightful, dreadful, 'Horrible', meaning exciting horror, tending to make you shudder was often in use in descriptions of the view in those days. As was 'awful', meaning causing dread, and often used of sublime views (and for the definition of that word, see page 39).

From the seemingly arid arguments over the meaning of 'sublime' and 'picturesque', there emerged through Wordsworth and others, a romantic, mysterious depth to ideas about the countryside which we still take for granted. It is part of the picture, as it were, that English as a language is a treasure chest of emotive atmospheric words which can be used in this way. Gloomy, mist, dank, dewy, dusk . . . they seem a perfect match for what they describe.

Unique writers such as Wordsworth often use words in ways that others do not. It might seem obvious that words used by people with more than usual frequency could have a rather different meaning for them. 'Insight' for example is used neither by Keats nor Shelley, but often by Wordsworth.

Insight must have had an almost religious meaning for Wordsworth. And that brings us to another point. If we fail to respond to such feelings, fail to become enthusiastic (even in Gilpin's fashion), aren't *we* the ones who are missing out?

Picturesque became a powerful word, and Gilpin made it a word everyone could understand when his 'picturesque tours' of various parts of Britain began to be published, illustrated with his own sketches. He loved getting off his horse and getting busy with his pencil. His guide to the Lake District appeared in 1789, for example, but he also took in Wales, the Scottish Highlands and other places.

William Gilpin did not originate the idea of touring to admire the view. In the Lake District, Thomas West had already published his Guide in 1778, which included special 'stations', points from which the best views could be seen. But Gilpin did more than others to make the idea popular. He launched the fashion we now take for granted.

He was a parson. He believed that if a man admired natural beauty (beauty then being seen as a reality, a quality as firm as weight), then he would the more admire moral beauty, that is, virtue. Moreover, there was nothing wrong in his eyes in exciting the senses with novelty and with such things as grand views. Men had come a long way from Medieval times when such delight could be considered dangerous.

Gilpin's earnest enthusiasm laid him open to satire in that witty age. So here he is, appearing as Dr Syntax, words by William Combe, picture by Rowlandson:

> *Your sport, my Lord, I cannot take,*
> *For I must go and hunt a lake;*
> *And, while you chase the flying deer,*
> *I must fly off to Windermere.*
> *Instead of hallooing to a fox,*
> *I must catch echoes from the rocks,*
> *With curious eye and active scent,*
> *I on the picturesque am bent,*
> *That is my game, I must pursue it,*
> *And make it where I cannot view it.*

A cutting last line that. Gilpin for all his earnestness did in a way put himself in cloud cuckoo land. In his attempt to use the 'picturesque' as yardstick of a view, he had to suggest that nature was sometimes (if not often) less than perfect. If the actual view did not match up to its potential, he was not above improving it with his pencil, to bend it to his sense of the picturesque.

Above, Dr Syntax sketching the Lake, a cartoon by Thomas Rowlandson to match the lampoon by William Combe, 1812.

He could completely disregard even modest accuracy, and his guide book views could have such things as rocks literally cliff-hanging. The artist must correct 'nature's prentice essays'. 'We deviated into a mere scene of mountains,' he wrote once, 'Nature seemed to have attempted some mode of composition which she left unfinished. . . .'

In his eyes, Helvellyn looked a great deal better moved to the other side of Thirlmere lake.

There was the odd complaint. One by a certain William Mason: 'If a voyager down the river Wye takes out your Book, his very Boatman crys out "nay Sr you may lok in vain there, no body can find one Picture in it the least like. . . ."'

As the author of such popular guide books, Gilpin is important in the story of the view. Nevertheless, in his lifetime Sandby, Girtin and many others – even Thomas Rowlandson, an excellent landscape painter – were out as 'true' artists (as we understand the word today).

And the general direction of Gilpin's approach was perhaps not quite the dead end it might seem, for as we shall see, dynamic men of that age were already moulding the shape of the land to create views of their own design. When Gilpin wrote, Humphrey Repton ruled landscape fashion with his 'Red Books'. Gilpin was an echo of such Grand Designs on the view.

Gilpin, for all his eccentricity, had written the right books at the right time. He had stimulated travel and had given travellers something new – a kind of language with which to discuss views and the countryside. The foundations were laid for dramatic developments. In fact, it was rather as if a new play took over the stage; that play is enjoying a long run, for we today are among the audience.

WILLIAM WORDSWORTH

William Wordsworth is too closely linked to the Lake District to be met anywhere else in this book, although he did travel and live elsewhere. Tourists of his own day hoped also to catch sight of the Grand Man himself amongst the immensely varied scenery of these hills. His name brought the American Ralph Emerson, Charlotte Brontë and even Charles Dickens to visit. After his death his home became a national shrine.

The promoters of the beautiful and the sublime (and even the picturesque) underlined the fact that views could stir the feelings, and that 'imagination could feel through the eyes', and not only for artists. Wordsworth, for whom poetry was 'the spontaneous overflow of powerful feeling', linked poetry with nature in a way not done before.

Like Walter Scott, Wordsworth had been a country lad, bird-nesting over the fells with the best of them, free as the wind. The memory was strong. His *Ode on Intimations of Immortality from Recollections of Early Childhood* begins (and who is never stirred by these lines?):

1   *There was a time when meadow, grove, and stream,*
    The earth, and every common sight,
    To me did seem
    Apparell'd in celestial light,
    The glory and the freshness of a dream.
    It is not now as it hath been of yore;-
    Turn wheresoe'er I may,
    By night or day,
    The things which I have seen I now can see no more.

2   *The Rainbow comes and goes,*
    And lovely is the Rose,
    The Moon doth with delight

Look round her when the heavens are bare;
Waters on a starry night
Are beautiful and fair;
The sunshine is a glorious birth;
But yet I know, where'er I go,
That there hath past away a glory from the earth.

It is commonplace to claim we feel nostalgia for our youth, but Wordsworth was not indulging himself. Nature, which at first was merely the background for fun on the fells, had become for him something greater, something worth loving for its own sake. It offered spiritual uplift: it was 'bliss ineffable' to commune with 'every form of creature'. Man came 'trailing clouds of glory'; Wordsworth considered that he could only fulfil his promise if he recognized that he too was part of nature.

Some of his most appealing poems are set against what he called 'spots of time', real places to be seen amongst the cloud-varied hills, the streams and rivers and open lakes of the English Lake District. Here experiences such as trivial encounters come to reveal deep truths. Into many poems are studded insights into the people and happenings he saw. In his preface to Lyrical Ballads he declared that he would 'choose incidents and situations from common life – and relate or describe them throughout, as far as possible, in a selection of language really used by men; and at the same time throw over them a certain colouring of the imagination, whereby ordinary things should be presented to the mind in an unusual way. . . .'

It was a conscious attempt to grow out of hackneyed poetry and write from the heart, in sturdy direct language. And at heart, he thought the simple rural life to be the best, closer to the beautiful and permanent form of nature, and (to put it simply) whatever your pains or ills, nature grand and powerful could put you right!

This, Wordsworth's view of nature, was revolutionary and with it he changed the way we ourselves see the natural world. The Lake District became not just a place of fine views, but a place where satisfaction and solace could be found. And what was true for the Lake District was surely true for countryside everywhere?

For many of his best years, Wordsworth was aided, supported and fired by his sister Dorothy and by the poet Samuel Taylor Coleridge. In an earlier pact, he and Coleridge had decided on the division of their work: Wordsworth to take the natural, Coleridge the supernatural.

While Coleridge supplied philosophical stimulus, Dorothy had a superb eye for detail. Her own journals are always a fresh delight: 'Thursday 15th (April 1802). It was a threatening, misty morning, but mild. We set off after dinner . . . saw the plough going in the field. The wind seized our breath. The lake was rough. There was a boat by itself floating in the middle of the bay. . . . When we were in the woods beyond Gowbarrow park we saw a few daffodils close to the water-side. We fancied that the lake had floated the seeds ashore and that the colony had so sprung up. But as we went along there were more and yet more and at last under the boughs of the trees, we saw that there was a long belt of them. . . . I never saw daffodils so beautiful, they grew among the mossy stones about and about them, some rested their heads upon these stones as on a pillow for weariness and the rest tossed and reeled and danced and seemed as if they verily laughed with the wind. . . .'

And Wordsworth:

> *I wandered lonely as a cloud*
> *That floats on high o'er vales and hills,*
> *When all at once I saw a crowd,*
> *A host of golden daffodils;*
> *Beside the lake, beneath the trees,*
> *Fluttering and dancing in the breeze.*
>
> *Continuous as the stars that shine*
> *And twinkle on the milky way,*
> *They stretched in never-ending line*
> *Along the margin of a bay:*
> *Ten thousand saw I at a glance,*
> *Tossing their heads in sprightly dance.*
>
> *The waves beside them danced; but they*
> *Out-did the sparkling waves in glee;*
> *A poet could not but be gay,*
> *In such jocund company;*
> *I gazed – and gazed – but little thought*
> *What wealth the show to me had brought.*
>
> *For oft, when on my couch I lie*
> *In vacant or in pensive mood,*
> *They flash upon that inward eye*
> *Which is the bliss of solitude;*
> *And then my heart with pleasure fills,*
> *And dances with the daffodils.*

For Wordsworth poetry truly was (as he put it) 'emotion recollected in tranquillity'.

Capturing The View

BOX EIGHT

Wordsworth's *Guide through the District of the Lakes in the North of England* was so popular that it was republished many times. It first appeared in 1810 as an introduction to a printed collection of views, but reissues surprisingly not only lacked illustration, but failed to mention any painter at all, bar recommending a visit to Hardraw Scar in Wensleydale 'of which with its waterfall, Turner has a fine drawing.' So he ended up with something we would think odd today – a guide book without pictures!

In recent centuries, much ingenuity has been used to mass-produce landscape drawings and paintings and so make views and scenery popular and available (if at second hand) to a large public.

The oldest and simplest of these was (and is) the WOOD-CUT. A smoothed block of wood is chiselled away, inked and pressed against paper. The hollows print white. With care, fine lines can be produced.

With WOOD ENGRAVING, fine cutting can leave thin ridges to produce shading and so imitate pencil drawings. A very hard wood such as box is needed. It was a very popular method of producing pictures of all kinds in Wordsworth's day, and continued a flourishing profession until the 1880s, when it lost out to competition from new photo-mechanical methods of reproducing pictures.

Woodcuts and engravings could be coloured; either by hand or by reprinting the page with cut blocks using other inks.

A LINE ENGRAVING is rather different. Here the line, cut into a plate of copper or zinc, keeps the ink. The same principle is used in ETCHING. Here the plate is covered with wax, and the lines scratched through to the metal; the plate is then dipped in acid, and only the exposed metal is eaten away. Merging shadows can be created by stopping out, that is, by recoating parts of the plate before dipping it again in the acid. The wider, deeper lines and hollows hold more ink, and show darker when printed.

The search for better 'tone' of this kind led to the invention of the AQUATINT process. Resin dust is shaken onto a copper plate, warmed to make it stick and then scratched or drawn. The plate is then bitten by acid, which attacks the metal freed from the resin. The size of the resin grains can be chosen to give the coarseness or fineness of texture required, while the time in the acid gives the depth of tone.

Colours could be hand-painted onto the print, or printed with separate plates. All in all, aquatints could match water-colour paintings for luminosity – so they were very popular with the British.

MEZZOTINT was often used to copy actual paintings of landscapes and other subjects. A copper plate was rough-ened, and the 'burr' scraped smooth to give areas of light tones. Constable had his paintings copied in this way, while Turner published a series of landscapes, his *Liber Studiorum* making use of this technique.

In the earlier part of this century, there was a renewal of interest in the early art of wood engraving, used mainly for book illustration.

By now of course most books on views and countryside life were illustrated with photographs, which had arrived in Victorian times. Postcard photographs were powerful pub-licity for beauty spots. But although photographs tend to be topographically exact in what they show, a photograph as a whole can assume a theatrical simplicity, as we see in View 29.

The tourist industry in the Lake District was helped along very nicely by Wordsworth. Poetry apart, he also wrote his own guide book to the area, which tourists added to their library alongside those of William Gilpin and Thomas West and others.

However, in the face of this increasing flood of visitors, Words-worth becomes less than charitable. He wrote irritably to the *Morning Post* in 1844, against the proposed railway to Windermere – the forerunner of today's motorway spur which carries millions of visitors each year.

'A vivid perception of romantic scenery is neither inherent in mankind nor a necessary consequence of education. Green fields, clear blue skies, and all the ordinary varieties of rural nature find an easy way to the affections of all men, but a taste beyond this is not to be implanted at once.' Neither he claimed could 'rocks and mountains, torrents and wide spread waters be comprehended' without 'processes or opportunities of culture to some degree habitual'. It was, he argued, of no benefit to bring tourists wholesale to the Lakes; 'rather they should make excursion with their families into the neighbouring fields. . . .'

He concluded his letter: 'Yours angrily!'

The railway was built!

Whatever you may think of the rest of the letter, Wordsworth ends on a good point. If real nature is admirable, why do you have to go to the Lake District to admire it? Nature down the road is just as real. Isn't it just as good?

More people meant that more people found new ways of enjoying what was fast becoming a national asset, and colourfully nutty some of them could be. John Wilson, who wrote as 'Christopher North', could lay on some soppy prose: 'Oh, Coniston, Old Man, there is some snow, like soap on a beard; but thy chin is a Christian chin – and that cove is a pretty little dimple which gives sweetness to thy smile.' But he could also with gusto bathe in all but every stream and lake, take his horse over the tops and swap wopping lies with the locals, when he wasn't wrestling with them in the old Cumberland and Westmorland style.

Although Wordsworth thought nothing of walking 15 miles to deliver a letter, here was the idea of purposefully adding exertion to the heady mix of scenery and the feelings it evoked. Many were finding it fun to sweat up to a view.

Later in the century, rock climbers arrived to joke as they swung below the crags – sometimes in Latin (the first of them were usually University people). Towards the end of the century, towards the end of the Victorian era, the rambling holiday was well-established.

This too was something rather new. Previously a visit to the Lakes had meant, if not following well-worn paths, at least not consciously avoiding them. From one viewing station to another, on the pilgrimage to Wordsworth's house at Grasmere, on the train, on the lake – there were crowds, people like daffodils, everywhere. Rambling meant a touch of un-togetherness, it became the best way to get away from it all, and armed with Wordsworth's legacy, face empty nature itself.

There was by now quite a lot to get away from, of course. The towns had mushroomed in Victorian times, but more than size was involved. The immense vitality of the booming industries and the growing cities and towns pulled public attention back from the countryside.

Excitement lay in gas street lights and other new inventions, in problems too that had to be solved. Cholera and typhus bred in the slums but paid scant regard to street names. The need to deal with disease stimulated the start of strong, local, elected government. *Punch*, the world-famous satirical magazine, started in 1841, but there are no jokes about the picturesque for many many years: its staple was the world of trains and bricks.

The countryside became somewhere to escape to when town life became wearisome. It was something to enjoy, to take great gulps of of. You had to make sure it gave you your money's worth of pleasure. Holidays as we know them today started at about this time.

Also by 1880 came the start of the struggle to protect fine views and scenery.

Wordsworth himself had coined the term 'national property' for an area as strikingly beautiful as the Lake District. Another local celebrity in Lakeland, Canon Rawnsley, carried the idea further, to a 'national resting ground' open to all, for the benefit of all. On Skiddaw lie the remains of a drinking fountain, a memorial to the day that he led Keswick people up the mountain to demolish a footpath obstruction. Rawnsley wrote sonnets as well as supporting innumerable causes in defence of Lakeland views. One famous battle (lost) was against plans to dam Thirlmere and raise its level to provide clean drinking water for Manchester.

Rawnsley was also one of the founders of the National Trust.

Here then, amongst the cloud-dappled hills, along the tumbling streams, in the woods and by the glorious open waters of the Lake District were born and tested many of the notions we take for granted today. In several ways the English Lake District is a place without match in the whole world.

WATER – THE EYE OF THE LANDSCAPE

ater is the eye of the landscape. Its gleaming surface, turbulent or passive by turns, hides a world apart, but nonetheless a world without which views of many kinds would be the poorer.

Wordsworth of course had a splendid choice; the Lake District has plenty of water of all kinds – rain, stream, river, waterfall, lake. Here is one of his 'spots of time':

> *I thought of thee, my partner and my guide,*
> *As being past away. Vain sympathies!*
> *For, backward, Duddon as I cast my eyes,*
> *I see what was, and is, and will abide;*
> *Still glides the stream and shall for ever glide;*
> *The Form remains, the Function never dies;*
> *While we, the brave, the mighty, and the wise,*
> *We Men, who in our morn of youth defied*
> *The elements, must vanish; – be it so!*
> *Enough, if something from our hands hath power*
> *To live, and act, and serve the future hour;*
> *And if, as toward the silent tomb we go,*
> *Through love, through hope, and faith's transcendent dower,*
> *We feel that we are greater than we know.*

Yes, rivers are particularly *satisfying*.

That early traveller, Celia Fiennes, had a delightful eye for water in the view. In the Lake District in 1698, she described tumbling streams: 'little currents of water from the sides (of the hills), . . . which makes a pleasant rush and murmuring noise, and like a snowball is increased by each spring trickling down'. She used the word *falls* of water, but never that word 'waterfall'. Today of course no author of a guide book could avoid using it; waterfall is part of the accepted language of viewmanship.

Waterfalls are counted jewels in a view, something worth a long walk, a hard climb. Ford's *Guide to the Lakes* of 1839, one of the early pocket guides, had a picture of a waterfall to front it, chosen instead of a lake or mountain!

Artists found that a waterfall makes a powerful picture. Amongst others, Turner delighted in placing waterfalls in his views. His *Morning amongst the Coniston Fells* matches a tumbling fall to the rainy sky which bred it. This picture is recognizable as visual poetry – but without a voice. It is interesting that when first shown, at the Royal Academy in 1798, he tagged it with a passage from Milton's *Paradise Lost* beginning:

*Left, Morning amongst the
Coniston Fells, painted by
J. M. W. Turner after his tour
of the Lake District in 1797.
The tumbling waterfall
excitingly echoes the wet sky
which bred it.*

*Ye mists and exhalations that now arise
From hill or steaming lake. . . .*

and perhaps lines of poetry can add something to the pleasure of a

55

painting – as the mind interprets what the eyes see, it can double its enjoyment in this way.

John Ruskin was an influential Victorian writer who in matters of painting and much else trained the eyes of a good many. He wrote about art, economics, religion, new social relationships and many other subjects besides. Slade Professor of Art at Oxford, he once had his students out with pick and shovel: 'making a road is the most worthy thing for men to do'.

He too must also have found particular meaning in waterfalls; he chose to be painted against one for his well-known portrait by John Everett Millais in 1853.

Ruskin had visited the Lake District when young, and the memory continued to burn. The very first thing he remembered in life was being taken, when he was five and a half years old, to the viewpoint on Friar's Crag, Derwentwater. 'The intense joy mingled with awe that I had in looking through the hollows in the mossy roots over the Crag into the dark lake has associated itself more or less with all twining roots of trees ever since . . . at the creation of the world for *me* in Friar's Crag.'

It was on an undergraduate tour of Italy in 1837 that (he reported) he felt for the last time the youthful love of nature which had seemed to Wordsworth to hint at immortality: 'It is a feeling only possible in youth, for care, regret, or knowledge of evil destroys it, and it requires also the full sensibility . . . the conscious strength of heart and hope.'

He had once claimed that mountains were the beginning and end of all scenery. Later he wrote: 'I find that by keeping long away from the hills I can in great part still restore the old childish feeling about them, and the more I live and work among them, the more it vanishes'. However, he did retire to live on the shores of Lake Coniston in the Lake District!

. . . He so hated industrial civilization (like William Morris having a nostalgia for an ancient England of cottage industries) that he refused ever to travel to the Lakes by the railway that had been built to Windermere.

His views on the sprawling growth of Victorian industry helped strengthen the growing taste for countryside which remained unchanged by it.

What makes a good lake?

William Wordsworth: 'The form of the lake is most perfect when, like Derwent-water and some of the smaller lakes, it least resembles that of a river.' But he did mention that some lakes such as Windermere are so long that they look more like a broad river. However, 'the appropriate feeling is revived' because their shape is winding! His favourite lake was Ullswater, 'perhaps the happiest combination of beauty and grandeur which any of the Lakes affords . . .'.

Thomas Gray: 'shining purity reflecting rocks, woods, fields, just ruffled by the breeze enough to show it is alive'.

And surely an island or two? Islands in a lake offer a hint of a world apart, as mysterious as the deep pupils of an eye. They were chosen for clan burial grounds in Scotland and Sir Walter Scott seized on their symbolism, featuring Ellen's Isle on Loch Katrine for his *Lady of the Lake* – and so (as usual) popularizing them.

And in our own very different century and for a very different readership, Arthur Ransome, in *Swallows and Amazons* and other tales, had his rather smug children sail amongst islands, alert to threat from the formidable Nancy and Peggy, teenage pirates in their own dinghy. Quite apart from the astonishing stirrings of sex unfulfilled that these books could evoke in the breasts of far distant schoolboys (and girls), Ransome sited many of these stories in the Lake District. By doing so he must also have ignited an equally strong longing for his Lakeland setting in the breasts of his young readers.

Many must have fallen in love with the large lake long before seeing one for the first time. (Today, with reservoirs everywhere, and more holiday travel, the exhilarating sight of a large body of water is familiar to all.)

ROMANCE IN THE VIEW

istory spells romance. Sir Walter Scott (amongst many others) built his home on the proceeds. But 'romantic' had and has meanings which, like that word 'nice', change with the age.

For the grand thinkers of two centuries ago, romantic could be defined more as a negative, an opposite to classical.

'Classical' notions reflected the lost ancient world of Greece and Rome, as recaptured, for example, in the paintings of Claude. His pictures were peopled by heroes and shepherds in scenery based on the Roman campagna with its marvellous mellow light. But there was more here than a nostalgia for antiquity. The classical world was seen as a world of certainty. Hero and shepherd both had a role in the drama, but both knew the part they must play. Idyllic scenery was the setting for the stately measures of their story.

This was rather different from today's holiday-snap fascination with ruins. It was rather an aristocratic, patriarchal attitude and it in fact echoed old English traditions. In the great castles and in the mansions of Elizabethan days, the retainers were part of the 'family'; lord and servant eating together in the Great Hall, for example. But by accepting their roles, even the brightest servants could rarely if ever become upstarts and dine at the high table.

In poems such as *Michael*, Wordsworth too had portrayed shepherds and the like. Though rustic, they were however described in their own right, as living people with valid feelings of their own and drama in their own lives. And here Wordsworth is a romantic.

For the classical man, the lot is cast; fate and role cannot be changed. The romantic still has a chance. He may pit himself against fate; he may fail. But at least his struggle is valid; he himself is an individual, worthy in his own right, no mere cipher.

Failure brings sadness – but this is a very different melancholy from the nostalgia for a lost classical world as shown in the pictures of Claude and Gaspard.

The romantic thrives on imagination and creativity, on mystery, too, and passion from the heart. He seeks the explanation of man – and nature.

The classical symbol of time past, of Arcadia Lost, is the stately colonnade and the cornucopia spilling purple grapes and other luscious fruits. The symbols of lost time for the romantic are ruins and ivy.

In the eighteenth and nineteenth centuries and the first part of the twentieth century there were plenty of both to be seen in Britain. The many different ruins of great abbeys or castles which we see today scraped clean, fenced and ticketed were then festooned with ivy in plenty. Trees would even grow from cracks. Ruins made a picturesque sight.

So it is worth hearing what that champion of the picturesque, William Gilpin, made of them: '. . . ruins are commonly divided into two kinds, castles and abbeys,' and 'The most beautiful species of architecture in which our ruins are composed is called the Gothic.'

Treating ruins simply as ornaments to the view is an attitude quite unlike the respect for history that our schooling and television programmes today teach us to assume is natural. Yet both he and we are in our different ways romantics.

Here is Gilpin again: 'It is not every man that can build a house who can execute a ruin. To give the stone its mouldering appearance, to make the widening chink run naturally through all the joints, to scatter heaps of ruin around with negligence and ease, are great efforts of art.' For the same reason he deplores the 'vandals' who restore ruins (in fact, he preferred British medieval architecture to that of Europe because more of it lay in ruins!).

A ruin became seen as such a positive bonus in the view that many were built – as follies crowning highspots. They took various forms, from castle keep profiles to simple isolated archways.

Many of these eyecatchers were in what came to be called Gothic style, which adopted both the pointed windows of the abbey and the battlements of the castle. It had nothing much to do with the real medieval buildings it was copied from – it was merely outside ornament, but it became the romantic answer to the classical colonnade of pillars.

Gothic was a style seen everywhere by Victorian times – town halls and semi-detached homes in the suburbs of the industrial towns, country mansions and railways stations. It has been said that 'Gothic gained the certainty of religion'.

In 1788 Hannah More, a writer of religious tracts amongst other things, was hoping to start a school for illiterates at Cheddar. A woman with her feet very much on the ground, her reaction to the famous natural gorge is revealing. The scenery was 'so stupendously romantic' that her 'imagination was delighted and confounded, was oppressed, and darted back a thousand years into the days of chivalry and enchantment at seeing hang over my head vast ledges of rock exactly resembling mouldered castles and ruined abbeys'. However, she thought that such emotions 'wind up the mind too high' for daily use; they were only suitable for poets or for the glory of God!

Moonlight, bats, owls, moss, gloomy pine trees, waterfalls, ruins – they were adopted as the furniture of the romantic (later often called Gothic) imagination. Tales as well as pictures played their part in feeding it. One such was *The Monk*, published in 1796.

The Abbot starts his downward path to rape and murder when he accidentally meets a woman disguised as a man in a grove in which stood 'a rustic grotto, formed in imitation of a hermitage. The walls were constructed of roots of trees and the interstices filled up with moss and ivy. Seats of turf were on either side and a natural cascade fell from the rock above. Buried in himself, the monk approached the spot. The universal calm had communicated itself to his bosom, and a voluptuous tranquillity spread languor through his soul. . . .'

The book is obviously going to be a good read. It echoed a growing delight in romantic visions and dreams of days gone by. Actual ruins made the dreams easier. Not that they suddenly leapt into view at this time – even Shakespeare in *Titus Andronicus* has a man of war, and a Second Goth at that, stray from the troop to gaze upon a ruinous monastery!

And if a real ruin could be brought into high romance, so much the better. Tintagel on the north coast of Cornwall is just one example. Legend says King Arthur was born here, and echoes of romantic Albion are easy to hear in the seas foaming at the foot of the cliffs below the castle ruins.

Poets such as Tennyson and Swinburne found it haunting. Little matter that the castle is Norman and Arthur not a real historical figure.

For us today, pleasure in ruins is a rather muted delight compared with theirs. Who can today accidentally come upon an *event*, such as a ruin by moonlight, where by chance someone is playing a flute – as happened once to Samuel Taylor Coleridge on a walking tour?

Sadly, our first-hand contact is cut down to daylight opening times. We tread neat gravel paths between neat trimmed grass, and the walls are bare. There are neither ivy, nor owls. With today's vast interest in the past, a major industry in its own right, things cannot be otherwise. But it is not the same.

So, the other message to be read into a pleasure in ruins is that they are not just eyecatchers adding something to the view. They can also evoke *feelings* – they are a kind of emotional drug. And if

the trumped-up folly could evoke the kind of sensations felt by Coleridge, could it not be possible to build the entire view to generate feelings? Indeed it could, and the art reached sophist-icated development in Britain, as we shall now see.

Above, Ruins of Holyrood Chapel by Louis Daguerre, 1824. Haunted moonlight indeed.

THE VIEW DESIGNED

A garden of Chaucer's time was a chatty affair, meant to be used. It was walled off from the outside world, and contained a good many different things in a small space. Highly scented plants were grown for nosegays – to combat the noxious stench of houses and streets – and for cooking. Food for thought lay in the choice of the flowers. Roses were popular; they represented love and charged the pergolas and arbours they decked with sexy innuendos. There were turf seats, damp to the bottom (wooden seats came later). There may well have been a lawn, a mini-meadow rather, its long grass brightened with white ox-eye daisies, purple pennyroyal and other blooms that grew wild in the fields.

As time went on, the walled seclusion of the garden remained, its internal intricacies multiplied. Entering it was like walking into a detailed tapestry. Alleys gave shaded walks; railings were painted emblematic colours. There were knots – entwined rows of scented, slow-growing thyme or rosemary – perhaps separated by coloured sand and sometimes enclosing plots of other herbs or flowers. Heraldic beasts could rage on the tops of their pillars like angry gnomes writ large. By Elizabethan times these had been replaced by horned moons and other symbols to smirk about.

By the late seventeenth century, garden ideas had been absorbed from places such as Holland. Such things as topiary in some places, a mania for tulips in another (in the story of gardening there is no one single plot!). The knot spawned the parterre, an elaborate geometrical pattern of low clipped box hedges usually occupying a flat terrace alongside the house. Here polite society walked, flirted, chatted scandal, did business.

In some places they walked further, for following the example of Versailles and other European palaces, some estates were being laid out with long canals and even a 'goosefoot' of straight, grand avenues radiating away across the park.

These promised novelty and interest, for amongst the regular spider's web of avenues and linking paths were studded fountains and other watery delights, arches, pavilions – each turn could hold a surprise. This was all in the European pattern, although nothing in Britain could match Versailles in scale.

Walking out onto the estate then became fashionable, which it had not been earlier. Samuel Pepys remarked how the wish to take the air had become a feature of life. The English weather helped here, not too hot to fever the brow, damp enough to grow refreshing greenery.

History of any kind is made of many strands. Charles II had at the Restoration saved a certain puritan John Milton from the revenge of the Royalists. As a poet, Milton was to become enormously influential. *Paradise Lost* published in 1667 told

> . . . *Of Eden, where delicious paradise*
> *Now nearer, Crowns with her enclosure green,*
> *As with a rural mound the champain head*
> *Of a steep wilderness, whose hairie sides*
> *With thicket oergrown, grottesque and wilde.*

('champain' means unfenced, open countryside)

Here was no exotic Eden, but a rather natural wild place which could by the sound of it be found in ordinary English countryside.

At the same time, worry was mounting about the future supply of trees in that countryside. For centuries there had been village coppice-with-standards management of woodland, a kind of rationing of the resource. But with a man-of-war of the time needing 2000 large timber trees, and Britain relying on her navy, there was concern.

In 1664, John Evelyn, diarist and contemporary of Pepys, published *Sylva, or a Discours of Forest Trees* – an influential book. One of his favourites was the hybrid lime, 'the proper and most beautiful for walks, as producing an upright body, smooth and even bark, ample leaf, sweet blossom, the delight of bees, and a goodly shade. . . .'

Sylva stimulated tree planting, and not only lime avenues. Soon, in 1682, the first plantation was set – of oaks in Windsor Great Park. 'The country wears a new face; everyone is planting their places. . . .' Planting trees became a fashionable thing to do.

There is one more strand to be woven in. At that time it was part of a wealthy heir's education to be sent abroad on the Grand Tour to Italy and back. Although he may have seen paintings by Claude and others hanging in the family home, Rome itself with its ancient columns was an eye opener (let alone the pretty women available for the evenings). Faced with its ruins, the pleasures, the magic light of the campagna, the Roman countryside, the classic past seemed only yesterday. Ancient Rome and Greece had the eighteenth century firmly in their teeth.

For those of romantic tendency, the journey across the Alps freshened it.

The scene was set. Very often the mansion itself was built anew or rebuilt (or even just refaced) in the columned 'Palladian' style first met in Italy. And the gardens and the estate were re-fashioned.

Those lines of Milton describing a natural Eden are inscribed on a hillside bench overlooking the grounds of Hagley Hall near Kidderminster. They directly inspired the way the estate below had been laid out, or that is what the poet, novelist and letter writer Horace Walpole believed. In his time Walpole (1717–1797) was a reliable guide to changes in taste and fashion.

It was becoming usual in Britain not only to plant up the inherited estate, but also to remodel it in a way very different from the formality that aped Versailles. This was now seen to have 'too much of art, all is formal, statues and vases sowed everywhere'. Intellectually now as well as politically, Britain had begun to scorn France with its despotic Court.

Britain began to see itself on the side of freedom; not yet the democracy we relish today, it was at least a land where there was contact between ruler and people. Looking back on the changes that took place in the park, they can be seen to be parallel – merging the cultivated authoritative world of the grand house with ordinary nature and the ordinary countryside around it.

For there seemed to be no need to shut out the countryside roundabout, rather the opposite. It was 'called in' as the poet Alexander Pope (Walpole's predecessor as yardstick of fashion) put it.

As it happens, earlier in 1712, the influential essayist Joseph Addison had advocated that '. . . fields of corn make a pleasant prospect, and if the walls were a little taken care of that lie between them, if the natural embroidery of the meadows were helped and improved by some small additions of art, a man might make a pretty landskip of his own possessions. . . .'

One useful device was the 'haha' – an odd name, supposedly from the delighted chuckles it evoked. It was a wittily simple way of doing without a confining wall. A ditch was dug instead, vertically faced with brick or stone on its inner side – cattle and commoners both found it an effective barricade. The haha was also an effective way of merging the older gardens around the house with the new-look estate beyond.

A new breed of expert, the landscape designer, became prominent. As with buildings, estates were often 'improved' – modernized by later designers fashionable in their own time. The well-known grounds of Stowe in Buckinghamshire are linked with the names of Sir John Vanbrugh, Charles Bridgeman (inventor of the haha), William Kent, Capability Brown!

Stowe and the other improved estates became studded with small buildings – the family mausoleum, or 'temples', often built in classical style. The round, arcaded Temple of the Sybil at Tivoli just outside Rome was often copied. These edifices were not simply charming eyecatchers in the view from the house or the gardens around it. They were meant to be visited (the estate was laid out in circuits) and when visited, were meant to evoke philosophic or other emotions.

Elsewhere, William Kent added ruins, and, in Kensington Gardens in London, dead trees to bring an air of pleasant melancholy. There is news that some even placed live hermits in their grottoes (but as the job meant being permanently engaged in thought for the benefit of any guest who might turn the corner, they were perhaps hard to find, and harder to keep).

Below, Aeneas at Delos, by Claude Lorrain, 1650's; a blueprint for Stourhead (see page 182) and many places else.

More seriously as Walpole said, 'Poetry, Painting and Gardening, or the science of Landscape will forever by men of Taste be deemed the Three Sisters, or the Three New Graces who dress and adorn nature.'

Stourhead Garden, a jewel of its kind, has been chosen as our VIEW 16; unlike most other estates it was designed by the owner himself and remains much as intended.

THE NATURAL LOOK

In England, the 'places', the estates, which were being re-fashioned were often old deer parks, hunting preserves. There, centuries of intensive grazing had produced a natural-seeming, rather open landscape, with expanses of closely cropped grass loosely set with trees.

The next development was the arrival on the scene of someone who would adopt this 'park' view and improve it. His name was Lancelot Brown. 'There are great capabilities here' he would announce with enthusiasm to prospective customers, hence his nickname 'Capability Brown'. In 1740 he was kitchen gardener at Stowe, but also showing the gentry, future clients, around the gardens.

He eventually redesigned well over 150 estates and became the Royal Gardener at Hampton Court. It was here that Hannah More visited him and he took her on a tour of his ideas. 'Now there [pointing] I make a comma and where a more decided turn is proper, I make a colon; at another part [where an interruption is desirable to break the view] a parenthesis – now a full stop.'

The vistas which have made Brown famous are each composed of nothing much else than sweeping turf, gentle slopes, clumps of trees and water. And, of course, the glorious cloud-capped skies of England. In fact they are seen at their best when the clouds mass overhead to match the bulk of the trees so carefully planted below. True, an occasional rotunda or temple (sometimes Gothic) or a boathouse might be seen, but by and large the view held only 'natural' things.

It was much like Burke's definition of the beautiful – gentle sweeps and curves. Even the lakes were serpentine, which happens automatically when a vale is dammed and the water fills the contours.

Included in the price was Brown's habit of bringing the park up to the mansion. The parterre and formal gardens were swept away, any coloured flowers were again put behind walls, and green grass grazed by deer lapped to the front door. Some of his work could be pure butchery: although he planted vast numbers of trees in clumps, he also felled ancient avenues, as being too formal. Around the Brown estate a belt of trees usually cut off the more distant view. Was 'nature' here too pure to be contaminated by the outside world?

It is interesting to ask *why* Capability Brown's natural look did become so popular. Was it a love of nature in its own right – before Wordsworth had explained how? Let's not try to lay the ghost, but to revive it with two conflicting possible explanations. First, the idea of 'liberty' – a scorn of French decadence and despotism, offering the possibility of fresh air between nobs and others – was at that time exhilarating. Such freedom could be seen not as just a lesson for human society, but as part of a greater respect for the real world, for individualism as well as for the whole of society (even perhaps for the peasantry), and also for nature. Trees, water, the movements of the clouds above were also worthy in their own right.

The second possible explanation is that with the increase in business wealth at this time any Tom, Dick or Harry could improve his holdings. Even small houses in Twickenham and other popular 'commuter' (by coach or horse) villages around London could adorn their grounds with a Stourhead grotto or a classic temple summerhouse. But only the really wealthy could transform the entire view from their front door in the way made fashionable by Brown. It only worked on the grand scale. It could be the snobbish thing to do.

The delight of history of any kind (and the basis of many incomes) is that there is never a last word.

Humphrey Repton (the first to call himself a landscape architect) took Brown's crown and reversed some of his predecessor's tendencies. He restored separate terraces to form a buffer between house and park. Though he disliked planting clumps on rises ('like bonnets') he too liked trees. He preferred, however, to cascade them down slopes rather than create Brown's commas, colons and full stops. He also used a greater variety of trees. He persuaded his clients with his 'Red Books' showing before and after views, which give us the chance to put ourselves in the minds of people of six or seven generations ago and see what they saw when admiring a view.

Brown had many detractors. One was Sir William Chambers who took a 'Chinese' line – he erected the pagoda in Kew Gardens, London. For Uvedale Price, Capability Brown was 'worse than ignorant. Anything he did is to be avoided.' Both he and Payne Knight were against Brown's 'clumping and belting'. But Payne Knight himself was so enthusiastic about the idea of the 'natural' that he once used a foreground of random boulders over the lawn, covered with brambles!

Thus Repton, though his successor, often stood as Brown's champion. So popular were the pair that their landscapes are no small part of today's countryside. Echoes are everywhere. Even seven trees atop a prehistoric burial mound, brushed into a porcupine by the winds sweeping across the downs, are in their way a memorial.

Below, from a Repton 'red book' – before (top) and after views – bound in red Morocco leather.

Today many of these classic landscape designs are in a sorry state. Apart from storms and natural disasters, they need upkeep, often expensive upkeep, just as any other kind of gardening. Few remain as their originators designed. And here too we have an

anomaly. Their designers could not see them in their prime, for trees take long to grow. We are the lucky ones.

In Victorian times, perhaps in reaction, the focus switched to colour. Rhododendron broke into the green clumps, while on a smaller scale gaudy ornamental bedding appeared – which still lives on in town parks, especially in seaside resorts. Later, the middle class 'cottage garden' was invented.

The noble attempt to bring nature into the grounds faltered. Instead the nature of the countryside gained its own respect.

But was it truly real nature that was seen in the countryside? Or were even the wildernesses as contrived in their way as any park?

THE STORY OF REAL NATURE

The countryside we are born to always seems natural. It comes as a shock to realize that home of nature though it may be, it is hardly natural at all. With few exceptions (such as cliff faces by the sea) man has had a hand in it all. Even the wildernesses are not what they seem.

The story begins with and after the ice age, when the warming of the ground meant that plants could grow. At first they were lowly growths, but in time trees appeared. No sooner was this wildwood in place, however, than the men of our first British farming communities were clearing it.

By Norman times woodland was decidedly patchy amongst the open ground, and it was being hard worked. Coppicing, charcoal burning, pasturing pigs and cattle, hunting with horns braying – people were bustling here, there and everywhere below the trees. These woods were not much like the old greenwood as we imagine it. Yet perhaps deep within the hunting forests enough of a feeling of wilderness did remain. Certainly the marvellous tales of Robin Hood, Maid Marion and the rest of the happy crew helped make the 'greenwood' seem the domain of freedom, a feeling which remains strong today. This is all very different from the outlook of medieval man. In his mind nature was hostile and the forest was a true wilderness, both moral and emotional, fit only for outlaws (which is what Robin Hood was).

In this context, what about our modern delight in the coloured woods of autumn? As might be guessed, admiration for the dying tints is a picturesque contribution to our senses. In the early eighteenth century, Alexander Pope notes that 'the very dying leaves add a variety of colours that is not unpleasant' – the fact of his mentioning it proving the novelty of the idea. Autumn became considered 'the painter's season'. One Sir George Beaumont thought there should be a brown tree in every landscape.

Copper beech, a garden-bred cultivar (cultivated variety) with handsome dark foliage, fitted the bill! It was one of the growing list of exotic trees to be seen on estates, joining such aristocrats as the Cedar of Lebanon, first grown in Britain 350 years ago.

The open countryside also saw many and varied changes. By and large, however, the English lowlands carry the marks of the 'Enclosures', seen in their neat grid of hedged fields, neat farmsteads and straight roads. Reaching a peak in Georgian times, innumerable private Acts of Parliament allowed the division and enclosing of the old, open, village lands.

What went was described by the Rev. James Tyler, writing of Northamptonshire in 1823. In his opinion, it was: 'distinguished by no beauty, a wide expanse of English soil; roughened by sluggish frost and strident winds the wide fields extended, and unbroken tracts strained and tortured the sight. . . . I have seen neighbouring districts stretching out their fields successively for twenty miles with no division. . . .'

Others, such as the poet John Clare, were to bemoan the loss of this openness, as we shall see.

But the delight of Britain is that each area of our countryside really has its own story. Such things as the way the barns are built can change by the village, certainly by the county. Everywhere ancient corners of countryside can be found, idyllically pastoral they seem. Some precious landscapes are seen in VIEWS 21, 23, 24 and 27.

They are precious, and their quiet beauty has in many ways been marred in recent years. Inevitable development in the shape of new roads, new buildings, power stations and power lines has scarred classic British views. Intensive modern farming has ripped out hedgerows to make larger fields for larger machinery; nor does farming have to acknowledge normal planning regulations in regard to giant sheds and other eyesores. Ancient woods have been clear felled to be replaced by ranked conifers.

The hedgerow elms which once clothed the lowland view and hid many of its scars, have been felled after succumbing to disease in the 1960s and have not been replaced.

Lastly, violent, tree-felling storms and other natural disasters from time to time strike at one region or another.

The wilderness areas – the mountains, moors and heaths – can also suffer visual catastrophes in the form of quarrying and conifer planting.

Today's landscape is very different from that which even our own parents knew when young. In fact, some writers point out that many parts of the English countryside of 1945, and certainly of 1939 before the start of the Second World War, would have seemed familiar to Queen Elizabeth the First. Some parts would even have been familiar to the Roman Emperor Claudius.

The Naturalist's View

BOX NINE

Amongst countryside writers have been some who kept nature dairies. Father of this school was the Reverend

Gilbert White. His letters to friends became *The Natural History of Selborne*, first published in 1789. When White was alive, the countryside was full of unsolved puzzles. Did swallows fly away in autumn or did they spend the winter in the mud of ponds, where indeed some were found? What were these unknown mice in the field? Popping them into a jar of brandy to preserve them, White described harvest mice for the first time in history! He makes a charming read.

Today, much of what puzzled him has been explained. A new science, ecology, has been bred.

So, one modern way of looking at a view is to see it as a patchwork of *habitats*. Our great-grandparents would have found the habitat a strange idea to spend much time on – all idea for nothing it seems – yet it helps us define what we see.

The word habitat itself simply means a living place, an area in which animals and plants live out their lives. A habitat is marked by the communities of plants which grow in it. That much is obvious, we know we are in a wood or on a heath by the vegetation around us. Similarly we expect certain animals to be associated with those plants. Nightingales nest and sing in woods, skylarks nest on open downland and sing above it – that too is obvious. But birds fly across one to the other. Out of the breeding season especially, the habitat boundaries for them become less marked.

However, for those caterpillars which eat oak leaves, exposure on a chalk downland is quick death. Not only is there no food (insects do not easily change their diet), but the tricks of camouflage and behaviour which protect them against predators in a wood fail them in the open grass. Within an hour or two the caterpillars will have had it.

So, from the viewpoint of an animal (or of a plant) a habitat has boundaries; and each type (species) of animal recognizes certain boundaries – a choice which is frequently as characteristic of it as its size, weight, shape and colouring and what it has for breakfast. For some animals (and plants) the wood is the universe; for others only part of their life may be spent within its confines.

Modern farming is a disaster for nature. It wipes smooth the variety which is part and parcel of a natural habitat. Being sprayed, the crops of modern grain and grass grow green in the fields, but nothing else grows. There are none of the many wild flowers which brightened old-fashioned corn fields and meadows. So there are no butterflies, few birds. Countryside green here betokens a sterile habitat.

Much the same goes for woodland. Oak woods are rich in wildlife, but plantations of sitka spruce and other foreign conifers are not. True, until they are shoulder high they do provide shelter (not food) for scrub-loving birds to nest, but in the end, they are as sterile as a barley field.

For wildlife, failing traditional habitats such as ponds in the fields (increasingly rare), old oak woods, old meadows and unploughed chalk downland, the remaining habitats are by and large the fringes – hedges, roadside verges, scraps of scrub on a slope too steep to plough.

Sadly, the sheer botanical and wildlife richness of old-fashioned countryside, so much part of the view of the past that it was taken for granted, is today largely found only in nature reserves and other protected places which have escaped modern 'improvement'.

Recent farming methods have also meant that the green of the countryside which has captivated innumerable poets and which keeps the view from the Malverns much as it looked centuries ago in Langland's time (see VIEW I), becomes in a way the vivid colour of deceit and betrayal. It may look much the same, but it is empty of real nature.

However, we are all children of our age. What we see when young is always the starting point. Tomorrow's landscapes with acres taken out of arable farming to reduce the grain mountains, with farm woods sprouting up and with new crops of many kinds will be rather different from those we enjoy today. . . .

NEW VISIONS OF THE VIEW

he changes wrought by the enclosures rippled through society at every level. The transformation of course was not simply of the view. An ancient way of country life was turned upside down. In many places a new breed of man took possession alongside the new breeds of livestock, a hard-headed yeoman farmer with his own farmhouse and barns standing proud amongst his own fields.

For those too poor to buy land or a tenancy, the prospect was bleak. In most cases they were stripped even of the traditional rights to graze in woods and common 'wastes'. To avoid starvation the choice was often a heartbreaking one: to be farm labourer hired at the yearly Michaelmas fair or to forsake the countryside to become a serf in the new workshops and factories of the town.

Some argue that those who did remain tied to the land even as farm labourers were better off; the improved farming meant that starvation was rare. Living conditions were still pretty appalling, however. There is a description of a Dorset village just over a hundred years ago where sewage ran down the high street and families slept four to a bed.

The poet John Clare saw the enclosures take place around him. Born on the fringes of the shires at Helpston in 1793, brought up in poverty, the son of a labourer, he nevertheless had published his first book of poems by the time he was 27.

> And note on hedgerow baulks, in moisture sprent,
> The jetty snail creep from the mossy thorn,
> With earnest heed, and tremulous intent,
> Frail brother of the morn. . . .

By now there was no shortage of poetry about the countryside – Wordsworth was getting into his stride – but here was a fresh voice.

John Clare had little interest in grand views and Great Designs. Nature, the countryside, was something to be loved tree by tree, flower by flower, beast by beast (he was especially fond of the sorely persecuted moles). For him the loss of the freely open countryside was enough of a heartache:

> Far spread the moorey ground a level scene
> Bespread with rush and one eternal green
> That never felt the rage of blundering plough
> Though centurys wreathed springs blossoms on its brow
> Still meeting plains that stretched them far away
> In uncheckt shadows of green brown and grey

Unbounded freedom ruled the wandering scene
Nor fence of ownership crept in between
To hide the prospect of the following eye
Its only bondage was the circling sky
One mighty flat undwarfed by bush and tree
Spread its faint shadow of immensity. . . .

Now. . . . Fence now meets fence in owners little bounds
Of field and meadow large as garden grounds
In little parcels little minds to please
With men and flocks imprisoned ill at ease. . . .

These paths are stopt – the rude philistines thrall
Is laid upon them and destroyed them all
Each little tyrant with his little sign
Shows where man claims earth glows no more divine
But paths to freedom and to childhood dear
A board sticks up to notice 'no road here'.

George Crabbe, slightly older, had also described the harsh reality of the countryside that was becoming so enthusiastically admired. A shepherd's life was not quaint

> *Can poets soothe, you when you pine for bread*
> *By winding myrtles round your ruin'd shed?*

. . . ask any hill farmer today for his modern version.

The view from the park was very different.

In literal terms, as the trees grew up in the hedges around the new enclosures, the countryside really did begin to seem like an extension to the park, wooded, delightful.

But the owner who could welcome this (and also allowed his estate to be landscaped in the new and 'natural' way) and who could earnestly respect art and life (and freedom) while walking its generous acres was also party to the most draconian game laws of all time. The Game Act of 1770 'layed on the lash' as William Cobbett put it. It was part of a tangle of legislation which brutalized the countryside, filling villages with spies. Poachers caught even with rabbits to feed their hungry children faced transportation; many were simply hung.

Jane Austen wrote some of the best-known of what could be called 'park' novels – using these country estates and their genteel life as settings. Sometimes she has her characters argue the toss. Edward Ferrars in *Sense and Sensibility*, for example: 'I like a fine prospect, but not on picturesque principles. I do not like crooked, twisted, blasted trees . . .'. He continues: 'I do not like ruined, tattered cottages. I am not fond of nettles, or thistles . . .'.

With mention of nettles and thistles Jane Austen here pokes fun at some extremes of picturesque viewmanship. Some, it seems, even grew them a 'purpose to lend true rusticity to their scene.

The point at issue here is that landscape now began to be used as a setting for literature. Some authors were (and are) more strongly authors of place than others.

Below, High Withens ruin as it was a few years ago at its most atmospheric. It has since been tidied up and had its roof removed – and with this went half its potency to prick the imagination.

For Emily Brontë, paradise lay in the empty moors around Haworth, Yorkshire. Here she set *Wuthering Heights*, perhaps basing the house on the now ruined farm of High Withens. 'Wuthering' was, in the words of her character Lockwood 'the significant provincial adjective descriptive of the atmospheric tumult to which its station is exposed in stormy weather. Pure, bracing ventilation they must have up there at all times. . . .'

The Haworth moors are still very much as they were when Emily Brontë roamed them. Her sister Charlotte wrote: 'Emily loved the moors. Flowers brighter than the rose bloomed in the blackness of the heath for her; out of a sullen hollow in a livid hillside her mind could make an Eden. She found in the bleak solitude many and dear delights; and not the least and best loved was liberty.'

It was Emily who tamed a merlin, a small wild falcon of the moors; the other family pets were dogs.

Wuthering Heights oozes with its setting. The setting enters everywhere. Even Heathcliff is 'an unreclaimed creature, without refinement, without cultivation; an arid wilderness of furze and whinstone . . .'.

Although we are now well-used to scenery being used as a setting (even thrillers rely as much on place as story), Emily Brontë's stormy moor is not simply the background to emotional storms, but has a symbolic role. Here is another example, Cathy describing Linton and herself:

'He said the pleasantest manner of spending a hot July day was lying from morning till evening on a bank of heath in the middle of the moors, with the bees humming dreamily about among the bloom, and the larks singing high up over head, and the blue sky and bright sun shining steadily and cloudlessly. That was his most perfect idea of heaven's happiness. Mine was rocking in a rustling green tree, with a west wind blowing, and bright, white clouds flitting rapidly above; and not only larks, but throstles, and blackbirds, and linnets, and cuckoos pouring out music on every side, and the moors seen at a distance, broken into cool dusky dells; but close by, great swells of long grass undulating in waves to the breeze; and woods and sounding water, and the whole world awake and wild with joy. He wanted all to lie in an ecstacy of peace; I wanted all to sparkle, and dance in glorious jubilee.

'I said his heaven would only be half alive, and he said mine would be drunk; I said I should fall asleep in his, and he said he could not breathe in mine. . . .'

Today the moor still seems to be untamed natural wilderness, as it seemed in the Brontës' day. But as we see in VIEW 25, there are plenty of clues proving that even it was created originally by man long centuries ago.

Thomas Hardy also placed his characters in forceful landscapes. In *The Return of the Native*, Eustacia flees to Rainbarrow, stumbling over 'twisted furze-roots, tufts of rushes, or oozing lumps of fleshy fungi, which at this season lay scattered about the heath like the rotten liver and lungs of some colossal animal . . .', a description of 'Egdon Heath' which John Clare might well have relished.

Hardy's heath was based on actual splendid wildernesses, wide sandy heathery wastes. These were mainly in Surrey and in Hampshire and in Dorset, which became Hardy's Wessex, as is explained and explored in VIEW 26. Today these wildernesses are fragmented: perhaps 50,000 acres in Dorset alone have gone since *The Return of the Native* was published in 1878.

While in the eyes of that notable traveller, William Cobbett, rich farmland made a day on his horse a joy, barrens – heaths – could make him stutter with anger. Celia Fiennes was also less than enthusiastic! Hardy, however, made the heath work for him, and indeed other Wessex landscapes too in his other novels.

In *Tess of the d'Urbervilles*, Tess at one stage arrives at a starveacre farm, passing a landscape empty of trees (even those in the hedges being hacked), where 'the stubborn soil around her showed plainly enough that the kind of labour in demand here was of the roughest kind'. Elsewhere, in the lush Frome valley with its rich watermeadows and contented cattle she 'heard a pleasant voice in every breeze, and in every bird's note seemed to lurk a joy . . . the irresistible, universal, automatic tendency to find sweet pleasure somewhere, which pervades all life, from the meanest to the highest, had at length mastered Tess . . .'.

Elsewhere: '. . . walking among the sleeping birds in the hedges, watching the skipping rabbits on a moonlit warren, or standing under a pheasant-laden bough, she looked upon herself as a figure of Guilt intruding into the haunts of Innocence. But all the while she was making a distinction where there was no difference. . . . She had been made to break an accepted social law, but no law known to the environment in which she fancied herself such an anomaly.'

Hardy's view of nature, as forceful as that of Wordsworth, is rather different. Wordsworth's nature offers a relationship with man. Thomas Hardy describes a nature indifferent to man.

These thoughts of Hardy's might seem worth a curse or two when you view such Wessex idylls as River Frome at Woolbridge. Why does Hardy have to fill it with human misery – and fictional at that?

On the other hand, this is may be nearer to the truth about the countryside than indulging in 'nature worship', which is what Wordsworth's ideas can all too easily become.

Emily Brontë and Thomas Hardy are just two examples of authors who use the countryside we see. As we gallop up to our own day, on the wave from the explosion of literature in the last 150 years, there are few paths untrodden, few views undescribed, few woods unexplored somewhere in one book or another. Few emotions or enthusiasms remain to be tried out in (and on) the countryside, with or without the earth moving at the same time.

Many have added to the growing list of real places made familiar through books. Hugh Walpole with his *Herries* novels gave tourists a soap opera of the Lake District where they spent such a happy holiday last year. Laurie Lee describes his birth-place so vividly in *Cider with Rosie* that it is hard not mentally to adopt it while you read. . . .

And it is not only a matter of us humans.

The now famous world of Ratty, Mole and Toad in Kenneth Grahame's *The Wind in the Willows* seems as real as any. After reading *Watership Down* by Richard Adams, you try to recognize the first rabbits you see. Truer to reality, Henry Williamson a while ago wrote *Tarka the Otter* and could without whimsy describe how a peregrine kills a pigeon. Read Ted Hughes, modern Poet Laureate, on fish and fishing. . . .

However, the change has not simply been that we are now used to more settings, topics and descriptions. The way we see the countryside in our mind's eye has also changed.

For since Wordsworth's day man has usurped nature as the ultimate power on earth. Catastrophe in the shape of nuclear winter or global warming is now firmly in the hands of man. The mental adjustment has been aided by people such as Charles Darwin, whose theory of evolution published as *The Origin of Species* in 1859 proved, to the consternation of Victorian church-goers, that man was not a separate creation but a part of nature.

Today nature plays audience to man. Not only novelists and their readers but all of us plunder the countryside and in many ways. Very popular nowadays is raiding it for a lonely place, although a place cannot be lonely – and it is in any case quite familiar to the locals.

In the 1930's there were already weekend traffic jams (and train excursions and bicycle outings) – the summer Sunday traffic jams are worse today. The countryside is now news in the papers. Television too has arrived, to catch even those who don't read much and don't think much one way or the other about trees and grass. Most countryside and wildlife programmes are now immensely popular with audiences of millions. We are now the experts on everything from sheep dog trials to the habits of spiders to the fight to preserve the wild Caithness boglands. Seeing it all on TV, the library of *information* now lodged with us is vast.

In these new circumstances, could any view be voted The Best Traditional British View? It seems that maybe one does still fit the bill.

THE PERFECT PASTORAL VIEW

'He makes me call for my greatcoat and umbrella,' said Mr Fuselli, elected Keeper of the Royal Academy. 'He' was John Constable, whose weathery paintings have something in common with chalk and swans. They are all things that almost *everybody* can recognize and name.

Constable loved water. He himself wrote in a letter (and he was a hurried and copious scribbler): '. . . the sound of water escaping from Mill dams, so do Willows, Old rotten Banks, slimy posts, & brickwork. I love such things. . . . As long as I do paint, I shall never cease to paint such Places. . . .' In *The Haywain*, perhaps the picture most likely to be up on sitting-room walls across the nation, cart and horses stand splashily in the river facing across to Willy Lott's house.

Below, The Haywain, by John Constable, painted in 1821.

Through his paintings, skies became a romantic symbol in their own right – rainbows were especially important. For him they meant 'dewy light, freshness, the departing shower, with the exhilaration of the returning sun.'

Constable was born in 1776 and bred in the flat, unemphatic farmland of the Suffolk–Essex borders. 'I associate "my careless boyhood" with all that lies on the banks of the Stour; these scenes made me a painter, and I am grateful . . .'. Indeed his famous large paintings, his six-footers, are in a way souvenirs, nostalgic memories of that Dedham childhood. This resulted from the course his life took.

He showed enough talent to enrol as a student at the Royal Academy Schools in London in 1800, but his genius did not emerge for some time. He visited various places – including the north, where he did some picturesque pictures of sublime crags! Later he was to find mountains oppressive. However, during the early 1800s he spent much time back at his birthplace, making careful studies direct from nature, eventually making oil sketches from nature, which broke new ground. (It was during this period, around 1812, that rainbows began to fascinate him.)

Dashed and dashing, these sketches captured movement in the view – the clouds racing across the sky, the tumble of water at a weir, the sudden shine of the sun on a distant cornfield. 'I live almost wholly in the fields, and see nobody but the harvest men' he wrote in 1815. His art was 'to be found under every hedge and in every lane'.

They are not his more familiar pictures, but they are advanced works of art in their own right. These were the pictures that anticipated the breakthrough in art made by the French Impressionists.

Later Constable moved to London and tackled his six-footers. In his studio, he would paint a quick picture, sometimes based on open-air sketches. The composition thereby decided, he was ready to start the final version of the paintings so well known and loved today – *The White Horse* (1812), *The Haywain* (1821) and the *Cornfield* (1826) among them. A telling comment on them was made by his daughter when he took her back to his birthplace. 'When I told her we were in Suffolk – she, O no, this is only fields . . . .'

Although they seem such *accurate* pictures, with a cosy familiarity for us today, they are not, of course. Many have a viewpoint from 20 feet above ground! Others show vistas of a vale which cannot today and could not then be seen from any one place: Dedham Church moved around! The details too, of mildewed stumps, raggedy banks, a quaint old-fashioned tumbledown-ness about it all, is a whole world away from today's river-engineering.

Is it a countryside we would all secretly prefer? Concoctions of paints and imagination though they may be, they sometimes seem as achingly familiar as those blue remembered hills of Housman. For many, England is truly England in *The Haywain*.

Both Constable and his contemporary Turner had admired Claude and Richard Wilson ('he looked at nature entirely for himself' said Constable). Both then veered onto their own destinies. Turner became increasingly romantic. His paintings based on his observations of dawns, storms and other things verged towards *abstractions*. This too was new.

In this Turner set himself apart. His work was an early augury of 'art for art's sake', something which we take for granted today. By which is meant the use of catches of colour, shape and form to express (or lead or cheat the mind into) reactions, responses, feelings. In the process the picture may seem to lose contact with reality – that is, with what our own eyes see. It doesn't look anything like, in other words.

Constable died in 1837, Turner in 1851. But their steps towards 'modern art' were not followed up. Instead other things happened in the countryside painting of the time.

Ruskin trumpeted, against Salvator Rosa for one: 'a man accustomed to the strength and glory of God's mountains . . . can scarcely but be angered when Salvator has him stand still under some contemptible fragments of splintering crag.' He believed that nature does not need stage-managing to reveal infinite truths, and as every painting could teach a lesson, what was needed was to get down exactly what nature was showing.

The Pre-Raphaelites did show every leaf and twig! But there were other currents. Unlike novelists such as Charles Dickens, Victorian artists seemed loth to tackle visions of the mushrooming towns and industry of the time. Even someone of the calibre of Whistler painted atmospheric townscapes from memory – invented.

Nooky-and-cranny cottagey paintings filled the studios. So did vast views of Highland hills. Countryside became sheer escapism.

It is unfair to think of British artists of the time as ostriches with their head in the sand, but certainly the fresh air (and colour) brought by the French Impressionists seemed to pass them by. Later, the vision of the Post-Impressionists, of Cézanne for example, had more effect – it was clear that a landscape painting could be built upon a visual *and* mental structure.

The shattering effect of the First World War resulted afterwards in many 'artists' colonies', recapturing not only spirits but sometimes nerves too, deep in the countryside. Some British painters were now seeing what lay around them in a new way, seeing with the eyes and feeling with the mind a new structure in their beloved landscapes. Landscape for many artists was becoming a personal experience, an expression of themselves.

It was also becoming a private experience for most of us, as we have seen, but artists could capture what this meant for others to share.

And today, you can be sure, someone is doing the landscape in milk bottle tops.

THE SEA, THE SEA

The sea view merits a book in its own right. It is so very different from the land that even an edge of it on the horizon changes the prospect.

Appreciating the beauty of the sea and the coast is largely a legacy from the Romantics. For people in earlier times, the sea meant peril for the traveller, even on a short crossing to France, and even more for those who made a living from it. A century ago, a year could see 2000 wrecks, many of them drowning the crew.

But attitudes changed. Seaside resorts offering carefully clad bathing for the sake of health became popular in Regency days. The sheer scale of the cliffs of the rocky coast, their measured repetition into the distance and the added frisson of their evil reputation meant that some places became immediate meccas for poets and others of romantic mind.

Below, atmospheric Tintagel Castle on the north Cornish coast. Such ruins became tourist meccas in Victorian times.

VIEWS TWENTY-EIGHT & TWENTY-NINE

Tintagel was one. Steep drops surround the castle ruins, the legendary birthplace of King Arthur. Our chosen cliffscape, VIEW 28, is further up the coast from Tintagel. Here the restless Atlantic thunders, and its roar is carried inland like a dying sailor's cry.

There are also the remains of a Celtic monastery on Tintagel – there has always been a strong link between early religion and the sea, and we see this in our VIEW 29, on a coastline of very different appearance.

In one other important way, a fine coastal view is rather different from a fine view inland. More likely than not it is *protected*. Many fine inland views do have protection, but not all that merit it by any means. We see on page 88 what is implied in protecting a view.

THE LUNAR LANDSCAPE

'Slagheaps have as big a monumentability as any mountains' so said Henry Moore, sculptor extraordinary to the world.

aniel Defoe and other early travellers saw little wrong with industry in the view (see page 21). Of course, in those now distant days the British countryside was scarcely changed by industry. It was the exception – it nowhere occupied the whole prospect. Nor was there any dereliction. Industry meant a new busy-ness, it was a novelty bringing welcome wealth to many different people.

Furthermore, some aspects of industry make a fine view in their own right – whether judged by our eyes today or by the yardstick of those who did try to define views in the past. Even William Gilpin, that apostle of picturesque scenery, could admire industry.

A railway viaduct swinging out across a valley can be *beautiful* – certainly as elegant an addition to the landscape as any imitation Greek temple.

Industry can also be *sublime*. The poet John Clare already thought that 'to a knowing eye, a quarry is as beautiful as nature'; but the vast slate quarries at Dinorwic in Snowdonia rival even Gordale Scar, that classic of the natural sublime (see VIEW 7). The cooling towers of our power stations have a sheer height, shape and massive weight with which they rule the view around them.

And *picturesque*? The empty shells of mine engine sheds can match a castle for atmosphere. Industrial archaeologists now have long lists of protected sites. Canals are reckoned as attractive as rivers. Dereliction can add charm to abandoned chalk pits in Kent, gravel pits in Berkshire and iron workings in the Midlands.

Last century, scenery was both being blanketed and created by industry. By exploiting the cheapest supplies of water or coal or whatever, industry did localize itself. A whole world was created within a tight area, a world with its own way of life and its own landscape – and a landscape which could be as immediately recognizable as any of the 'natural' landscapes in this book.

One example is seen in our VIEW 30; others are to be seen in South Wales, South Yorkshire. Others, such as countryside of Stoke on Trent, Burslem and the other 'five towns' of the Potteries have had face-lifts and become greened in recent years.

George Orwell (who first coined the phrase 'lunar landscape') detested slagheaps not simply for their ugliness, but because they

were simply planless dumpings. He likened them to the emptying of a giant's dustbin.

The issue raised here is really that of *contempt*, of development powered solely by profit for its own sake heedless of its effect on the quality of life of its people. Both Ruskin and Wordsworth had hated industry, not only for its effect on the scenery, but as much for its effect on the people. Orwell felt the same, and Charles Dickens.

Possibly, if Victorian industry had adopted a different social mode, mine tips would not have received such a bad press!

Above, Coalbrookdale at night, by de Loutherbourg, 1801. Industry seizing the Romantic imagination.

SAVING THE VIEW

ast century's industrial boom created a new energetic class in society – the factory managers and their like. Another result of the boom was squalor for those who worked on the factory or mill floor. In 1820, life expectancy in Salford with sewage running raw in the streets was only 20 years. This was not squalor that the new middle classes could ignore. The first cholera epidemic struck the slums in 1830. By 1840 typhus was also raging. Such diseases spread.

As Dr Samuel Johnson said, the prospect of execution clears a man's mind wonderfully. The emergency forced changes, and by the end of Queen Victoria's reign industrial towns with more go-ahead local government (another Victorian innovation) were supplying their people with things we take for granted today – sewage disposal, clean drinking water, also public libraries, education for all (in primary schools at least) and town parks.

In 1895, the National Trust was founded, to take both property and land into protective care. Although not a government agency, it can ony be stripped of its holdings by individual Act of Parliament.

Normally, however, the open countryside which can spring the unexpected view on even the most bored of car passengers is not under such benevolent, tree-counting ownership.

Concern for it was mounting rapidly in the first part of this century. The threat was not simply from industry and had much to do with the growing scale of its popularity.

Not only were more people than ever using the countryside for holidays and relaxation, but towns sent tentacles of ribbon development out along the newly tarmacked roads. It seemed only a matter of time before London, already gobbling miles a year, joined up with Brighton.

At the same time there was social engineering of a kind. Some dreamed of brave new worlds standing amongst fields; new suburbs and new towns were created – greenly spacious places with houses and factories, but they too ate up the acres.

It was not until the end of the Second World War that development was brought under control. The very name of the Town and Country Planning Act of 1947 spoke for itself – town, countryside and planning were for the first time joined as one. The idea of 'green belts' around cities was germinated.

Totalling Up Protected Views

BOX TEN

The membership of the *National Trust* is now over 1½ million and it now manages around 1% of the total land area of England and Wales and Northern Ireland (Scotland has its own National Trust). Its gardens and parks are maintained as they stand. Its farmland is run on modern terms; it is Trust policy to accept new property only if the estate can generate income for it. However, in some areas such as the Golden Cap estate in Dorset, traditional farming is subsidized to maintain the old field patterns and their wildlife.

Green Belts have been established around London, Tyneside, York, West Riding cities, Sheffield–Rotherham, Merseyside, Manchester, Wirral–Chester, Stoke on Trent, Nottingham and Derby, Birmingham and Coventry, Gloucester and Cheltenham, Bristol and Bath, Oxford, Cambridge and the Hampshire Coast.

The *National Parks* of England and Wales are neither parks nor national, but areas of great scenic beauty within which development is subject to special planning controls – the aim being to retain productive communities *and* scenery at the same time. National funds may be available. Our present 10 National Parks occupy about 9% of England and Wales. Scotland does not have National Parks, but about 6% is covered by similar Area Orders.

Areas of Outstanding Natural Beauty cover around 9% of the area of England and Wales. Unlike National Parks, they may have local planning restrictions but no national grants.

There are now over 2000 *Nature Reserves*. Some are officially owned, by national and local authorities, others by voluntary groups such as the county Nature Conservation Trusts. They total over a million acres. By protecting a wood or an area of old downland, a nature reserve also protects the view. In addition there are some 4000 Sites of Special Scientific Interest (SSSI), totalling some 3½ million acres, in which proposed changes have to be notified to the Nature Conservancy Council and agreed in advance.

In addition, views can be protected on *Commons*, which are privately owned, and open under byelaws or (as with Epping Forest) Acts of Parliament. Council-owned commons are usually freely open to the public.

Shortly afterwards National Parks were established in England and Wales. Then Areas of Outstanding Natural Beauty were designated. Many more nature reserves were established – by protecting a wood or an area of old Downland they also protected the view.

In recent years the reclamation of derelict land has transformed the Potteries; in South Yorkshire some once-black tips are now green and have sheep grazing on them. Local and national tree-planting programmes are now commonplace. Many of these are under the auspices of the Countryside Commission, for purely visual reasons. Landowners, farmers and foresters all plant trees for other reasons – but their plantings too are often 'landscaped'.

Anomalies remain, however. Roads seem to take precedence over much else. Electricity pylons are not subject to normal local planning control, not even in green belts; nor are modern farm buildings subject to such control. A good many giant silos and shelter sheds damage many views – unlike 'traditional' buildings they do not match their locality. And farming is still completely out of control as regards the protection of hedges, trees and woods – without which the view often loses all charm.

'Is then no nook of English ground secure from rash assault. . . .' So trumpeted William Wordsworth against the proposed Kendal–Windermere railway. But assault lies in the eyes of the beholder. Odd changes take place. In the Lake District National Park, white static caravans are now painted green, while white cottages are admired. It was Wordsworth who held that white cottages were eyesores on the view.

As we have seen in our journey through the length and breadth of Britain, the view of the view changes with the age. The views of tomorrow would make another book.

KEY TO MAPS

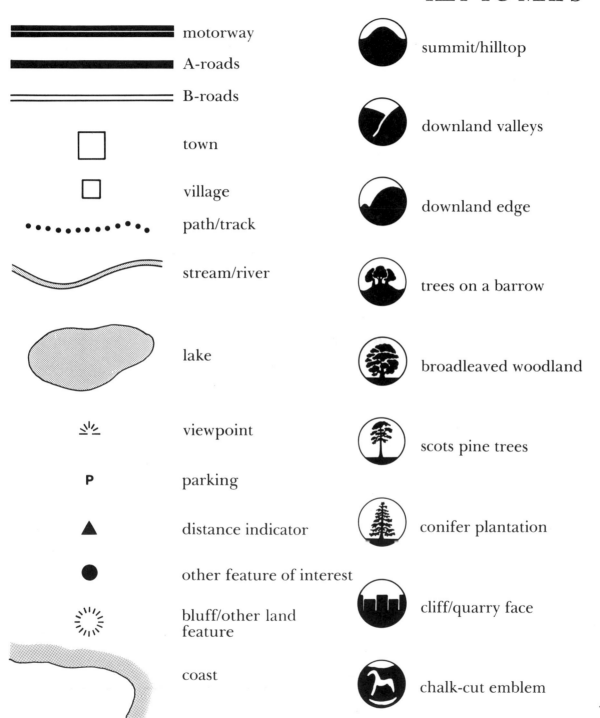

motorway

A-roads

B-roads

town

village

path/track

stream/river

lake

viewpoint

P parking

distance indicator

other feature of interest

bluff/other land feature

coast

summit/hilltop

downland valleys

downland edge

trees on a barrow

broadleaved woodland

scots pine trees

conifer plantation

cliff/quarry face

chalk-cut emblem

THE VIEW THAT DREAMS ARE MADE OF

The view from the ridge of the Malvern Hills is chosen for three reasons. First, it is outstanding, stretching far in every direction. Second, when you stand here to admire the view, you may stand on some of the oldest rocks in England and Wales. And third, the land below the hills also seems touched with magic. These views are such as to dream over. These Malvern Hills (surely one of the most evocative place names in the English language) have conjured visions for many people, a poet to rival Chaucer and a world famous composer among them.

The paths on these hills can freely be walked at any time of day or night.

The Malvern Hills are a miniature mountain range, some six miles long, and as that early traveller Celia Fiennes said 'in a Pirramidy fashion on the top'.

In her day they were known as the English Alps; and to be sure they offer the finest ridge walks in England. The difficult choice is where to head for amongst these 40 square miles of outstanding natural beauty, and which of the many well-marked paths to choose. But visit first one of the two prime viewpoints: Worcestershire Beacon 1994 feet high, from which we take our VIEW 1 or Herefordshire Beacon at 1114 feet, contoured by 'British Camp', an Iron Age hillfort.

This 'camp' is one of the most impressive in the country. It presents a splendid silhouette both from 'Elgar's Route' and (especially) when seen on the approach from Ledbury (recommended). From Chance's Pitch it spreads its deep ramparts across the slopes ahead. See also the dreamlike pastoral scenery of fields and brooks north of Chance's Pitch.

Parking is pay and display, but is easy to find everywhere on the Malverns, often in the now disused quarries, which are frequently landscaped. This is the work of the Malvern Hills Conservators, set up a century ago to protect local commons rights, and later to protect the actual scenery of the hills.

Gullet Quarry is recommended: here a wide pool reflects a towering cliff, a rock face worth a second glance, for here is something very unusual. Thrusting *upright* are slabs of extremely hard ancient Pre-Cambrian rock, amongst the oldest to be found in England and Wales. Alongside nudge deep *horizontal* layers of much younger rock. This is an impressive geological spectacle.

Though hard, this old rock apparently contains cracks; the rain drips and runs down

1

through countless thin fissures to emerge here and there as springs, and welcome springs they are. Their water is cool, and very pure, for the rock is too hard for its minerals to dissolve. You will often see a car parked by a handy spring, rows of plastic bottles alongside. And why not, when you realize that the water most of us drink has been recycled through several kidneys already. It isn't only the Queen who likes her Malvern Water.

And – oh yes, when driving here beware of sheep wandering from the slopes above: the notice STRAY ANIMALS means what it says.

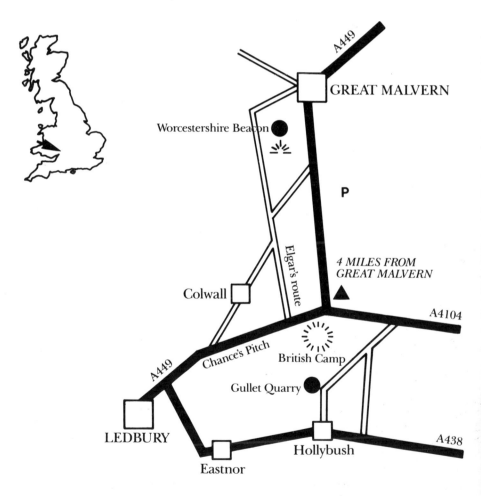

OS grid reference of viewpoint   SO 769452

The view south from Worcestershire Beacon

Here the Malvern Hills show themselves to be a splendid, narrow switchback of summits spectacularly heaved up from the country-side around. For such modest height, the views are generously sweeping. From the tops, the view stretches to the Brecon Beacons and the Black Mountains in Wales, north to the Wrekin and the Clee Hills, to the east to the Cotswolds lying far across the Severn Vale, to the south to the estuary of the River Severn. The western slopes that we see here are gentler than the steep eastern side.

High on the tops there is open grassland with some heather and bilberry. These tops must have been open for a good long time. The name Malvern comes from the Welsh words *moel-bryn*, meaning the 'bare hills'.

Over the flanks kestrels hover riding the updraughts. It is rarely that you can watch these birds from above as you can here.

Scrub and woodland blanket the lower slopes.

Over these clinging woods, rather pretty countryside can be seen, clear washed as if a shower had just that moment passed. Here lie deeply hedged fields, some edged by brooks running from the springs. This kind of countryside has an ancient feel to it; and indeed may have little changed its appearance for hundreds of years.

It might indeed seem familiar to William Langland who was born hereabouts. He lived at the time of Geoffrey Chaucer, and like Chaucer wrote poetry, the narrative *Piers Plowman*. Falling asleep by a stream amidst the pleasant lands below British Camp, the poet dreamed visions of the 'fair field full of folk'. Although its motif is the struggle to gain Christian salvation, *Piers Plowman* is still entertaining (in modern translation) in its freshness and satire.

The Malverns can be dramatic. A low sun adds a sharp cutting edge to the curves of the British Camp, a splendid warrior summit. It was this sight, incidentally, that stimulated the com-poser Sir Edward Elgar to write *Caractacus*, among the first of his more famous works. He too was born nearby, and loved playing on these hills. He returned in later life to write masterpieces at their skirts. Such hills, to be sure, can conjure dreams.

British Camp is haunted with other memories. It was built by Celtic warrior tribes in the centuries before the Roman arrival. The Welsh patriot Owen Glendower is said to have rallied his men here. In later ages it was the site of a beacon, part of a national network of warning fires. When in 1588 these beacons were lit as warning of the Spanish Armada, 12 counties saw the fires shining out from the tops of these Malvern Hills.

THE ANATOMY OF THIS BEST VIEW

• *A high viewpoint, giving a vast panorama. This 'Beacon' is 1394 feet (425 metres) above sea level. Many paths criss-cross the high ground in front of us, giving miles of fine view walks.*

• *A view across patterned, ancient countryside. Here we overlook countryside which may be much the same as when William Langland dreamed six centuries ago.*

• *The bonus of ancient remains and tales. Good views can always be seen by following the Red Earl's Dyke or Shire Ditch, running along the crest of these hills. Dug in 1287 it is still 12 feet deep in places. Its purpose – to solve an endless boundary dispute between the red-headed Earl of Gloucester and the Bishop of Hereford. The slope is on the Earl's side to prevent straying deer jumping back to the Hereford lands! And in the distance, the warrior 'British Camp' of Herefordshire Beacon.*

95

THERE IS MORE about Langland's narrative poem, and of the creation of Elgar's music, on page 14.

In Box 2 we see how rock underlies the view.

Who was the first person to climb a hill, just to see the view? On page 12 we begin our detective hunt for clues to explain why today we like a good view.

GAZETTEER ONE

TEN MORE TOP BEACON VIEWS

Here are wide, all-round views, from the sites of Armada beacons which may remain as piles of stones. The countryside below (or afar) is also first-rate. Most of these viewpoints are all a short walk from parking.

1) Beacon Hill, *988 feet, near Danby, North Yorkshire looks over the North York Moors and much else.*

2) Pendle Hill, *1831 feet, near Burnley, Lancashire. A beacon hill, and a hill noted for its witches in times past. Climbed by George Fox; who then went on to Sedbergh and spoke for three hours to 1000 seekers and went on to found the Society of Friends (Quakers).*

3) Alderley Edge, *600 feet, near Wilmslow, Cheshire. The medieval beacon remains as a pile of stones.*

4) Beacon Hill, *912 feet, SW of Loughborough, Leicestershire – fine views over Charnwood Forest.*

5) The Wrekin, *1334 feet, S of Wellington, Shropshire. Although a stiffish climb is needed to reach the old Armada beacon site on the top, this is the most all-encompassing viewpoint in Britain. Parts of 15 counties may be glimpsed.*

6) Wandlebury Ring, *on the Gog Magog Hills outside Cambridge, only 234 feet, but the view stretches far across the flat Cambridge and Suffolk lands, starved of hills.*

7) Ivinghoe Beacon, *807 feet, Buckinghamshire, offers an astonishingly wide panorama to the north. This is also the end (or start) of the Ridgeway Long Distance Route.*

8) Dunkery Beacon, *1705 feet, near Minehead, Somerset. Distance in every direction, and closer to hand a panorama of combes and contours and the sparkle of water.*

9) Butser Hill, *888 feet, S of Petersfield, Hampshire. The highest point of the chalk South Downs; a starfish of combes gives an impression of sheer bigness. A beacon stood atop it.*

10) Ditchling Beacon, *813 feet, near Brighton, Sussex – even the road up yields breathtaking views, including glimpses of the white cliffs of Seaford Head.*

But none from Wales, or Scotland? Well, which would you choose? There is no shortage of views fantastic from the hill roads.

SEEN FROM THE ANCIENT TRACK

PILGRIMS' WAY, BOX HILL

The counties of Britain are stitched with many old and historic tracks. One of the most ancient of them lies along the slopes of the North Downs. Routes such as these generally kept to the high ground, and so can be relied on to yield a whole succession of fine views today. Our view is not from the top of Box Hill, but from where the old path follows its flanks. Here we truly do walk in the steps of time.

Much of Box Hill is National Trust land, and freely open. Parking is pay and display.

Box Hill bluffly lords a cut through the chalk of the North Downs. The River Mole did the job, from here flowing north to the Thames.

Chalk (perhaps the only rock that certainly everybody can recognize and name) is soft, and exposures tend to slump down as they weather and quickly green over. But the face above the Mole is so steep that in places it remains white like a fresh graze.

The white scar is scattered with dark scrub, itself of great interest. Yew grows here, but also box – and Box Hill is one of the few places in Britain where native box grows wild. Well-known as hedging shrub from gardens, it is an evergreen with nostalgically scented leaves.

Box has a dense, fine wood which carves well. It was used for chess pieces amongst other things, but blocks of it were also used for wood-engraving, the main method of illustrating books and pamphlets in recent centuries.

One of the masters of the art was Thomas Bewick (1755–1828). His own success had a direct effect on Box Hill, for it meant that no fashionable book was complete without engraved illustrations of some kind. So do we blame him for abetting the wholesale stripping of the box trees, even though he was famous for his country scenes? There are far fewer now than in his day.

On the road up to the top, we pass many yews standing solitary in steep pastures. We have here one of the few places in southern Britain which sports a mountain road. Real hairpin bends through shadowed woods of yew, hawthorn, cherry and beech face the car on the way to the top.

On the top of Box Hill, the chalk is overlain with a clayey soil containing many flints. Woodland grows here, mainly beech, and carpeted with bluebells in spring. Car parking lies hidden away amongst the trees. Also hidden away up here is a fort, one of a chain built early last century to protect London

2

should Napoleon have chosen to invade.

The summit look-out point has a fine view, but no view guide (the white triangle in front of it is an Ordnance Survey Trig Point).

The 'North Downs Way' passes up here, but walk down to join the old Pilgrims' Way. This ancient track is not on the crest, where the clay-with-flints make sticky going in winter, but on the dry chalk flanks. Both North Downs Way and ancient track meet, however, at the River Mole, which they cross with stepping stones.

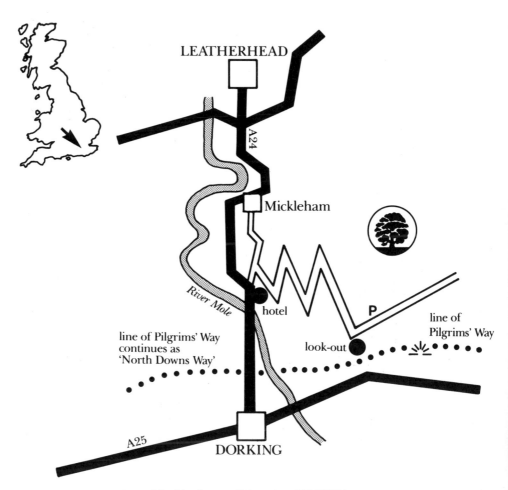

OS grid reference of viewpoint   TQ 180511

*View along the line of the old Pilgrims' Way on the
southern flanks of Box Hill.*

A prehistoric track originated at the cliffs of Dover and Folkestone
and then swung inland following high ground up to the North
Downs. It then led on to Salisbury Plain.

Giving a dry line above the tangled wet wilderness of forest and
swamps of the lower ground, this route was most probably
regularly used by our first farmers, the people of Neolithic times
who began to settle here in Britain around 6000 years ago.

In those early days, these tracks were not the hedged paths we
see today, but widely open; and not so much well-defined paths as
directions that warriors, tinkers and herdsmen and their cattle
and sheep took across dry ground. It was not until Roman times
that roads to compete with them were laid out in the valleys.

In time, as valley towns and villages grew, old tracks such as this
lost their importance. Many remained in use, however, as drove
ways. Along them the farm stock was walked across country to
market (as had to be done everywhere in the days before railways).

Salisbury Plain, with its stone circles of Stonehenge and Avebury was a religious centre in prehistoric times matching in
importance any in Europe. Echoes lingered: this old route became
known as the Harrow Way or Hoar (Holy) Way. The stretch from
Winchester to Canterbury on which Box Hill lies became known
as the Pilgrims' Way, for the journey to the shrine of St Thomas à
Becket in Canterbury.

In those days, the view south from Box Hill would have been
across thickly wooded countryside which clothed and hid small
towns and villages. Today, sprawls of suburbs lie scattered below.
Both Dorking and Reigate are queens of London's commuter
country.

If you get tired of living in the midst of bricks and traffic, an
overview helps soothe the troubled breast. People in large numbers regularly drive (sometimes walk) up here to sit and relax, and
leave worries and the mortgage behind.

For all of us, views are part of the ritual of time off. But it was
not always so. In the past, a view could stir stronger feelings.

Indeed, here are some less than immortal lines written by one
eager Edward Beavan in 1772, once he had got the customary
larks and nightingales out of the way:

> *Beneath you chalky Hill, see REIGATE's town;*
> *Lo, ruins tell its abject venal state,*
> *Cot[tage] after cot in sad succession drop*
> *For there despotic reigns the mouldering power.*

THE ANATOMY OF THIS BEST VIEW

● *An ancient track. Here the
'Pilgrims' Way', part of the
Harrow or Hoar (Holy)
Way.*

● *An ancient feel. Compared
with the age of this route, the
hedges in the view are
youngsters. They are dated in
centuries while the track is
thousands of years old.
Though many lengths of the
Pilgrims' Way are hedged,
we here have something of its
ancient character. In its
heyday the path would have
braided itself out across the
hillside, then entirely open.*

*These hillsides have never
been ploughed. So here you
walk admiring the view,
surrounded by wild flowers.*

● *Lavish views. Here the
view extends to the South
Downs, the cousin of these
North Downs.*

101

In his day it was the fashion amongst some poets to climb to a view to pontificate on the world below.

THERE IS MORE about the way views stirred poetic breasts on page 16 and about hill poets in BOX 3.

GAZETTEER TWO

MORE ANCIENT TRACKS

Valleys were generally marshy and well-nigh impassable in prehistoric times; lowland settlement was by lake or river highways. The higher ground was often first settled – and the fact that these tracks cleverly maintain the high ground with its extensive views is a sign of their age.

Today many authentic ancient tracks have been linked with lesser footpaths and bridle paths to form Long Distance Routes for walkers.

1) The old road crossing the Corrieyairack Pass on the way from Fort Augustus to Laggan Bridge is one of several known as General Wade's Military Road *– he improved them after the Highland uprisings of 1715. The first to benefit from this one was Bonnie Prince Charlie, who trod it at the start of the '45 rebellion.*

2) Many border routes were ceaselessly used down the centuries, not least when the Scottish borders were a home-grown Wild West, with cattle rustling the way of life. The Romans would have found these tracks ready made for their own advance. Clennell Street *is one, leading north from Alwinton to Wholehope.*

3) The old Craven Way *crosses the slopes of Whernside in North Yorkshire from Dent south to Ingleton. It runs sandwiched between white stone walls.*

4) Blackstone Edge, *west of Ripponden, Yorkshire. This Roman road runs towards Rochdale. The intact surface can be seen near Littleborough.*

5) One of the tracks known as Portway *runs across the White Peak limestone uplands from Ashford south to Wirksworth, Derbyshire.*

6) Mountain Road, *from Abergwesyn, Powys, to Tregaron SE of Aberystwyth, Dyfed. Once used as a drove road taking cattle to Midlands markets, this spectacularly crosses the 'Great Desert of Wales'.*

7) Sewstern Lane *from Stenwith Bridge near Long Bennington, Lin-*

colnshire, to Sewstern. Maybe not so high – but then neither is the land hereabouts. A classic deserted green lane: keeping to the highest ground available between the Rivers Trent and Welland indicates its age.

8) The Ridgeway *strides the chalk ridge from the Thames at Streatley to Avebury Stone Circle. It once extended further – onto Salisbury Plain on the one hand and across the River Thames (as the 'Icknield Way') to the flint mines in Norfolk. The Ridgeway also passes the famous chalk-cut White Horse, near Uffington. Good viewpoints are from above the White Horse.*

9) Exmoor Ridgeway. *This runs from Wheddon Cross near Dunkery Beacon to Chapman Barrows – many burial mounds and other relics nearby reflect its great age.*

10) The Abbot's Way, *from Buckfast Abbey to Princeton, Devon. Like the Pilgrims' Way, this track striking across Dartmoor served Stone and Bronze Age settlements long before Christ was born.*

FROM BROADWAY TOWER

With an overlook of 12 counties on a clear day, the view from Broadway Tower must be admired for its sheer distance. The charm of the countryside in the view, and the charming countryside atop these Cotswold hills multiply its magic. There are quaint oddities to observe, not all of them in Broadway Tower.

The Broadway Tower Country Park (a private park) is open April to early October. The entry ticket includes entry to the tower. However, the view can be sampled from nearby public footpaths at any time of year.

It's worth having a look at the local stone walls. They're made of Cotswold stone, a light coloured limestone which weathers to rich and varied tints of brown and yellow. It even colours the fields, shattered by the plough so that in Spring they seem to contain more rubble than soil. Yet, with dressings of factory fertilizers, they grow grain enough. In the days before artificial fertilizers, of course, such ground made poor ploughland, and was only suitable for grazing the famous Cotswold sheep.

Cotswold stone walls edge the fields, the stone for them dug from shallow quarries often extending along roadsides. These walls lend a delightful fitness of colour and pattern to the countryside here. The local buildings can make geologists of us all!

Throughout the Cotswolds we find different kinds of limestone. Shelly limestones (ragstones) break irregularly, and are used for field walling. For buildings, granular oolites (freestones) are preferred, because they are more easily dressed to smooth shapes. Thinner splitting beds of limestone, known as 'slates', were used for roofing.

The Country Park contains some fine examples – Tower Barn was rescued from a site further down and rebuilt here.

Here in the Country Park are shaggy Highland Cattle and other traditional breeds. There is a small flock of Cotswold sheep, heavy fleeced animals. Although so familiar to travellers in the past, they have now become an endangered breed, not often seen.

The Tower is our goal. It was built in 1790, a folly with battlements and curved windows, not quite gothic in style (for the import of that remark see INTRO page 7). Following the then romantic fashion for a 'dark tower', it is not built of local stone!

A visit to the tower is well worth the trouble. There are photographs explaining the view and a telescope to use. On the way up (a spiral staircase)

3

other interests are on view, exhibitions of an unexpected kind.

PS – and have a look at another relic – the coachman's signpost at the corner of the Chipping Campden road. Well over the height of today's cars (but breast high for a coachman), the arms end in fingers, the distances in Roman numerals. There was time to work these out as you trundled past in your horse-drawn coach.

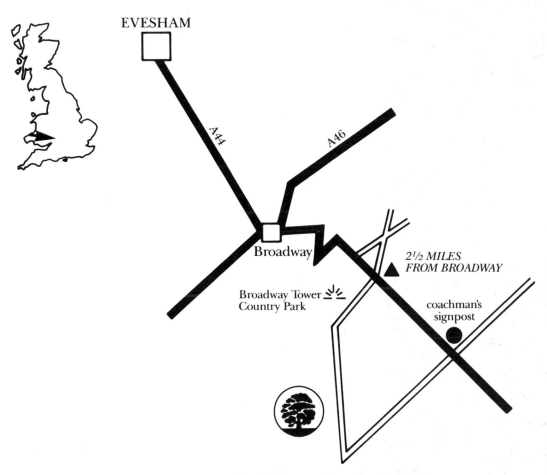

OS grid reference of viewpoint   SP 112360

View from Broadway Tower

The 65-foot prospect tower above Broadway was built by Lady Coventry in the 1790s. She was responding to a fashion for admiring views, by then growing strongly. Fashion in her day was as gripping as it is in ours; being fashion, all in your circle did it, quickly.

And so the country rather suddenly sported these lookout towers built by the owners of the stately homes nearby, spreading 'like beacons of good taste' across the nation.

But of course a fashion by definition must bring admiration in its train. These towers were built to be admired not only by the owner's pals and acquaintances. Very often they (and even the grand houses themselves when the family was not at home) were open to visiting strangers 'of breeding'.

For in those days, the new improved turnpike toll roads armed with novel aids such as coachmen's signposts were beginning to carry travellers of a new kind – excursionists out to view. The first trippers if you like.

A prospect tower was not only a quaint addition to the landscape, but also in its way an imposition on it, a stamp of ownership. In those days the circles for whom views were fashionable could very often actually *own* a large part of the view they admired.

Broadway Tower has more interest. Early last century one of its owners, the founder of the famous Phillips library of Medieval manuscripts, installed his printing press in it. It was later let out to Oxford tutors, and their friends used the tower. Amongst these were William Morris, Edward Burne Jones and Dante Gabriel Rossetti – founder members of the Pre-Raphaelite Brotherhood.

From here William Morris wrote the letter sparking off the *Society for the Protection of Ancient Buildings*, the very first British conservation group. And later the family Hollington lived in the Tower for 40 years – on the three floors which now house the exhibitions of Morris designs and other items.

What is a view? Deductions can be made here. We stand with our feet firm on hard Cotswold limestone. Below us stretches the red English plain – a countryside of black and white cottages and red brick – brick made of clay dug from the fields around.

But Bredon Hill and other outliers give us the clue. They show that our Cotswold limestone once extended far to the west, on in front of us, covering those clays.

In the slow course of time those deep layers of missing Cotswold

THE ANATOMY OF THIS BEST VIEW

● *A framed view, from a tower expressly built for the purpose!*

● *A fine view. This view from Broadway Beacon, 1024 feet, covers almost as many counties as the champion, the view from the Wrekin. North from here we look across the Vale of Evesham, a land of orchards, core of Britain's apple industry. The soils here are often reddish.*

To the west, the eye is carried into Wales, with the Black Mountains on the horizon, 50 miles distant.

This magnificent panorama includes Worcester Cathedral, Tewkesbury Abbey, Shakespeare's Stratford and Warwick Castle.

● *The chance of some geological detection. There are shapely hills not too far away, Bredon Hill capped with a dark wood lies near to hand. We will see what this implies.*

limestone have weathered away. The outliers remain, not yet eroded like the ground around.

So this view is a *negative* of a kind. And it gives us an overwhelming awareness of the slow immensity of geological change.

THERE IS MORE about early travellers and what they thought of the view from high spots such as this on page 20 and BOX 3.

GAZETTEER THREE

MORE TOWERS IN THE VIEW

All those steps. . . . Although some were erected in commemoration, many of these look-out towers cost good money for no profitable use, hence they are often known as follies. A true folly, however, is a sham or shell – anything from a mock castle tower one wall deep or just a single arch, erected as eyecatchers on a rise, to embellish the view from a nearby mansion.

1) Outlook Tower, *Castle Hill, Edinburgh. This contains a camera obscura – a delightful artifice to present easily viewed live images from roundabout; built in 1850.*

2) Mow Cop *is an odd place in more than one way. A 'ruined castle' built on a hill 1100 feet above sea level, 5 miles south of Congleton, almost on the Staffs–Cheshire border – on May 31 1807 an open air prayer meeting held within it lasted 12 hours and led to the birth of Primitive Methodism.*

3) Edge Hill Folly. *Also known as Edgehill or Radway Castle. At the Civil War battle, 1642, Charles I unfurled his standard at this spot – 100 years later this octagonal folly was built – now part of a hotel!*

4) Faringdon, *Oxfordshire. A prospect tower notable for being the last built – 1935 – to provide work for local unemployed.*

5) Leith Hill, *Surrey. In 1764 this hill was topped with a tower built to take the height to exactly 1000 feet above sea level. Then in 1864 someone added battlements and raised it to 1029 feet, the highest point in the south of England.*

6) Pepperbox Hill, *near Salisbury. This has fine views across the chalk expanse of Cranborne Chase. The 'pepperbox' is quite early, 1606, six-sided. Was it erected as an early folly or to watch hunting on the chase?*

7) Lansdowne Tower, *Bath. 130 feet of eccentricity – but in its way a monument of stature. It was built by eccentric William Beckford – with fine views of Wales, Severn, the Mendips. Often mistaken for a water tower.*

8) Glastonbury Tor, *Somerset. Looks from afar to be crowned by a folly – the tower is a relic of a church which once stood here, however.*

9) The Hardy Monument, *near Weymouth, Dorset. Not the novelist Thomas Hardy, but Hardy of 'Kiss me, Hardy' renown – Nelson's flag-captain. One of the most eyecatching of erections.*

10) Paxton's Tower, *Llanarthney, near Carmarthen. Built to commemorate Nelson, overlooking the Tywi valley.*

BLUE REMEMBERED HILLS

THE EILDON HILLS

Here we have a direct view of nostalgia. Sir Walter Scott lived nearby. Prolific author, he popularized Scotland, its past and the majesty of its mountainous countryside. He would regularly drive here, to draw his carriage up and sit motionless watching the changing light mould new folds into the soft blue contours of these Eildon Hills.

Scott's View lies alongside the road, with adequate parking. There is a viewing table. A visit to Dryburgh Abbey nearby and of course to Scott's own home at Abbotsford are recommended.

Scott's view is a dramatic viewpoint overlooking the River Tweed. The best view is probably not from the viewing table itself, but from the field under it; the Tweed's tight meander is better seen from here.

The Tweed is one of the famous salmon rivers, of course, and in early Autumn if you are lucky to be up here when the leaves begin to smoulder, many pools may hold a solemn figure waiting for the take. There are complaints that things are not as good as they were – too many people are netting salmon at its mouth, and too many are fishing the Atlantic feeding grounds. Both of which are true. And poaching is thriving.

Those musings aside (a good spot for musing this), there is delightful countryside hereabouts.

It is a lowland countryside, unlike the bare hills which accompany the younger Tweed only a few miles upstream.

These Eildon Hills are separated from these. Indeed part of the appeal of the Eildons lies in the way they rise abruptly from the land around them.

Of the three summits, the north, closest to us here, is the more interesting. On its hidden flank, the open ground sweeps down to the edge of Melrose.

This steep-sided summit was an ancient settlement site, an acropolis reminiscent of those of ancient Greece. At its top are the remains of a ramparted camp, enclosing countless hut circles (with binoculars, traces of the banks can be seen from Scott's View). But the Romans took it, and erected a signal station in it. Strangely, a tribute to them, often decked with flowers, lies alongside the road from Melrose.

'*Here once stood the fort of Trimontium,*' it reads, '*Built by the troops of Agricola in the 1st century AD. Abandoned at least twice by the Romans and ultimately lost by them after one hundred years of frontier warfare.*'

OK, a delightful oddity of the kind our countryside is so full of. But why the fresh flowers? Whose nostalgia

4

works here? Perhaps this still is a real frontier.

Dryburgh Abbey is not far away, partly ruined, with neat lawns and explanatory plaques on the remaining walls. A scatter of gravestones surrounds it; on the walls now hang others, some quaint in language.

Sir Walter Scott and some of his kin are buried within a still-roofed transept. Nearby is the grave of Earl Haig, of first World War repute. Bemersyde House was his family home.

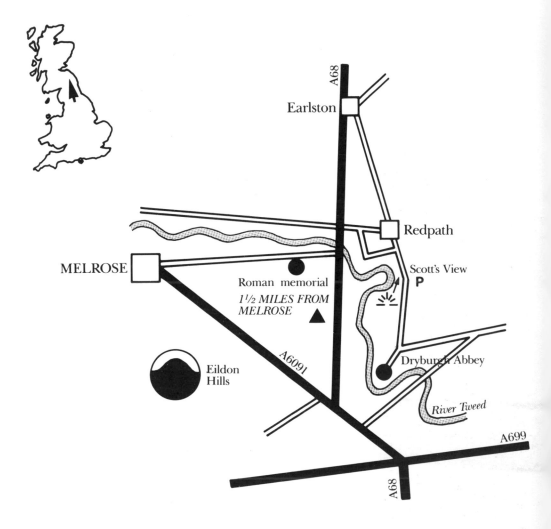

OS grid reference of viewpoint   NT 595343

The Eildon Hills from Scott's Viewpoint.

The Eildons, isolated and prominent and forming a landmark on the Borders, that once no-man's-land between Scotland and England, have three summits.

Legend has it that these hills were once one, but were split into three when a Michael Scott, a noted wizard, was faced with the dilemma of finding work for a demon. To keep him occupied Mr Scott set three tasks. The first was to dam the Tweed, done in the space of a night. The second was to split the Eildons, with the result we see today. The third was to spin ropes of seashore sand. At which (since we haven't seen much of him) the demon is presumably still busy.

Sir Walter Scott, born 1771, died 1832, retold this story, one of the many Border tales that he first heard sitting listening by the local hearths when he was a lad in this countryside. Its history fascinated him; he boasted that he could stand on the Eildons and point out 43 places famous in war and verse.

His historical, heroic stories and narrative sagas have titles (*Waverley, The Lay of the Last Minstrel, Ivanhoe*, etc) which are still very familiar, although the works themselves are rarely read today. In his lifetime they were an enormous and sensational success.

So successful were they, in fact, that those with Scottish settings set in train the nostalgia for the Highlands which is still so very strong. When *The Lady of the Lake* was published in 1810, for example, there was an immediate flood of tourists to view Loch Katrine, its setting.

Sir Walter Scott, that able conjurer of the past, indulged himself in nostalgia in another way. He used his royalties to build Abbotsford House, adding a new room with each new success. In their walls were embedded fragments from older buildings, while he tried to pack in the Middle Ages with his growing collection of swords, armour and other relics.

As befits such a man, he is buried in the ruins of the four-times plundered Dryburgh Abbey. It is said that at his funeral, Scott's carriage horses drawing the hearse paused out of habit at his viewpoint, allowing their master to enjoy his favourite view for the last time.

Near Scott's View is Bemersyde House, once home of Earl Haig, famous (or infamous for those of other viewpoint) from another, closer war – the First World War of 1914–18. He retired here in 1921, and immediately set about recreating the gardens that

THE ANATOMY OF THIS BEST VIEW

● *Blue hills. They need not be so very far away to assume this hue. The Eildons are closer than the photograph suggests:. 3½ miles by the viewing table. Being blued strengthens sense of distance.*
● *Some historic feature underlines their appeal. An ancient settlement lay atop the north height to the right.*
● *A strong vale. As with all the best views of hills, the vale itself is of visual interest.*
● *The vantage point of personal interest: Scott's view.*

Henry VIII had himself designed for Hampton Court. A touch of nostalgia here of yet another kind.

Blue is the colour of nostalgia; and the Eildons are usually that splendid hue. But if perchance not (maybe rain is nearby with a bleak low light) such is the strength of suggestion that they will certainly remain blue in your memory.

THERE IS MORE about Sir Walter Scott and Highland nostalgia on page 29 and about blue in the view in BOX 4.

GAZETTEER FOUR

BLUE REMEMBERED HILLS

The criterion here is hills that mean something in the breast of those who view them. Such a choice must be personal, but here are some starters.

1) Robert Burns country, backed by the *Carrick Hills. His birthplace cottage at Alloway, South of Ayr, Strathclyde, is now a museum.*

2) The Lake District, *not the crags but its gentler southern hills. Beatrix Potter lived at Sawrey, in Hill Top Farm, bought with the proceeds from her children's stories of Peter Rabbit* et al. Her property in Sawrey and elsewhere, some of it very beautiful, she left to the National Trust – and to us.

3) Wenlock Edge *runs from Craven Arms, Shropshire to the Severn Valley.*

> On Wenlock Edge the wood's in trouble,
> His forest fleece the Wrekin heaves.
> The wind it plies the saplings double,
> And thick on Severn snow the leaves.

Lines by A. E. Housman. Vaughan Williams set Housman's poem A Shropshire Lad *to music in* On Wenlock Edge.

4) Black Mountains, *Powys. Tight amongst these, in a shut-in valley, Eric Gill, firm opponent of industralization, set up a typical artists' colony of the 1920s, sharing in milking, bread-making and farming.*

5) The Chilterns, *Buckinghamshire. These were the 'Delectable Mountains' of John Bunyan, Nonconformist author of* The Pilgrim's Progress *(1678).*

6) The Berkshire–Oxfordshire Downs *seen from Badbury Hill, near Faringdon. Here the downs seem a country apart. Richard Jefferies knew and loved them. He lived at Coate, now part of Swindon. In* The Story of my Heart *he describes flinging himself down: 'I was utterly alone with the sun and the earth. Lying down on the grass, I spoke my soul to the earth, the sun, the air. . . .'*

7) The Quantocks, *Somerset. 'The most shapely of hills,' thought Dorothy Wordsworth.*

8) The South Downs *around Arundel. Nobel Prize-winning author John Galsworthy – author of* Strife *amongst other things – lived at Bury, and each night at around 11 o'clock he would stand and stare at the Downs before making for bed. He allowed himself two hours a day to walk and ride over them.*

THE AWESOME PASS

There is much to be said for the old-fashioned habit of being put in awe by mountains. And where better than in a steep-sided valley or forbidding pass. And if it is alive with ghosts, then so much the better. Hence the choice of Glencoe.

A road runs through the Glen.

The Glen proper is about 7½ miles long, with a col or pass which stands at about 1000 feet above sea level. But the name Glencoe is often given to the whole valley, all 15 miles of it to Kingshouse.

A good road built in 1935 now traverses Glencoe, but there are older ones. Signal Rock (from which legend has it that the signal for the massacre was given early on February 13 1692) is reached by the old road which diverges from the new and runs higher and to the north of the River Coe.

At the head of the glen, at Altnafeadh, a zig-zagged 'devil's staircase' crosses to Kinlochleven. This is in fact an old drove route, along which the MacDonalds presumably drove a good many cattle. Around 1750 it became upgraded as a military road, one of a network then being imposed on the Highlands after the failure of the Jacobite rebellion.

As were the Lake District Hills, and the heights of Snowdonia and the Brecon Beacons in Wales (and some areas of the Pennines) the Scottish Highlands were deeply sculpted by ice during the Ice Age. Glencoe is a fine example of a valley deepened by the glaciers of the time.

Like a gigantic tongue, these glaciers slowly rasped the rock away (and how ice, which melts with pressure, can rub away rock is another story). A main glacier cut the Glen, subsidiary feeders joined it, as was often the case. These side glaciers scalloped out the Three Sisters.

Apart from the steep-sided valley, another clue to glaciation lies in the scratches found on some of the exposed rock faces.

The Ice Age at an end and the glaciers melted away, the tumbling streams could then begin to cut their own channels. They haven't yet had enough time (geologically speaking) to make very much of an impression.

5

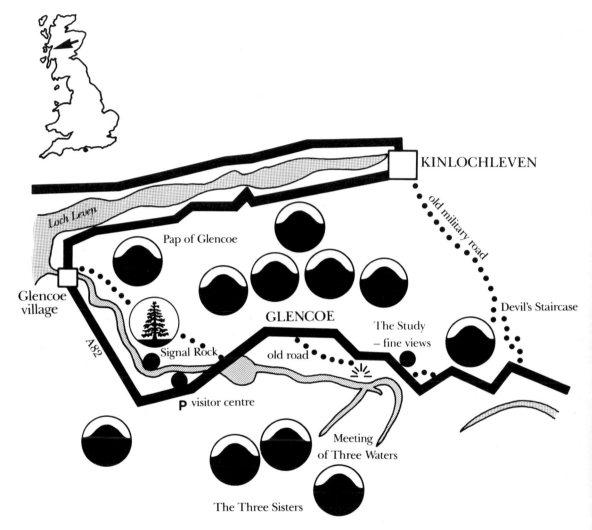

OS grid reference of viewpoint NN 180565

Glencoe

An awesome, empty place of angry rock and torrential streams. Yet the MacDonalds once lived here. It echoed with their voices and the shouts of their children. The Glen now seems to brood at all times of day and at all times of year, as if never to forget the grudge it bears for the infamous massacre. It gives us a view straight to the troubled heart of the Scottish Highlands.

By accident of mistaken instructions, the MacDonald chief was a few days late registering his acceptance of the English king William III. This paltry opportunity was seized.

A detachment made up largely of Campbell soldiery was marched into Glencoe. In the Highland tradition, they broke bread with the MacDonalds in their homes – for near a fortnight.

At 5 o'clock in the morning of February 13 1692, well before dawn, the massacre began. It is said that a fire was lit on Signal Rock to instruct the redcoats to begin killing. Few saw it, for a snowstorm raged.

Of the 200 MacDonalds, 40 were shot or bayoneted outright. Most of those that fled died of hunger and exposure on the hillsides, their homes looted and burnt behind them. The authorities largely succeeded in keeping this infamous savagery from the world.

The MacDonalds were typical of their time, their story is now almost a physical part of the highlands.

The frontier of these Scottish Highlands lies along a fault, a massive rock fracture running from the Firth of Clyde to south of Aberdeen. North of it lie ranges of mountains, some huge, truly meriting the name mountain (though Scotsmen themselves refer to them as hills).

Settled in early times, a people called the Picts eventually held much of the territory. They faced the Romans (though never tamed by them), but in time were mastered by Scots crossing from Northern Ireland, and later suffered Viking attacks.

The clans (based usually on glens) were established by medieval times, and tartans may also have been established by then. Life relied on cattle and small patches of oats alongside the croft. And in fact one important activity was rustling cattle. Though the glens had been wooded with pine and oak in places up to the tree line, much of this forest disappeared, fired for grazing, fired in raids and reprisals and fired to drive out wolves.

The death of the last wolf coincided with the collapse of the Jacobite rebellions in 1745 and the end of Highland independence from rule from lowland Scotland and London. The infamous clearances were imposed, Highlanders being stripped of their crofts for widescale sheep farming. They could only seek a new life far off in town or colony.

The crofts crumbled. Nimble sheep kept the already impoverished soil bare of trees. In few other places in Britain is a wilderness view so closely linked with actual history as it is in these Highland glens.

THERE IS MORE about Highland tradition on page 29.

THE ANATOMY OF THIS BEST VIEW

● *The route lies down a steep-sided valley. Here we see a brooding, glacier-cut valley of a kind common in our western and northern hills, and in Scotland known as glens. A glaciated valley of this kind has a U-shaped cross-section, with steep sides and flattish bottom.*

● *Streams are a feature. Although turbulent with frequent rains, they have not had time enough to sharply deepen the valley floor and have made only a nick in it.*

● *Quite a bare place. Originally, with the Ice Age over, the glen floor was probably wooded. Centuries of firing and grazing have destroyed its tree cover. A relic tree or two however is the clue that these valleys would naturally carry forest.*

● *The road winds, taking the easiest route. This makes its line apt. Modern roads sadly tend to create scars in the valley.*

● *History in the view. Plenty of that here.*

● *Mist – to further the brooding nature of the scene.*

119

GAZETTEER FIVE

THE ATMOSPHERIC PASS

There aren't a lot of these in East Anglia: none in fact. But other places in the south, even the soft countryside of the chalk downs, can yield steep-sloped coombs.

Glencoe is supreme in its documented story. For some others we have to rely on our imagination to people them.

1) Pass of Killiecrankie, *near Pitlochry, Tayside. A nightmare until General Wade – he seems to have been a one-man Department of Transport up in Scotland – traversed it with a military road. Here in 1689 Jacobites led by Bonnie Dundee routed William III's army.*

2) Dunmail Rise, *carries the road from Keswick to Ambleside, Cumbria. Its scale in the Lake District context makes it worth including; it is capped by a cairn (to King Domhnall). A modern dual carriageway now sweeps past it – worth pausing to wonder how this happened in a National Park. The road now visually wrecks this once atmospheric pass.*

3) Trough of Bowland, *in Bowland Forest, SE of Lancaster, Lancashire. Few trees here: and for why hunting forests need have no trees see VIEW 19. A bleak road in many weathers across glaciated countryside.*

4) Giggleswick Scar, *an atmospheric series of cliff formations broods over the steep road running from Settle to Clapham, North Yorkshire.*

5) Wade's Causeway, *on the North York Moors. This is by origin a Roman road crossing the bleak tops. From it the strange sight of giant golf balls – the Fylingdales Early Warning radar station.*

6) The Snake Pass, *North Derbyshire. Of all the passes across the real Pennine moorland, this is king. It is sheer delight, all the more when you remember its summit is but half an hour from either Sheffield or Manchester.*

7) Winnats Pass *between Chapel en le Frith and Castleton, Derbyshire. Wild and craggy, the name means 'windy gates'. Now much busier, as a neighbouring pass below Mam Tor, the shivering mountain, has had to be closed.*

8) Aberglaslyn *in Snowdonia. A rugged tree-planted pass; the railway roused furious protests from John Ruskin and others.*

9) Burrington Coomb, *an atmospheric route leading into the Mendip Hills. This coomb is dotted with small caves.*

10) The Down Gap at Lewes, Sussex. *One of the passes through the South Downs created by a river escaping from Weald to sea and, like many, guarded by a fine castle. Lewes had, according to that early traveller Daniel Defoe, 'the most romantic situation I ever saw'.*

THE NOBLE MOUNTAIN

SNOWDON FROM LLYN NANTLLE

**S**nowdon is an aristocrat of a mountain. Like all British summits, she is not so very high (3560 feet;), but accidents of geology mean that some approaches provide marvellous views magnifying her grandeur. We have chosen one of the best, which frames her summit above a lake. An artist's view this – and one moreover which played a part in the history of viewmanship.

Even for those who have never yet visited her, Snowdon is an evocative name. She has long been a tourist goal. The summit is easily gained by a broad, gently sloping track from Llanberis (and by a mountain railway all the way to the top). There are other, steeper paths.

But our view is *of* the summit. Lying on the B4418 as it does, this viewpoint is easily visited.

This view, like many in our uplands, is of a glaciated landscape. Here we see steep mountain faces, especially in the cwm (the Welsh word) or corrie (the northern name).

A cwm is a large rounded gouge found below a summit. Nowadays it often holds a deep pool, but it was once the birthplace of a glacier. Here the fallen snow became compacted into ice, to pluck more rock from the cwm face as it did so. As a result, a cwm has sheer walls, and its crags offer exciting rock climbing. It is not for nothing that Snowdon was the birthplace of that sport in the 1850s.

Seen from Llyn (lake) Nantlle, Snowdon seems saddlebacked. Do not take this for granted, it is a symptom of some incredible geology, for the rocks at the summit of Snowdon as we see it today once lay at the *bottom* of a trough (a syncline) of rock layers. It was perhaps once the bottom of a valley, with heights rising up on either side. That vast mass of rock has been weathered away.

Those rocks were once volcanic ashes which had settled at the bottom of some ancient ocean. Finding fossil shells at the top of a mountain puzzled many early visitors. Could they have been left by Noah's flood?

Snowdonia is a National Park; look out for the symbol. In keeping with British verbal eccentricity, this name does not mean that it is a park or nationally run. But it is an area where planning regulations favour the protection of the scenery, while allowing farming to continue and other work and some development to take place.

Snowdonia is noted for its birds. Watch out for ravens,

6
___

flying (surprisingly) upside down when doing aerobatics. Peregrines and buzzards are also quite common, and ring ouzels – a kind of white-necklaced blackbird.

And notice the rhododendron in Snowdonia. In spite of its splendid banks of purple flowers in late spring, it is now a considerable nuisance. A favourite garden shrub in Victorian times (as it is today) it has naturalized itself in Snowdonia. Its growth and dense foliage swamp all other low vegetation and take over ground, even encroaching into the fragments of ancient oakwood which remain in some valleys here. Naturalists would like to see it eliminated.

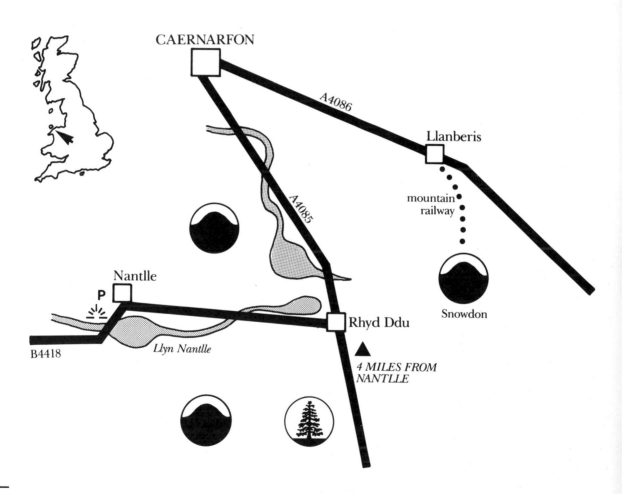

OS grid reference of viewpoint SH 510530

Snowdon from Llyn Nantlle

Snowdon is part of Welsh heritage, and Celtic Wales has a proud past. Whether or not they had a religious centre on Anglesey (white-robed druids are a Victorian invention), the Welsh remained a thorn in the side of the Romans, even with legions at Chester and Caerleon. This old identity echoes in the Welsh name for Wales: *Cymry*, translateable as 'people like us, comrades'. The English 'Wales' is from a Saxon word meaning 'foreign'. It stayed a place apart in later times. Offa's Dyke was a Dark Age frontier and the separation was underlined when William the Conqueror empowered his marcher lords to hold absolute authority over the troubled borders.

Edward I swept into Wales to build castles to quell the Welsh. A century later, Owain Glyndwr (Owen Glendower) struggled bitterly and failed, leaving Wales devastated. But the Tudors, victors of the Wars of the Roses, had a tinge of Welsh blood. Henry VIII's Act of Union removed the privileges of the marcher lords – and in fact Wales was loyal to the English Crown in the Civil War.

Later, in the nineteenth century, Welsh identity blossomed again with the Methodist chapels, which also became a meeting place for those fighting the shabby conditions that industry brought to Wales. This national link of socialism and chapel lasted up until today.

Sir Walter Scott wrote to revive Scotland (VIEWS 4, 5); but national identity can be aided by art as well as words. In 1771 the splendidly named Welsh patriot, Sir Watkin Williams-Wynn, invited the English artist Paul Sandby to tour North Wales with him. It was part of a campaign of propaganda for Welsh interests and was the first time an artist (rather than a poet) had been invited on such a jaunt. It was rather like taking along a photographer!

However, another artist of note was already linked with Wales. In the 1760s Richard Wilson painted Snowdon from our viewpoint by Llyn Nantlle. It was a milestone of a picture.

Wilson was one of the first to paint Welsh landscapes, but he was also an artist who helped bring to British landscape painting some of the prestige it enjoyed in Europe.

At first sight, his painting (page 34) seems similar to what we ourselves see today, but we have to understand its context, its point in time. The way the picture is composed with mountain, lake, trees and figures and side 'curtains' of trees framing the view owes a great deal to Claude Lorrain and Gaspard Dughet, earlier masters of European landscape painting.

THE ANATOMY OF THIS BEST VIEW

● *A shapely pile of rock! This is true mountain scenery with frowning crags.*
● *A frame for the view. The twin slopes could not be bettered. Rising between them, Snowdon presents itself posed for a picture.*
● *An interesting middle ground. Water in the view.*
● *Interesting weather. Snowdon is known as 'The Cloud Breeder'. Here we see another aspect of her year.*

By adopting their formula Wilson tried to impose order on this natural scene. He caught in paint the feeling of agelessness, the inviolate quality of the mountain. This view becomes timeless – and noble.

All artists strive to impose visual order. Although Claude was a man of his age, he had great influence on later artists. In fact, many still compose pictures in his way. His paintings even played a part in British landscape designs, as we shall see.

THERE IS MORE about Richard Wilson, Gaspard and Claude Lorrain – and parks – on pages 15 and 62.

GAZETTEER SIX

FACING THE HEIGHTS

Real heights are only to be found in the West and North of Britain, but we can get some of their atmosphere elsewhere.

1) Torridon Mountains, *Ross and Cromarty. Loch Torridon has the magnificent red sandstone Liathach at its head. This is almost a lunar landscape.*

2) Ben Nevis, *the highest mountain in Britain, rising to 4406 feet. It is rather lumpen in shape, the great cliffs are on its northern side – so it is best viewed from Banavie and further north of there.*

3) Lake District. *The best view of the heights? One of Wordsworth's own recommended views is of the Langdale Pikes from the hamlet of Skelwith Fold, near Skelwith Bridge, Ambleside. From the Langdale valley, they loom overhead.*

4) Pen-y-ghent, *seen from Horton in Ribblesdale, amongst other places. This is the most distinctive peak in the Pennine range. Nearby are Ingleborough and Whernside – all three over 2000 feet.*

5) Cader Idris, *the Throne of Idris, presents a vast ice-plucked face rising to 2927 feet near Dolgellau, Gwynedd. Richard Wilson painted its cwm with cwm lake, choosing a high vantage point.*

6) Charnwood Forest, *Leicestershire. Yes, we are not in the high country now, but this craggy area does have a touch of mountain about it. You can console yourself with the fact that you stand on a buried mountain chain; only a few hundred million years of erosion and it might appear again.*

7) *Eastern* Black Mountains, *between Brecon, Powys and Abergavenny, Gwent. Wild seclusion and deep valleys with heights of over 2500 feet ranged above.*

8) Brecon Beacons, *rising to 2900 feet, sculpted by glaciers.*

9) Butser Hill, *south of Petersfield, Hampshire. Chalk, but with great steep slopes. It forms part of the Queen Elizabeth Country Park.*

10) Hay Tor, Dartmoor. *Not bad for the smoothed south. This, 1491 feet high, is the most accessible of the moor's 150 tors, about a mile from the road. The highest are Yes Tor (2030 feet) and Great Willhays (2038 feet).*

THE SUBLIME

GORDALE SCAR, YORKSHIRE

he village of Malham is at the heart of some of the most extraordinary scenery in Britain, and of it all, Gordale Scar is the prize. The Scar makes us catch our breath. It amazed people in past centuries too, when they travelled from far and wide to be awed by it. It was counted *sublime.* **On top of all this, Gordale Scar is the subject of one of the largest of all British landscape paintings!**

The scar is freely reached by a footpath. Parking nearby may be difficult in summer. But at any season, why not leave the car in the village and walk – it is only about 1½ miles, half an hour. It is a delicious walk, along a charming northern lane set with pale stone walls and stately ash trees. Halfway there, the edge of the cliff appears ahead, a foretaste of what is to come.

The path to the Scar is well signposted, with a gate in the road wall and a display explaining the name, Norse in origin. *Gore* or *geir* means an angular area of land and *dalr* a valley (dale). *Scar* means cliff.

Set out on the path across the green meadow to reach the stream. This flows clear, braiding itself across the valley. Note the lush growth in the water, including wild watercress flowering white at any time from May to October. This plant likes the limey water.

The path then moves to one side of the valley. There are some scree slopes in places.

Note the dark yews on the slopes; they too like the limestone soil.

As you walk, the valley sides are steepening, closing in. The stream begins to echo. It is indeed becoming a right powerful gorge. You turn the final corner.

It is as if your eyes were suddenly plucked open. Nothing on the way has prepared you for this. It is more dramatic than entering a cave as tall as a cathedral (and the Scar was once just such a thing before its roof collapsed). The fact that it is open to the sky multiplies rather than diminishes its size.

It is, in one word, *sublime.* Not that you will hear that word spoken nowadays.

'Quite impressive isn't it? Aren't you glad you came?'

'Mmmh.'

You are guaranteed to hear that or something like. Gordale Scar is guaranteed to evoke emotion – even on a dull day.

On the way back, look at Janet's Foss, a charming water fall. There is an excellent National Park Information Centre on the Skipton exit in Malham village. A small but good exhibition of photographs and

7

other material explains what you have seen.

It is also worthwhile travelling on to see Malham Cove: a bulging bone-white amphitheatre over 350 feet high with a spring of water gushing from its foot.

Also for the specialist are the areas of 'limestone pavement' which lie on some hills roundabout – natural rock gardens of a now rare kind.

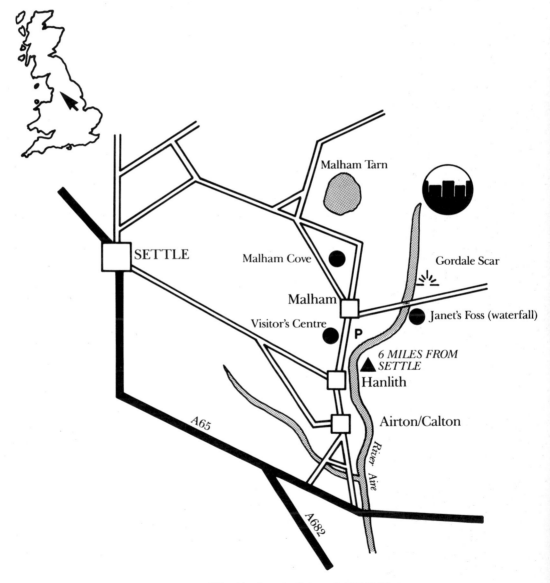

OS grid reference of viewpoint SD 91 63

Gordale Scar

Here is a colossal cleft.

The rock is carboniferous limestone, dating from around the same time as the coal swamps. Its layers are jointed or cracked, and the rain finds its way through the soil and down into these cracks.

They become widened because the rain water is slightly acid and this enables it slowly to dissolve the limestone, year by year. (If a piece of limestone is dropped into a stronger acid such as vinegar, it actually fizzes.) In the course of time channels are created, and caves are eaten out.

Gordale was once a large cavern: its roof collapsed some long time ago, shearing away at the joints. A fragment of its roof still overhangs.

Ever popular today, Gordale Scar was also the goal of countless tours in the previous two centuries. The Scar allows us to experience directly what they meant in the past when they talked of *sublime* in scenery and art.

Together with *beautiful* and *picturesque*, the word had a definite meaning in landscape appreciation.

Beautiful meant smoothness, a small scale, delicate colouring and light. 'Beautiful' scenery could most easily be found amidst lowland valleys. 'Sublime', on the other hand, meant that it could create awe – massive in scale, sometimes with sharp lighting or gloomy recesses.

Later, 'picturesque' also became a much used word – meaning paintable, making a good picture.

And in fact, Gordale Scar was painted by John Ward in 1814, as an example of the sublime. This painting can be compared with the view we see today.

Its size alone would guarantee it respect: nearly 14 feet long by 11 feet high, it is the largest landscape painting hanging in London's Tate Gallery.

Although Gordale Scar is already striking, it is clear that Ward (page 40) was more interested in creating a dramatic scene than in photographic accuracy. The viewpoint is an invented one, so that certain features such as the looming height of the rock faces and the overhangs can be magnified. This multiplies the awesomeness, even the terror, evoked by the scene.

He uses codes to heighten these primitive reactions – the stags locked in battle, the bull radiating massive primeval power. They are window-dressing of a kind.

THE ANATOMY OF THIS BEST VIEW

● *Sheer rock. This is the finest limestone gorge in the country. On the approach the valley steepens and closes in, a theatrical curtain-raiser. The gorge here at the end is sheer drama.*

The rock is rugged. The limestone has sheared away along joints (cracks) in the massive layers to give vertical faces; some even bulge out.

● *The echo of water. The stream which falls as a waterfall is only part of the flow which cut the Scar; the rest now sinks underground further up, but its new channel leads it to surface again near the mouth of the gorge.*

● *Dramatic lighting: chiaroscuro. In such a narrow cleft one side only catches the sun, depending on the time of day. The rest is deeply shadowed.*

● *The cleft gives one the idea of going somewhere.*

● *The scene is bare. Bar a hanging bush or two, there is little else but rock, water, light and shade. A notice board would visually cut such a scene dead.*

131

That the sublime could be pictured in this way meant that it could be understood. And in time language matched it. Today we accept that cliffs can *frown*, gorges and chasms *yawn* open with dreadful hunger.

Cliffs do not frown, of course, nor do rock faces yawn. But now they do in our mind's eye. Thanks to paintings like this one of Gordale Scar, our imaginations have been bred to accept such ideas.

THERE IS MORE about the sublime on page 38 and the picturesque on page 42.

GAZETTEER SEVEN

THE SUBLIME

In the lowlands we usually have to fall back on quarries to give us what is essentially bare rock view. Genuine feelings of amazement are, for example, easily evoked by Swithland Quarry *in Charnwood Forest, Leicestershire. The deep quarry, steep-sided, is drowned in still, blue water.*

1) Corrieshalloch Gorge, *Highland, south east of Ullapool. This is a stupendous gorge; there is a slight suspension bridge over the tumbling falls which forms part of its splendours.*

2) The millstone grit of the Pennines sometimes weathers into sharp cliffs, such as Great Alms Cliff *near Ripon. Hard though this gritstone seems, it is in time grooved and worn by windblown grains. Odd shapes may result – as at Brimham Rocks near Ripley, and the Bridestones.*

3) Kilnsey Crag, *Wharfedale. An impressive bulging cliff, towering over the road here.*

4) Dovedale, *Derbyshire, where the river runs through a narrow limestone gorge with steep walls, worn away in some places into fantastic shapes. There are others, less well-known,* Chee Dale, *for example, bordering on Millers Dale. Here a magnificent gorge winds below 300-foot cliffs.*

5) Snowdon, *of course, was also considered a sublime view. There are splendid close viewpoints (closer than our VIEW 6). One is Cwm Idwal, off the A5 road between Capel Curig and Bethesda. Below the great slab rock faces are plenty of glacial features in the way of scored rocks and moraines.*

6) Llanymynech Hill *near Oswestry, Shropshire. This is now owned by the Shropshire Trust for Nature Conservation, and is a nature reserve. Towering quarry cliffs loom over spreads of grassland.*

7) Cheddar Gorge, *Somerset, of course. A must in days gone by for tourists searching for the sublime. Rather spoiled now by its road and the Caveman Tavern and other tat around the cave entrances at the foot of its 450-foot cliffs at the bottom of the gorge. The top of the Gorge is better. The best way to arrive is from above, on the B3371 road from the top of the Mendips. Here it can still strike that sublime spark.*

8) High Rocks *to the west of Tunbridge Wells, Kent. Crags of sandstone. Not bad for its position so far south. See also Harrison's Rocks, Groombridge. At* Rocks Wood *at West Hoathly, in West Sussex, there are oddities such as the curiously shaped 'Great upon little' Rock, the larger almost completely undermined, resting on a thin bed of clay.*

9) The Valley of the Rocks, *Lynton, Devon. A cragged valley curiously running parallel to the sea cliffs.*

10) Lydford Gorge, *West Dartmoor, is a deep and narrow chasm off the A386 Tavistock–Okehampton road.*

THE PICTURESQUE

RYDAL FROM WORDSWORTH'S VIEWPOINT

An argument over the best view in the Lake District would last a century or two, and never be resolved (for in the meantime, the rules would have changed and tastes as well). This view is chosen, not only because it is perfectly picturesque, but also because it is on William Wordsworth's doorstep. He in fact recommended this view from Nab Scar.

As the Scotsman said of the Lake District: 'Take away the hills, and wha' ha' ye got?' What indeed?

There is no way of approaching this viewpoint *without* passing some of the world-famous Lake District hills or seeing some prospect of them, Skiddaw above Keswick in the North, the Langdale Pikes past Windermere if you approach from the South. Or perhaps the best entry to the Lake District is from Penrith and then along the shore of Ullswater, past the spot where the Wordsworths saw their daffodils, set against the majestic hills over the water.

The lakeland hills tower high. They seem remote, unreachable, but this is partly optical illusion. Distances are much closer than they seem. There is on record a mistake made by a Swiss Alpine guide over here for a holiday; local lore has it that he set aside half a day for a climb that takes an hour or two.

Happily (just as in the Alps) the fells are usually common grazings, and by custom free to all, to walk where they like with only the sheep for company.

The sheep are often Herdwicks (pronounced Hardwick), thought to be the old 'native' sheep of the region. They are small, agile animals with white faces; only the rams have horns. Swaledales are also commonly seen. They are dark-faced with a light nose; both rams and ewes are horned.

Stone walls stride everywhere, even across the hills, and they are worth a detailed look, especially where they climb a steep slope. Some surmount rock outcrops and even crags.

These walls are of various ages. Those on the valley bottoms and lower slopes around the 'inbye' fields are usually the older (and the oldest of all often made of smoothed surface stones).

But the enclosure movement reached here too a couple of centuries ago, and some higher fells were also taken in with intake fields. Walling gangs did the work, using sharp stone quarried from a nearby bluff. One gang's length between the 'wall ends' can differ noticeably from another's, in skill, in the number of 'through stones' (these can make stepping stones), and in other ways.

8

Many of the Lake District fields are awash with bracken. It is a weed, though an attractive one in some lights, texturing the view.

Here bracken is really a sign of land let go. In the old days, farmers kept more cattle, which trod the bracken down, and which ate the young fresh bracken shoots in May and June. But the sheep do not damage it and do not nibble it. Bracken and tumbled walls are signs that intensive hill farming is ending on the fells.

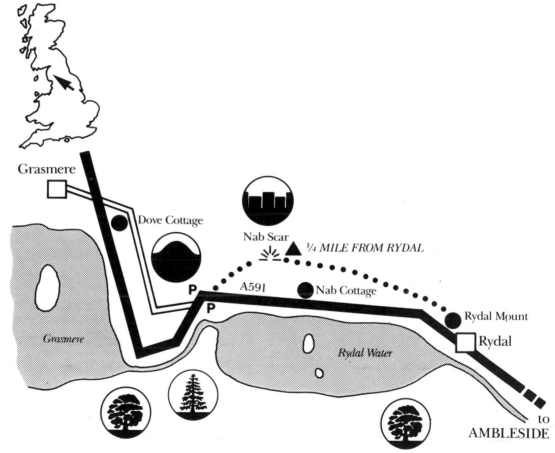

OS grid reference of viewpoint NY 355066

THE ANATOMY OF
THIS BEST VIEW

● *Sky. Lakeland and light theatrically partner each other. As we see it here, the light can be amorphous,*

View across Rydal Water

Our viewpoint is close to what have become international shrines to William Wordsworth. Dove Cottage was his home from 1799 to 1808. Here he wrote some of his best-known lines, yes, even those on the Ullswater daffodils, see p. 48.

The Wordsworths later lived in Grasmere but later moved to Rydal Mount. Here William Wordsworth wrote a good deal more and became Poet Laureate. He died in 1850.

They left Grasmere because they could no longer bear to see from their windows the graves of their two children in the churchyard nearby. The entries of birth and customary early death (from diphtheria, measles and other illnesses) in the family bible are heartbreaking.

We forget now that family men and women who made their mark in the past had to cope with strains quite unknown to us today. Their stature becomes even greater.

William Wordsworth transformed our view of nature. In his hands it became something to stir our feelings. This was not just the simple awe of 'sublime' views such as Gordale Scar. Simple things, even flowers by a lake, could conjure emotions. After Wordsworth things were never the same again.

When Wordsworth wrote, the notion of the 'picturesque' view was in fashion. Tourists sought it out. In Wordsworth's own day, the two waterfalls at Rydal were attracting regular queues. A garden house was even built in the grounds of Rydal Hall, from which the lower cascade could be seen framed in a window, picturesquely, literally as if it were in a picture. These falls can also be seen from Rydal Mount.

And the gardens of Rydal Mount with terraces and vistas through trees remain much as they were when Wordsworth himself designed them.

In his own *Guide to the Lakes* (published anonymously in 1810 and an immediate best-seller) Wordsworth wrote: 'the Waterfalls of Rydal are pointed out to everyone. But it ought to be observed here that Rydal-mere is no where seen to advantage from the main road . . . a foot road passing behind Rydal Mount and under Nab Scar is very favourable . . . .'.

We took his advice. The view is very fine indeed.

FOR MORE about William Wordsworth, his famed poetry and his guide book to the Lake District, and about the odd characters who hunted here for the picturesque, see page 42.

yielding only the barest hints of the clouds above. On more clear-cut days, the sun can dapple the distant fells with cloud shadows.

● *A background of bare fell. The high hillsides erupt in rocky bluffs. These hillsides were fashioned by the glaciers of the Ice Age.*

● *A quieter middle distance and foreground, gentler slopes with pastoral beauty. The hillsides were once tree-covered; native oaks often remain picturesquely scattered or in enclaves on lower ground.*

Centuries of sheep grazing aided by changes in climate in the past have destroyed the higher trees and left the fells open. Trees could still grow – the occasional single tree or securely fenced plantation proves that.

● *Water. High on the fells, the tumbling becks have not yet had time (since the retreat of the ice) to cut deep channels. But here we have the beauty of a limpid lake, together with the bonus of an island as eyecatcher. In other lakeland views the white cottages also make attractive eyecatchers.*

● *All in all, aided by its deceptive scale, the far, middle-distance and foreground elements in this view balance each other to perfection.*

● *The bonus of the first touch of Autumn in the scene.*

137

GAZETTEER EIGHT

THE TEN BEST LAKE DISTRICT VIEWS

Some of these are recommended by William Wordsworth himself.

1) From Brantwood, the view of the Coniston Fells across Coniston Water. Brantwood was Ruskin's home.

2) From Ashness Bridge, looking across Derwentwater to the mass of Skiddaw.

3) From Low Wood, the Langdale Pikes across Windermere.

4) From Friar's Crag, the view across Derwentwater.

5) From Gowbarrow, on Ullswater, looking across the lake to Martindale. Here grew those famous daffodils.

6) Amongst the hills at Tarn Hows.

7) From the road near Wasdale Hall, looking up Wast Water. Perhaps the most 'sublime' of all Lake District views with clean sweeping lines of scree slope dropping straight down to the lake. This forms the emblem of the Lake District National Park.

8) Stock Ghyll Force waterfall, Ambleside. Magnificent double falls.

9) The view from Hardknott Pass, with the Roman fort.

10) From the western side of Lake Windermere. As Wordsworth says: 'To one who has ascended the hill from Graithwaite, the Promontory called Rawlinson's Nab, Storr's Hall, and the Troutbeck Mountains, about sunset, make a splendid landscape.'

THE NOBLE RIVER

THE RIVER WYE

ere we have an intriguing glimpse of one of the finest rivers in the country, the Wye, winding a boundary between Wales and England. But as we shall see, those windings are themselves an insight into some odd geology.

This noble river provides us with a surfeit of fine views. A good direction to approach our particular viewpoint is from the north, on the A466 from Monmouth.

But whilst in the Monmouth area, visit the Kymin – a road winds up a steep hillside to bring you to a hillock crowned by Round House Tower, built in 1794 for a local dining club. Nearby is a temple celebrating fifteen admirals. It was much admired by Lord Nelson (who happens to have a museum devoted to him in the town). Surprising, really, for this is scarcely a naval port!

Plenty of military history, though, for we are now in the borderlands between England and Wales. Monmouth has its keep surviving; it was an important strongpoint – whoever held it could control the entire south of Wales. Chepstow also has a fine castle bossing it on a bluff over the Wye.

Driving south from Monmouth, the river soon begins to loop splendidly, on one side shouldering steep wooded slopes, with a shallower flank of fields on the other. Much of the woodland is deciduous, but there are plantings of larches and other conifers which on this magnificent stage do not look amiss.

We cross the river into Welsh Gwent and soon pass ruined Tintern Abbey (its setting inspired some of the best lines of William Wordsworth). Such is the aura of the river that parts of Tintern village have a definite seaside air to them. The road then climbs the slope above the river and Wynd Cliff is reached with its car parks. There is a good view from the lower viewpoint; Eagle's Nest still lies a walk away.

For this walk we can park (free) in Quarry car park, and set off along a trail through a yew wood – some of the trees are really ancient, gripping the bare rock with roots gnarled like veins on a grandmother's hand. The wood is loud with bird song for much of the year. We then reach the '365 Steps'. Here we follow in the footsteps of famous poets, writers and gentlemen (and ladies) of leisure who toured such wild places when the Romantic Imagination was being born, over 150 years ago.

The 365 Steps were laid out (or rather up) in 1828. Some are giant steps too with treads a couple of feet deep. They take us to the top of Wynd Cliff, and the short stroll noisy with rooks to the magnificent viewpoint of the Eagle's Nest, 700 feet above the river below.

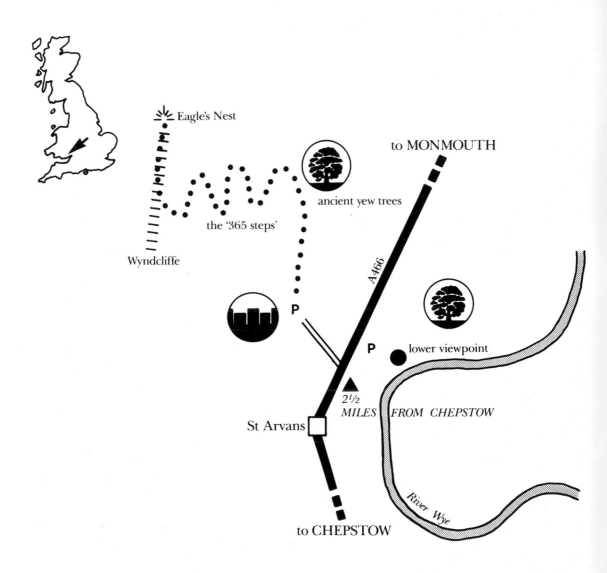

OS grid reference of viewpoint ST 525970

River Wye

In the main our rivers are of three kinds or 'ages'. They are young where they rise in the hills, tumbling past rock and boulders. They become middle-aged where they run in sight of the first cornfields, but they are still powerful enough to cut themselves deep valleys. When old they wind snake-like across a flat plain on the final stage of their journey to the sea.

But, of course, some rivers running from the western and northern hills do not become old – they tumble straight down to the sea. For eastern rivers there is no mountain birth. In the south, chalk rivers have a character of their own. Chalk streams rising as they do from springs have an even flow – they rarely flood and their banks are slight.

Clay rivers on the other hand (and most of our lowland rivers are clay rivers) scour their bed deep when in spate.

We usually see these rivers in gentle flow – only partly filling their steep-banked flood path.

And in our view, we see another factor – the sloping muddy banks tell us that the Wye here is tidal, as are all rivers within reach of the sea.

So – here we have a tidal old river snaking its way on the last leg of its journey to the sea. Yet all is not as it seems, for clearly the Wye is here cutting itself down through hilly ground.

Its story is this: originally the Wye snaked its way across a flat plain. Slowly the land began to rise, but the Wye kept to its old tack, cutting itself the steep-sided valley we see. Meanwhile not too far away, the River Severn became a powerful force, sweeping out a vast wide valley. This can be seen in the background of our picture, past the final range of the Wye's cliffs.

In fact, further north, the Wye actually leaves the shelter of the hills, turns, and enters them again!

It would be unusual if a river valley as lovely as this were *not* part of literature in some way. It was much admired by Dorothy and William Wordsworth when they visited the area in 1798. The greatest of his early poems resulted – '*Lines composed a few miles above Tintern Abbey*'. However, these dealt more with tall rock and deep and gloomy wood, ignoring the abbey ruin. With this poem he began to express his appetite for nature.

There is more about Wordsworth's view of nature on page 46.

THE ANATOMY OF THIS BEST VIEW

● *'Water is the eye of the landscape' – as the imaginative landscape designers of the past had it. Here we see the River Wye classically composing a view in its own right.*

● *The river twists as energetically as a caged snake. It does represent considerable energy and in time where the water runs faster at the outside of the bends, it cuts itself cliffs.*

● *The far cliff seen in this view is interesting. Beyond it lies the flat vista of the Severn estuary. The cliff remains like a fragment of a castle wall. We will interpret this below.*

● *The wooded slopes create an idyllic setting. Though seeming wild, in the past even such steep woodlands may well have been coppiced. Alder trees and trees of the willow tribe will grow at the water's edge, with oak, beech, ash and other trees on the drier slopes above. In places further up the valley groups of larch and other conifers have been planted in Victorian and later times.*

143

GAZETTEER NINE

THE RIVER

Britain's rivers are of various kinds. Here we present a selection – young, middle-aged, old. Chalk rivers have their own distinct character.

1) The River Tay *at Aberfeldy makes a popular visit. The bridge was built by General Wade in 1733.*

2) There are many fast running troutbecks to be seen in the Lake District. At Ashness Bridge, *near Keswick, we have a classic stream view.*

3) The River Greta *at Greta Bridge, County Durham was the subject of many beautiful and original watercolours by John Sell Cotman at the start of the 19th century. They are reckoned amongst the best of English landscape art.*

4) The River Derwent, *North Yorkshire. This rises near the coast north of Scarborough then swings right round and does not approach the sea until it meets the Humber. This river is rich with wildlife. One of its most picturesque stretches is through Forge Valley Woods, near Scarborough.*

5) The Ouse Washes, *Cambridgeshire. This was once an impenetrable marsh, until a Dutchman, Cornelius Vermuyden, dug parallel cuts to straighten the meanders of the River Ouse. The plan was to use the meadowland in between to take the winter flood water, in order to protect the surrounding rich fenland soils. These 'washes' are now a paradise for winter bird watchers.*

6) The Thames at Port Meadow, *Oxford. Here the majestic Thames glides past a gigantic ancient grazing meadow, still dotted with grazing cattle and horses as it always has been in the past.*

7) The Thames again, from Richmond Hill, *London, the subject of well-known paintings. The fact that London now spreads way beyond does not detract from the idyllic quality of this scene of the great swing of Old Father Thames across the flat ground below.*

8) The Teifi, the loveliest of Welsh rivers, with many faces. From flowing deeply in tight gorges, it widens within a few miles into a broad estuary and enters the sea at Cardigan.

9) The River Meon, *Hampshire, a typical chalk stream full of trout.*

10) The River Dart *has a vast estuary for its size. In fact it runs into a valley flooded by rising sea level.*

THE FORCE OF NATURE

HIGH FORCE WATERFALL, TEESDALE

his is by far the most dramatic waterfall in Britain, tumbling, peat-stained water set in a delightful wooded gorge like a natural theatre. One of the rock layers exposed here is also rather special – the quaintly named Whin Sill.

A waterfall is a mysterious, powerful thing, but like all nature, it obeys certain rules. Here we discover its secrets.

Tickets have to be bought for both parking and entry to the path leading to High Force waterfall.

On assignment to powerful High Force waterfall, most routes pass by splendid open moorland.

The B6277 road coming from Alston is particularly fine in this respect. After miles of breathtakingly empty grass moor, lower ground is reached with a scattering of pure white farmsteads each set neatly in its own fields.

And from this direction, a short diversion to Cow Green Reservoir is well worthwhile. Flooded in the early 1970s, Cow Green carried unique collections of arctic tundra and alpine flowers which had first bloomed here at the end of the Ice Age, and remained established, flowering here year after year ever since.

Mountain pansy, saxifrages, spring gentian – they can all still be seen, however, on a fascinating nature trail in what is now the Upper Teesdale National Nature Reserve which enfolds the reservoir. A track also leads to Cauldron Snout, another major waterfall just below the reservoir.

Cauldron Snout is, incidentally, England's highest cascade, 200 feet high.

The car parked and the parking ticket bought, you cross the road for the path and another ticket at the hut. No use complaining – they have been charging entry here since 1897. The path runs through woods, at first of dark fir, then opening out, half a mile in all, and with plenty of seats along it.

As the gorge closes in, the slopes steepen. The side opposite across the water becomes a natural rock garden, attractively studded with shrubs and small trees. The path skirts a bluff of rock. Its lower half is cracked into small horizontal ledges, like a loose pile of books. *Jum 83. Del was* (was what?). Just the place for names – and there are plenty scratched up.

Above this slight echo of immortality, set in rather sturdy rugged vertical columns is the famous rock of the Whin Sill. But more about it overleaf, here you get a close look at it.

It is worth continuing past our viewpoint of the waterfall. Steps to the right lead on to-

10

wards the top of the falls. Here you can stand on the Whin Sill itself and look down at the surging peaty water, tossing with white foam.

This path leads out into the National Nature Reserve and gives a glorious vista of the upper stream tumbling down from the open moorland beyond.

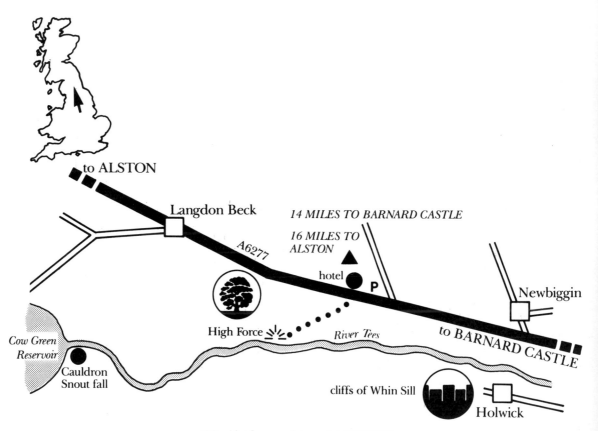

OS grid reference of viewpoint NY 880284

High Force waterfall

Our most dramatic waterfalls cut themselves back into steep-sided gorges, and High Force is a perfect example. In fact this tendency is part and parcel of the reason for the waterfall in the first place.

As it flows, a stream or river in time cuts itself a valley, and takes the debris of the rock layers with it on its run down to the sea. The valley is steeper, the faster the flow of the water.

The rock of a valley is not often of the same quality throughout. There are harder beds which resist erosion, and here waterfalls occur.

Sometimes the fall sluices down rapids – the harder rock steepens the river's bed. But where softer rock underlies the harder, this softer rock is in time gouged out. The harder capping is undercut and falls in.

So a vertical fall is created, and this wears away at the same tight path, creating a nick which enlarges into a narrow gorge, as we see here.

Here the harder band is an exposure of the Whin Sill. It is dolerite, a rather coarse lava which when molten exuded itself between other rocky layers.

The thickness of the Whin Sill varies from place to place – 200 feet in some places. It is also exposed by the sea at Bamburgh on the Northumberland coast – the castle stands on it.

It creates the craggy inland cliffs on which the Roman Wall runs at Haltwhistle, north of the Tyne. (Such crags can also be seen from the road south from High Force.)

As we see in the photograph, the rock of the Whin Sill has a columnar appearance – rather like a smudged version of the famous Giant's Causeway, in fact. Both were created when the molten lava cooled slowly enough to allow a gigantic crystalline structure to develop.

For a long time now, waterfalls have been among the best-loved of tourist traps. They are as invigorating as the sea – and the reason may not be wholly visual. There was a theory a while ago that the churning water struck ozone from the air around, ozone which was thought to give the lift to a briny sea breeze (it doesn't).

They may indeed have had ancient worshippers. Although there is no proof that waterfalls themselves were sacred, the Iron Age 'Celts' who fought the Romans worshipped certain springs.

In fact, their temples were groves of trees rather than buildings, and they worshipped natural things such as sacred oak trees and the hare.

THE ANATOMY OF THIS BEST VIEW

● *The water falls straight and deep into a foaming plunge pool. The waters of the young River Tees here tumble through portals of Whin Sill rock, then fall past softer rock to the swirling pool 70 feet below. They tumble with ceaseless roar.*

● *The fall is set back in a dramatic defile, this defile itself lying at the head of a narrow gorge.*

● *Hopes of immortality? Not only does the rock by the path bear initials, but so does any handy branch.*

149

With their endless, effortless demonstration of power, their thunder and their (usually remote) setting, waterfalls contain the essence of the picturesque.

THERE IS MORE about the picturesque on page 42. Waterfalls were as they are now, a must for the first guide books. They attracted painters of all kinds and still do.

GAZETTEER TEN

THE WATERFALL

The geological factors that create a waterfall mean that dramatic falls are only to be expected in hard rock, in hilly country where active erosion of the land surface is still continuing (or to put it another way, where the valleys are steeper). Down in the south we have to rely on weirs for the thunder of the waters. Some waterfalls have strong literary or artistic links.

1) The Falls of Glomach *can be counted the highest in Britain. There is one plunge of 330 feet, then another of 60 feet, in a ravine near Loch Torridon, Highlands.*

2) The fall that makes it into the Guinness Book of Records is Eas a'Chual Aluinn, *which drops 658 feet down the slopes of Glas Bheinn in these Highlands – but this is braided down over the rock face.*

3) The Falls of Clyde *were painted by Turner. There are three falls in all in a spectacularly stepped, wooded gorge.*

4) Grey Mare's Tail, *Borders. There are others of the name; this 200-foot dramatic fall is seen from the road from Moffat to St Mary's Loch.*

5) There are many fine falls in the Lake District. The Lodore Fall, *for example, just off Derwentwater. See also VIEW 8.*

6) England's highest fall is Cauldron Snout, *near High Force, but again this is no sheer leap.*

7) The highest English sheer fall is Hardraw (Hardrow) Force, *1½ miles north of Hawes, North Yorkshire.*

8) Swallow Falls, *Betws-y-coed, Gwynedd. Still impressive although the surroundings are not.*

9) Pistyll Rhaeadr *highest in Wales, 240 feet, in two leaps. Near Llanrhaeadr ym Mochnant on the road between Oswestry and Lake Bala.*

10) Scwd-yr-Eira, *Porth yr Ogof, south west of Brecon. A curtain of water behind which runs a path; one of several fine falls in this area.*

THE ENCHANTED LAKE

LOCH LOMOND IN SULTRY LIGHT

No true guide to the best British scenery could omit the Bonnie Bonnie Banks o' Loch Lomond. And here they are, for Loch Lomond must be a prime contender for the title of most beautiful lake – partly for its setting, partly for the shapely islands which adorn its surface.

The western road is busy: the eastern is not, and it makes a delightful drive or walk.

Glasgow is a fine city; but city it is and it points the contrast with Loch Lomond. This lake, within a short drive of Glasgow and thickly populated central Scotland, miraculously retains its wild charm. The road up the eastern shore is by far the more interesting of the two.

The Loch is met first at Balmaha, a pretty little harbour. From here mail boats make circuits of the islands, and crossings can be made to the isle of Inchcailloch, splendidly wooded and part of the Loch Lomond Nature Reserve. Its name means 'women's island'; it bears the remains of a nunnery. It was also the burial place of the MacGregor clan – just the spot to tune into the mysterious ghost of Rob Roy (but more of him anon).

Loch Lomond is the largest inland water in Great Britain. It was once a sea loch, a deep inlet of salt water, a limb of the Firth of Clyde before its mouth became silted up. It is now a freshwater lake.

Along the road to Rowardennan you will pass a rather reedy inlet, covered with water lilies. This, a university field station, is a clear example of the doom facing all fresh water lakes. Shallows are invaded by reeds which trap sediment brought down by the feeder streams. The banks encroach into the open water to create a marsh – and in time the lake dries up. It takes a long time, but it does happen, as dead flat valleys found amongst the hills show. (In fact a large marshy area now lies to the south east of Loch Lomond.)

The lie of the large islands of Inchcailloch and Inchmurrin holds another geological story. They strikingly mark the line of the Highland boundary fault – a gigantic fracture of the rocks which forms the division between the Highlands and Lowlands of Scotland.

This line can be seen from the ridge on Conic Hill, above Balmaha. Another striking view is offered further up the lake. The road ends at Rowardennan, but from here a path climbs Ben Lomond. This, at 3194 feet, is the southernmost of Scotland's *munros* – mountains (or hills rather, as the Scots call them) over 3000 feet high.

11

It is not too arduous, and in fact Ben Lomond is the most-climbed real height in Scotland. Numbers of visitors could exceed those climbing Helvellyn, the popular summit in the Lake District.

Also recommended on the way home – a visit to the salmon leap at the Pots of Gartness. Here between August and October, if the stream is full enough, these valiant fish can be seen jumping the falls on the way to their spawning grounds.

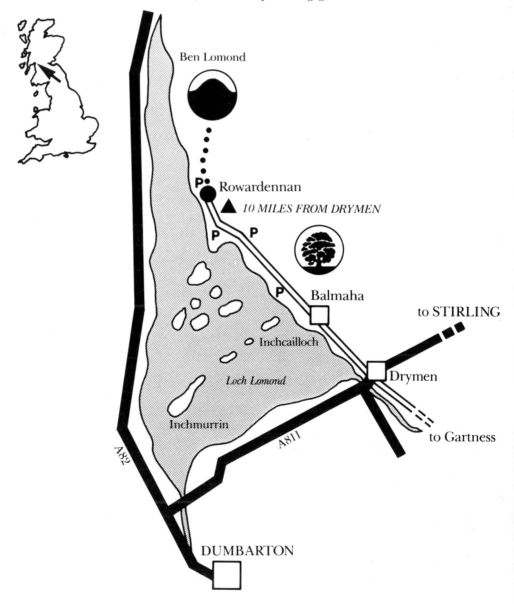

Loch Lomond

Scottish names ring throughout the world. Who hasn't heard of Loch Lomond? And where is it they live who haven't heard of its bonnie banks? And hummed the tune without ever visiting the place?

> *By yon bonnie banks and yon bonnie braes,*
> *Where the sun shines bright on Loch Lomon';*
> *Oh, we twa hae pass'd sae mony blithesome days,*
> *On the bonnie, bonnie banks o' Loch Lomon'.*

(Chorus):

> *Oh! ye'll tak' the high road and I'll tak' the low road,*
> *An' I'll be in Scotland before ye;*
> *But wae is my heart until we meet again,*
> *On the bonnie, bonnie, banks o' Loch Lomon'.*

No, it is not a dirge spawned in the music halls when Victorian tourists first began to flock here and to the Trossachs, the first part of Scotland to be discovered after Sir Walter Scott's popularizations. It seems that it was written over two centuries ago by a Jacobite supporter of Bonnie Prince Charlie, languishing in a prison cell in Carlisle. Scotland is nothing if not history.

Do Scotland's views always creak with nostalgia? Hereabouts was MacGregor land.

The name Rob Roy also means something internationally.

Rob Roy MacGregor was a kind of Scottish Robin Hood, for the poor and against the rich – or in his case for the ancient Highlander life against the Lowlanders and the English redcoats.

Rob Roy was a real person, born around 1650, perhaps in Glen Gyle which comes down at Ardlui at the narrow head of Lomond. His mother was of the Campbell clan, the assassins at Glencoe (VIEW 5), but that was still some years off. He was a chieftain, but his clan, the MacGregor, was being squeezed out of their lands, outlawed, and even forbidden the use of their name and tartan. Sir Walter Scott in his novel *Rob Roy* popularized his life and stirring deeds.

The result is, as they say, history. When a few years ago a service was held to commemorate his memory, 200 delegates from MacGregor Societies in the USA – including eight Mexicans – flew over to join in.

It is the real history of such people as Rob Roy which gives added dimension to Scotland's views. As we found at Glencoe,

THE ANATOMY OF THIS BEST VIEW

● *A lake is more dramatic when its shores are fretworked or when islands create edges and stepped vistas down its length.*

● *Very often the shores themselves make a delightful visit, with small cliffs, beaches – the coast writ small.*

● *Amongst its setting of hills, the light is ever changing. Loch Lomond is best seen by moonlight (but that does not produce a good photo). Here we see it spectacularly, in the brooding light of an approaching storm.*

155

nowhere else is the view we see today so unchangingly linked with actual historical dates and figures. In many cases, today's view remains as they saw it then.

THERE IS MORE about Best Lakes – and Wordsworth's reckoning of them, on page 56.

GAZETTEER ELEVEN

LAKES (WITH OR WITHOUT ISLANDS)

Lakes are a feature of the hills. In the lowlands we have to rely mainly on flooded gravel pits or other diggings or on reservoirs. But some modern lowland reservoirs are so vast that they make fine views in their own right.

1) Loch Maree, *Highland. This runs close to Lomond in the votes for Scotland's most beautiful lake. It has numerous small wooded islands.*

2) Kielder Water, *Cumbria. Set in the largest man-made forest (of conifers) in Europe, this yields a magnificent expanse of water.*

3) Ullswater *was William Wordsworth's favourite Lakeland lake, but he wrote rather hesitantly of it: 'As being, perhaps, upon the whole, the happiest combination of beauty and grandeur, which any of the Lakes affords.'*

4) Ladybower, *near Sheffield. If reservoirs we must have, this is charming in some of its reaches. Like all reservoirs, the drop in level in dry weather exposes very unnatural shores, stark bands of mud. Drystone walls of the old fields disappear down into these hill reservoirs, and in years of drought, ruins appear in Ladybower.*

5) Lake Vyrnwy, *Powys. A giant reservoir close-set with conifers, it is sometimes used by British film-makers wanting Alpine Swiss settings!*

6) Rutland Water, *vast with a shoreline 20 miles around, this incredible reservoir has been landscaped so that in places it is edged by lagoons used by large numbers of wildfowl. 210 different bird species have been seen here.*

7) The Norfolk Broads. *In origin, one of the most unusual collections of open waters in Britain. Everywhere shallow, of more or less even depth, in the best spots bordered by thick reed beds, the Broads are in fact the flooded hollows left by medieval peat diggers.*

8) Bewl Bridge Reservoir, *near Tunbridge Wells, East Sussex. Rare open water in the Home Counties.*

9) Sutton Bingham Reservoir, *on the Somerset–Dorset border south of Yeovil. Woods and fields bordering this serpentine, out-of-the-way reservoir make this a charming place.*

10) Colliford Lake, *Bodmin Moor, Cornwall. A reservoir, just down the way from the old smugglers' Jamaica Inn on Bodmin Moor. Dozmary Pool, at 1000 feet above sea level, is nearby. Great views.*

THE POWER OF STONE

CALLANISH CIRCLE, WESTERN ISLES

Of the thousand or so prehistoric stone circles still standing in Britain, this is the most simply dramatic. From a distance it is as enigmatic as the best of them. But on close approach its stones glisten and its puzzles multiply. For it is not a simple circle, but includes both a cross-like alignment of stones and a stone avenue. Accessible at all times, without payment.

Today's landscape here is largely flat and empty. There are trees at Stornoway (a wood was planted around the castle a century ago) and it is interesting to wonder if the island of Lewis was as bare when the stones at Callanish were dragged upright.

The silhouette of the main circle frowns on the low horizon above Callanish village, rather whitish from a distance – it is called Fir Hreig, the pale men. But when caught by the sun, it can glow as brilliantly as an iceberg.

Close to, the circle shows itself to be made of stones of a local 'gneiss' (pronounced 'nice'), a granite-like rock, one of the oldest found in Britain. This is streaked white and grey, rather attractively, and spotted with lichens.

There are other places of interest not far away. At Dun Carloway stands a broch, in its way as mysterious as this stone monument.

There are brochs to be found in many places in the west and north of Scotland, but this is one of the best-preserved. Opinions differ as to whether they are Pictish, and built against Roman slavers, or from later times and a defence against the Norsemen. Or indeed if the first, then probably both.

The broch at Dun Carloway is a circular stronghold, its outer wall still towering 30 feet high. This wall is hollow, its outer face sloping in, the inner face vertical. Within it is space in which presumably the people slept in troubled times, their animals in the open courtyard, here 25 feet across.

Not far away again around Breasclete lies a collection of black houses. These were the style of housing most families lived in throughout the Highlands. They are single-storied, thatched dwellings with not much if anything in the way of amenities of the kind we take for granted today. There was not even much in the way of a chimney for the fire. Hence (from the smoke) the name. Those that survive are converted; some have been museumized, restored to their previous state.

For the wildlife addict, no visit here is complete without a trip to view the machair. This lies along the western side of

12

many of the Western Isles – a wide, open shelly flat strip alongside the sea, which has for centuries only been lightly grazed or cultivated.

As a result, many wild flowers brighten it, and many wading birds nest in it. But sadly it is threatened by changes in traditional farming. Catch its delights while you can.

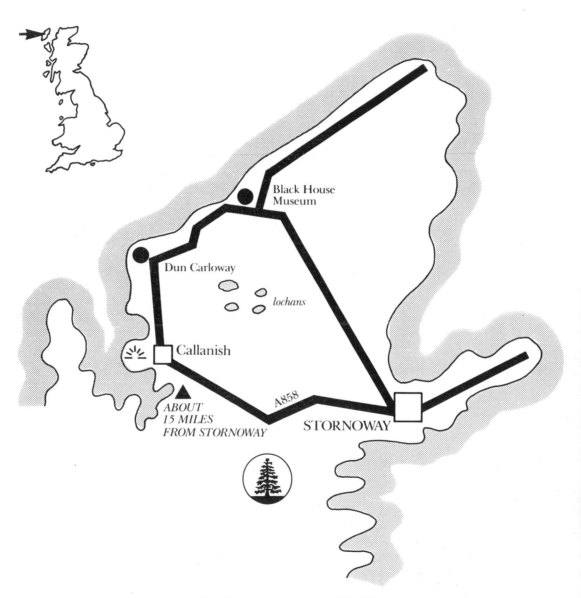

OS grid reference of viewpoint NB 213330

Callanish Stone Monument

Structure and situation combine to make Callanish the most haunting of our prehistoric stone circles. Impressive Stonehenge, gigantic Avebury – they have tamer ghosts.

Callanish is complex in plan. It may have had overlapping and varied uses at different times in its long life – as is true of today's churches.

There were burials here: chambered tombs, such as often stored the bones of corpses that had been left out to be picked clean by the ravens and other scavenging birds beforehand.

The stone avenue is more puzzling. There is also one running from Avebury, while Stonehenge had an earth-banked avenue. They were clearly ceremonial ways, and it is interesting that Corsica has stone rows, some scored with pictures of swords, some even with faces, perhaps representing dead warriors.

Such monuments, both in Britain and in Europe, were often started in late Stone Age times, but enlarged into what we see today somewhat later in Bronze Age times.

Callanish itself had become almost swamped with peat (the staining can still be seen). It was dug clear last century, and seeds found in the bottom soil showed that grain was once grown here. Around 2000 BC a timber structure was put up here, to be replaced by the central stone pillar and circle. The tomb was added later. The age of the avenue is not known.

Between the stones, Bronze Age people dug pits, presumably again for some ritual. But by 1000 BC Callanish had probably fallen out of use, its power lingering on only in tales of myth and magic.

And this is true of all our stone circles. Once their original function had been lost, their builders and even the language they spoke forgotten, myths and legends took over, which lasted until recent times. What is interesting is that several are common enough to suggest they echo original beliefs.

Betrothal vows were made at Callanish (and a first bedding amongst the stones ensured a happy marriage). Men were changed into stone – for anything from dancing on Sunday to upsetting the local witch. Story had it that the stones of Callanish were giants turned into stone by St Kiaran for refusing Christianity – a memory perhaps of a warrior caste long gone. Along with other sites such as the Hurlers in Cornwall and Long Meg in Cumbria, the stones were said to be uncountable, never twice giving the same total. (There were magic numbers linked with stone circles – 3, 7, 9.)

THE ANATOMY OF THIS BEST VIEW

● *Vast standing stones. Some weigh many tons, and heroic feats must have gone into their erection. Although steady, their weight can almost be felt.*

● *They stand in stately measure. But their seemingly confused arrangement multiplies the hints of rituals forgotten long ago. Callanish stone circle is in fact a multiple monument consisting of circle, tomb, avenue and stone row.*

The 16-foot tall central monolith forms the 'headstone' of a small and partly ruined tomb chamber. This is surrounded by 13 tall, twisted pillars arranged in a ring 40 feet across. Three short rows of standing stones radiate out to east, south and west; while to the north-northeast runs an 'avenue' of parallel lines of stones, pointing to the distant mountains of Harris.

● *Tricks of light multiply its aura. Dawn, dusk – or maybe moonlight – when did its makers use it?*

A common tradition, though not told of Callanish, is that the stones of the ancient circle move in the night, often to go and drink at a nearby stream or spring, or to dance.

Whatever they get up to, they are firmly back in place by cock crow.

THERE IS MORE about the ways that such ancient monuments gripped the romantic imagination and became essential visits on a tour on page 58.

GAZETTEER TWELVE

THE STONE CIRCLE

And other prehistoric standing stones and other relics. There are very many to be seen in most counties except those towards the east and southeast of England.

1) Cairnholy, Creetown, Dumfries and Galloway. Here are rings of standing stones, clearly the remains of courtyard cairns and other burials.

2) Castlerigg stone circle, near Keswick, Cumbria. In a splendid mountain setting, at midsummer sunset the tallest stone casts a 1/2 mile shadow to a spring in the valley.

3) Arbor Low, SE of Buxton, Derbyshire. Oddly, the stones of this circle do not stand, they lie atop the ground – but with no lessening of atmosphere thereby. Stunning views.

4) Anglesey was a centre of learning for the prehistoric Welsh priesthood; it became known as the Island of Druids. A superb menhir, a standing stone, just north of the Menai Bridge gives such a superb view of Snowdon that it must be the reason for its siting. Four miles southwest of here, is Bryn Celli Ddu a vast temple-like prehistoric tomb, which originally stood enclosed within four circles.

5) At Rudston, in the churchyard, near Flamborough Head, North Yorkshire, is the tallest standing stone in Britain, 25 1/2 feet high.

6) Rollright Stones, a stone circle on a bleak ridge just north of Chipping Norton, Oxfordshire. A malevolent feel to this circle. Its other names include the Whispering Knights – turned to stone.

7) Stonehenge, *near Amesbury, Wiltshire. With roads and barbed-wire fenced fields of modern Wiltshire downs all around, this monument still keeps its grandeur – just. It looks surprisingly modest from the distant view. Not long gone are the days when you could park the car alongside and walk around the stones by moonlight.*

8) Avebury stone circles, *west of Marlborough, Wiltshire. Counted by many to be more impressive than Stonehenge, this giant banked complex of rough stones engulfs half a village.*
    Such places aroused academic interest in the past. One of the first antiquaries was William Camden, whose Britannia of 1586 was a survey of ancient places. John Aubrey was another. In 1663, Charles II took him as a guide to Avebury. 'His Majestie commanded me to digge at the bottom of the stones . . . to try if I could find any humane bones; but I did not doe it.'

9) Winterbourne Abbas, *Dorset; a small but atmospheric stone circle stands in trees alongside the Bridport road.*

10) There are many stone rows and standing stones on Dartmoor, a circle, Scorhill Circle, *near Gidleigh, for example, with its tallest stone 8 feet high.*

THE PROUD CASTLE

BODIAM, SUSSEX

Set in a wide moat, its battlements reflected across the placid water lilies, this is surely everyone's dream of a fairy-tale castle. Rather unexpected is the way it is situated in its attractive surroundings.

Parking and entry to the castle ruin are both (separately) free to National Trust members. Otherwise you pays your money.

This castle has many surprises.

Quite apart from its stateliness, it is remarkably whole – or so it looks from beyond the moat. The outer walls stand as they were designed, more or less complete, without later changes or additions.

With no gaps, either. Although Bodiam was taken twice, it was never subject to cannonades. It was yielded without resistance in the Wars of the Roses and then in the Civil War, when it was gutted.

So its air of completeness is a mere shell. Little memory remains of the rabbit warren of tight-packed rooms and roofs which gave living space inside the walls. But the interior is well worth visiting, a lively plank bridge walk across the moat. The well of fresh water, vital to the castle's life, is quite impressive. Fed by a spring, it can brim high, almost welling out you might say. As impressive to those with a nose for historical detection are the numbers of fireplaces left in the walls, the floors they warmed long since decayed and fallen. This must have been a very *snug* castle.

But maybe not snug in the way we like today. It had few horizons. When it was built, the lord of the castle also possessed almost complete power over the local neighbourhood. In fact a castle like this would have been its pivot. If his wife, children, cousins, stewards and personal retainers lived here permanently (he himself was often away on state business), so did any number of now forgotten local miscreants. As well as home, this was also courtroom and gaol.

So perhaps while the children played, unfortunates were regularly strung up on the ancestors of the oaks that now line the moat. Life for the peasants then was nasty, brutish and short.

Such sobs and cries have now been forgotten; so have the smells that once permeated the structure. As well as a goodly number of fireplaces, this castle also had a rare number of privies, lavatories, 33 in all and all with shafts draining directly down to the moat.

However, tantalizingly little has been found in the mud, considering the 300 or so years

13

it was inhabited. Some finds are shown in the museum opposite the castle's gateway. No costly jewellery, sadly – not for its value, but for its personal links. All we have are fragments of metal, spear heads and the like, and bits of pottery of course.

Another surprise is the position of Bodiam Castle. It is not located at the bottom of a valley as its deep moat would suggest, but up a slope away from the river (which carried a harbour when the castle was built).

166

Also of interest is the vineyard on the slopes above the castle. Climates change as well as rivers. Vineyards were quite common in southern Britain when Bodiam was built.

Bodiam Castle across its moat

Castles can hardly avoid being a major part of the view. Built for defence, they often crown a high spot. Here a spring-fed moat has led the castle to be placed on a sloping hillside, overlooking what was a harbour on the River Rother.

This narrow and banked river was once wider and deeper, and a likely high road for French privateers – the reason for building the castle in the first place.

Its simple design adds to the fairy-tale quality of this castle. It was one of the last to be built, by which time a Royal licence had to be obtained to crenellate (that is fortify). A copy of it is in the museum.

Its fairy-like appearance was not art, but down to earth sense. Everything we see had a *reason*. Even the arrow-slit windows; they were usually widened inside to give archers elbow room. But this also (aerodynamically) stopped breezes whistling in through the gap. Which is why 'archer's slits' are also found in farmyard barns. The round towers – all the better to see you with, in every direction (square towers have blind areas).

Lord Curzon rescued the castle from galloping decay. 'At Bodiam' he wrote '. . . no trace of the modern world appears to invade the ancient and solitary beauty of the scene, and it could hardly surprise anyone, were a train of richly clad knights, falcons on their wrists, and their ladies mounted on gaily caparisoned palfreys, suddenly to emerge from the Barbican Gate. . . .'

As we have observed, the traffic might just as well have been peasants being led out to be hung (or worse).

Castles were not pleasant places. One of the nastiest auras in Britain inhabits the oubliette – from the French word meaning 'forget' – below Harlech Castle. It is green now with ferns growing in the light coming through the broken floor above. There was no light then.

The fact that such horrors can now be admired is our debt to the romantic imagination, which in Britain seized on the ruined castle and the abbey. Victorian taste in fact went one better – it used a bit of one (the crenellations atop the castle tower) plus a bit of the other (the arched windows of the abbey) to create the Gothic style.

THE ANATOMY OF THIS BEST VIEW

● *Castle walls entire. Although it looks complete, it is but a shell. The inside was 'slighted' (that is destroyed) by Cromwell's Roundhead troops in 1644, nearly 300 years after it was built.*
● *But the romance of the ruin is not lost. The windows gape wildly with the sky behind.*
● *Some goodly towers. Originally the round towers may have carried steeply pitched, real fairy-tale roofs. None remain in England, but they can be seen in Europe and Scotland (and in one fake medieval castle in Wales).*
● *A romantic moat – here with occasional mats of waterlilies.*

167

And here we have a small proof of the strength of that debt, even today. Bodiam Castle is justly admired; on the path up to the moat is a Second World War concrete machine-gun pill box, built for the very same reason, defence against invaders. Both are now historic. But watch how many people on the path notice the latter.

Perhaps another debt to the romantics is our belief that yesterday is never as interesting as the day before.

THERE IS MORE about the pleasure of such ruins on page 58.

GAZETTEER THIRTEEN

THE ANCIENT CASTLE

Many have been restored; some such as Windsor and the Tower of London have never been uninhabited. There are many Highland castles, and literary castles. Yes, there is a Cawdor Castle in the Highlands – Shakespeare made Macbeth its thane. It is a spine-chilling place. But it is as ruins that we enjoy almost everything older than a few centuries. Here are some more of our most atmospheric, empty castles in some state of ruin.

1) Kilchurn Castle, *Argyll. The finest baronial ruin in Scotland with an awesome setting on Loch Awe.*

2) Conisbrough Castle *near Doncaster, South Yorkshire. The elegantly sweeping lines of the 90-foot white keep in a countryside of black coal-tips. Sir Walter Scott wrote* Ivanhoe *while staying nearby (pub names recall this) and set one scene in the castle's wall chapel.*

3) Harlech, *Gwynedd. This most cruel castle was one of those built by Edward I to impose his will on the Welsh. It stands on a crag 200 feet above sand dunes (there was originally a harbour at its foot). It has been attacked countless times. It houses an infamous oubliette, now derelict.*

4) The ruin of Peveril Castle *glowers on a cliff over Castleton, Derbyshire, unassailable on three sides.*

5) Goodrich Castle, *Hereford and Worcestershire. A classic marcher castle, built to control its share of the Welsh borders.*

6) Kenilworth, *Warwickshire. A stately dark-red ruin, open to the sky. A vast pile with many historic connections (yes, Queen Elizabeth I did sleep here).*

7) Castle Rising, *near King's Lynn, Norfolk, is a magnificent relic keep within gigantic earthen ramparts.*

8) Richborough Castle *and fort, near Sandwich, Kent. An old one, this – Roman in fact. It was one of the forts of the Saxon shore – and our best preserved Roman fort, with 12-foot thick Roman walls still standing strong. Within them was built a later keep.*

9) Corfe Castle, *Dorset. There are truly romantic glimpses of this from any of the approach roads: shape and size create its allure plus the necessary amount of dilapidation – including watch towers now at a slant.*

10) Tintagel Castle, *Cornwall. Here is High Romance, due to its supposed links with King Arthur – see VIEW 28. The castle sits on a crag falling to the sea in a very picturesque way.*

THE ROMANTIC RUIN

RIEVAULX, YORKSHIRE

cale and setting put Rievaulx into a class of its own as a monastic ruin. Added to this, Rievaulx can be viewed from above, from a terrace giving splendidly composed vistas of the ruin and its setting, a grand introduction to the Grand English Art of planned viewmanship.

Rievaulx Abbey ruins are in the care of English Heritage, while the terrace and its two temples are in the care of the National Trust. Admission charges for the abbey and terrace-temples, separately. Car parking by ticket for the former, free for the latter.

What is the best time of year for a visit? In late spring when the bluebells and wild orchids flower in the terrace woodlands? In autumn when the foliage colours? Or in sultry summer, when the clouds brood high above?

Rievaulx has a dramatic enough setting – a tightly wooded valley, Rye Dale, leading down to the flat plain of York.

There are two prime views of this abbey. The first is from its own level, from the village lane which skirts it. There is even a handy field gate or two to lean over, though it is worth buying a ticket to actually wander through the ruins themselves.

From this lane, splendidly set against the wooded hillside the ruined abbey presents a colossal face – much of the walls of nave, transepts and choir are seen to remain.

Then on to the next view. We climb the hill, park the car, pay our money and (as advised) go for a stroll through elegant woodland. This half-mile path leads out to the southern end of the wide grassy expanse of the Terrace, near to the round 'Tuscan' temple. An oddity of architecture gives it this name – it has (Greek) Doric style decoration above its columns, but they stand flat, without bases in the Tuscan way.

This temple can be viewed and walked around, but not entered. So we leave it to stroll along the Terrace on well-mown grass. And here we see that the trees along its edge are cut back from time to time, to give a series of glimpses of the valley below and the country beyond. The Terrace curves, and after a while not only does another Ionic temple come into view, but the Abbey below comes into sight, posed in the gaps in the trees. You choose your favourite glimpse, for the perspective of the arches changes from sighting to sighting as you walk.

This is not all. The squarish Ionic temple with its fine columned portico also has surprises. It was built for dining; a

14

table ready-laid is on view, beneath a ceiling ornately painted with stories of Aurora and other classical themes. Around the walls stand elaborate tables, settees and other furniture in ornate style.

That is not yet all. The basement of this Ionic temple where the food for the banquets was once prepared now houses exhibitions. One tells the story of the Duncombe family who created this marvellous Terrace. The other shows how it sits in the story of landscape design in Britain.

You get more than you bargained for in this terrace view. And it's all included in the price of one ticket.

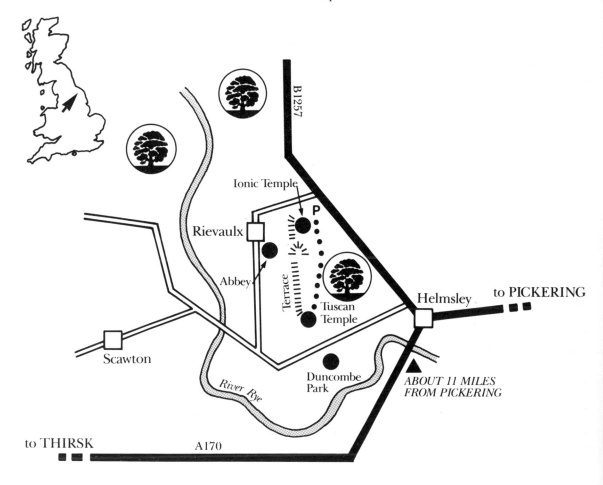

OS grid reference of viewpoint SE 580850

Rievaulx Abbey, from Rievaulx Terrace

Although practicalities such as a powerful patron nearby accounted for the choice of this vale, the siting of the abbey follows the Cistercian tradition. Twelve brothers settled here, primitively, in 1131, to remove themselves from the temptations of town life. The order which had arrived in Britain under Henry I chose secluded sites, often in such remote wooded valleys.

They were anything but dreaming hermits, however. They organized farming, especially sheep-ranching, on a grand scale, in control of thousands of tails. (In places, the widespread grazing of these mega-flocks may have changed the look of the countryside around.)

Profits accrued and paid for this tremendous building, once at the forefront of architectural development, which housed 140 monks and 500 lay brothers.

Unlike castles, which fell into ruin in every age, our abbeys became ruined all at about the same time. The result of Henry VIII's quarrel with the Pope and Catholic church of Rome; the Dissolution created instant ruins.

The Terrace is altogether another story. It was created in the 1750s, and it was a momentous novelty in its day.

It is very 'natural'. There is nothing rigid in its lines. The flowing curves of nature are followed although the edge of the terrace had to be graded and the trees cut, the better to reveal the abbey ruins below.

Even its two temples are not forced into the view as dramatic eyecatchers, but placed like buildings discovered accidentally during a walk in a foreign land. The curve of the terrace in fact means that they gradually come into view as you walk from one to the other.

Gentry would gather here to admire the abbey and the valley beyond. For the Duncombes who owned it, the Tuscan temple was for solitude, the Ionic for parties.

The cleverly cut vistas enthralled Dorothy Wordsworth when she visited. Turner painted one or two pictures. The poet William Cowper wished to stay for ever.

Arthur Young, one of Britain's early and doughty travellers (see page 22) visited during a six-month tour of the north country and wrote extensively about the Terrace. 'Exquisite' is only one of the adjectives he uses. Here is what he says about our own viewpoint:

'Before you arrive at the portico, the scene is much varied;

THE ANATOMY OF THIS BEST VIEW

● *The ruin is strongly patterned. The empty windows and fractured arches create bewildering, visual echoes.*

The most dramatic sightings of the abbey are from close to the Ionic Temple, where it is almost directly below.

● *Its skeleton is graceful. Much more so than a castle. Our collective culture now accepts the 'Gothic' as a prized ruin.*

● *A picturesque setting – again, we admire clothings of trees as a result of our collective romantic imagination.*

hitherto an edging of shrubby wood along the brink of the precipice hides its immediate steepness from your eye, but here it is broken away, and you look down on the abbey in a bolder manner than before; the trees are wildly scattered, and all the other objects seen in great beauty.'

THERE IS MORE about ancient-monuments on page 58.

GAZETTEER FOURTEEN

THE RUINED ABBEY

Unlike castles, our abbeys by and large all fell into ruin at one time with Henry VIII's dissolution of the monasteries and his seizure of their lands and wealth. Cistercian abbeys tend to lie in remote, picturesque sites.

1) Crossraguel Abbey, *Ayrshire far enough from the border warfare. This has only time to blame for its slow decay; ruins in an excellent state!*

2) Fountains Abbey, *near Ripon, Yorkshire. One of the mightiest monastic foundations in Europe in its day.*

3) Whalley Abbey, *near Blackburn, Lancashire. Setting for many local stories, including Harrison Ainsworth's* The Lancashire Witches *– required reading for anyone visiting Pendle Hill (see gazetteer 1).*

4) Coventry Cathedral. *Unlike all the others chosen, this is not in a countryside setting. It was chosen because it recaptures feelings – but from our own time. Starkly this ruin stands, a moving memorial to the bombing in the Second World War. Its replacement, largely built in the 1950s, stands nearby.*

5) Valle Crucis, *near Llangollen, Clwyd. Isolated and atmospheric. The name means Vale of the Cross – the latter (now a stump) erected in memory of a Celtic prince who fought the invading Saxons.*

6) Llanthony Priory, *Gwent. Founded by a William de Lacy who saw the sun rising over the Black Mountains and decided to remain, as a hermit. Walter Savage Landor eccentrically planned to found an ideal community here, but quarrelled with all around him and left. Later he penned these lines:*

> *Llanthony, an ungenial clime,*
> *And the broad wing of restless Time,*

Have rudely swept thy mossy walls
And rockt thy abbots in their palls.
I loved thee by thy streams of yore,
By distant streams I love thee more;
For never is the heart so true
As bidding what we love adieu.

7) Tintern Abbey, *4 miles north of Chepstow, Gwent. Thanks again to Wordsworth for immortalizing this place, though his lines dwelt more on the nature round about (see VIEW 9).*

8) Castle Acre Priory, *Norfolk, with a magnificent west front.*

9) Glastonbury, *Somerset. Here, it is said, Saint Joseph buried the Holy Grail used at the Last Supper. Once one of the richest monasteries in Britain. Now in complete ruins, from which there is a unique view across a unique part of Britain, the Somerset levels.*

10) Waverley Abbey *(nowhere near Walter Scott's view), near Guildford, Surrey.*

HAMPTON COURT GARDENS

ith the Palace at Hampton Court we have a splendid Tudor building which has been enhanced with architecture by Christopher Wren. The two sit together well. So it is with the extensive gardens and park – amongst the greatest in the world; they provide a dictionary of views and other outdoor delights from more than one period in the past.

Hampton Court Palace and Gardens are in the care of the Department of the Environment. Foot entry to all gardens is free; all else is payable.

Hampton Court Palace presents an immensely wide face to the road. And it gives the impression of being spaciously placed, if not in open countryside then certainly not in town. It is insulated from the miles of London's suburbs which engulf it by the River Thames on one side and parklands on others. No modern office towers rise behind it, as they do with other London palaces.

We can reach the Formal Garden by various routes. Why not start with a visit to the famous maze – as puzzling still as it was when it was first laid out. Records show it being planted with yew in 1690. And yes, there is a simple trick to get to the centre and out again.

Not far from the maze is 'Wilderness House' where the landscape architect Capability Brown lived when he was appointed Master Gardener here in 1764.

Brown was noted for his vast designs – landscapes of miles of grass, trees and little else; he is equally noted for his butchery of many formal gardens, lapping the grass right up to the mansion.

He seems to have been muted here at Hampton Court, but he has left one marvellous sight, in the shape of the Great Vine, which he planted as a cutting in 1768. Its main stem now has a circumference of slightly over 7 feet at ground level.

An old print shows us that the ground between the broad walk and the circling canal, still to be seen in part, was once a swirl of plantings. Not much remains of these – the area is now largely trimmed plain grass (well-nigh too neat for eyes used to our own back lawns) dotted with trimmed lollipops of trees.

But if these foreground details of the past have gone, the longer view does remain – down the full, majestic length of Long Water to a horizon hazy with distance, or so it seems. There is scarcely a glimpse of the suburbs pressing beyond the far reaches.

It is worth walking out into

15

the park. The great gale of October 1987 uprooted many trees, but this was not the first damage of the century; Dutch elm disease eliminated many trees here.

Our goal, however, is the restored Formal Garden.

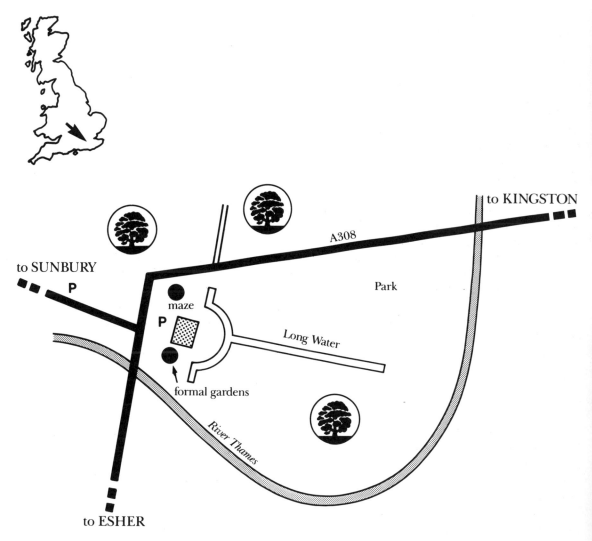

OS grid reference of viewpoint TQ 160682

The garden in seventeenth-century formal style, Hampton Court

The history of the gardens at Hampton Court is as interesting as that of the palace buildings.

The palace was built by Cardinal Wolsey and on a grand scale. Too grand for safety perhaps; at any rate he later decided that he had better believe that he had built it for his master, Henry VIII, who took it.

In Wolsey's time, the gardens were probably small, including kitchen and herb gardens to the north and to the south, and others in simple floral arrangements.

Henry put in hand his own designs, and these can be guessed at from itemized accounts of the time. £49 went on carving thirty-eight stone statues of kings and queens, together with a number of lions, dragons, greyhounds and unicorns. There were posts and railings painted in green and white, the Tudor colours – and sixteen brass sundials.

These would surely have conspired to make his privy garden as solemn and constrained as the royal chapel. Today we assume a garden should be colourful, a free and airy place.

Gardens of mansions of the time were often built up in a squared grid, with a fountain central to all in some way. One 'box' could contain an orchard, another was set aside for vegetables. One was often a 'knot' garden.

The small knot garden was laid out to a formal pattern. Closely clipped low evergreen shrubs could be used – and the frequent clippings yielded a regular supply of sweet smelling cuttings to strew on the floors of the rooms as an antidote to the 'pestilent ayres' of the time. Sometimes the pattern was also picked out with sand or brick dust, or the spaces filled with herbs or flowers. The pattern was geometrically neat (although it could also be ornate).

An extension of the knot garden was as a 'parterre' – a much larger, geometrical design, also using low 'hedges', but large enough to relate to the house as a whole. Although the knot garden was usually enclosed, the parterre usually gave fine views out across the estate.

Somewhere in this development, mazes became fashionable. Few grand houses of the sixteenth and seventeenth centuries were without one.

Perhaps the hedge maze of the kind at Hampton Court was spawned by the parterre. But it is interesting that turf-cut mazes were then to be seen on many village greens. Shakespeare refers to them; in *Midsummer Night's Dream* Titania says: 'the quaint mazes on the wanton green, for lack of tread are undistinguishable.'

THE ANATOMY OF THIS BEST VIEW

● *Enclosure. This is the essence of a garden as opposed to a park.*
● *Intricacy. A garden of this kind is a completely formal thing, and the patterning underlines this.*
● *Colour. Here the strong skeleton is green – the green of neatly trimmed 'hedges'. Flowers add colour (which changes with the season of course).*
● *The walks are gravelled in a traditional way. This small paradise was laid out in 1924, in the style of one of three centuries ago ('paradise' comes from the old Persian word for garden, by the way).*

Mazes of this kind are still to be seen at a few places such as at Brandsby, North Yorkshire, Wing, Leicestershire, and Hilton, Cambridgeshire.

These village mazes provided a ritual or religious walk – a kind of mini-pilgrimage; knot gardens were also for walking in. But even though the view from the parterre could be admired, it was to be a while before people stepped out in the park itself. In fact Samuel Pepys notes that the habit was a new one in his day.

GAZETTEER FIFTEEN

THE EARLY GARDEN

Like all living things, gardens grow and change. Here are some early examples which remain somewhat in their original condition or were laid out to earlier designs. This gazetteer should be consulted together with those of VIEWS 16 and 17. These gardens are usually open for the summer months; some are open all year round.

1) Levens Hall, *near Kendal, Cumbria. A world-famous topiary garden, laid out in 1692, the shrubs now clipped into some very odd shapes.*

2) Bramham Park, *near Wetherby, West Yorkshire. Laid out in the French style of le Notre who designed the gardens of Versailles. Here we have the Grand Vista with grand avenues and rides radiating from temples and other focus points. It suffered in a great storm of 1962, but is recovering.*

3) Melbourne Hall, *Derbyshire. A famous early garden with long vistas, started in the 1690s. This is the only layout by the early designer Henry Wise to escape changes by Capability Brown.*

4) Chatsworth, *Bakewell, Derbyshire, has (apart from all else) a splendid cascade in pure seventeenth-century style.*

5) Oxburgh Hall, *near Swaffham, Norfolk. In the grounds of this moated mansion a parterre, laid out in 1845, on designs from the century before.*

6) Oxford Physic Garden, *The High, Oxford. This was laid out in 1621, the first of its kind in Northern Europe – a classic enclosed garden of a rather different kind.*

7) Westbury Court Garden, *Westbury, Gloucestershire. A formal*

Dutch-style garden laid out at the end of the seventeenth century, with canals and yew hedges.

8) Ham House, *Richmond, London. A restored seventeenth-century garden. Other London gardens of note are the* Chelsea Physic Garden *(1673) and of course the complex known as* Kew Gardens. *The latter has dated landscapes of various types and kinds. These London gardens all suffered to some degree or other in the great storm of October 1987.*

9) Painswick Rococo Garden, *Gloucestershire. An odd survivor of a brief fashion in the eighteenth century, now being restored to original designs.*

10) Ashdown House, *Oxfordshire. An unusual doll's house set in the Downs, with a parterre in seventeenth-century style.*

PLANNED ENTICEMENT

his is the most beautiful *designed* landscape in Britain – very little here is 'natural', not even the trees. (Many are exotic and Stourhead Garden is a fascinating arboretum.) It is all the more interesting in that it was created not by professional landscape designers but by its owners around 2½ centuries ago.

It is noble at all times of year – in May it is coloured with rhododendron and horse chestnut in flower, in summer (perhaps the time when it was meant to be seen) it is varied green, in autumn the leaves turn, and winter brings slow mists to drift between the lake and trees.

The garden is a National Trust property, open conventional hours throughout the year. Stourhead House is also open in the afternoons from April to end October on various weekdays. (Free to members, free parking.)

Stourhead is easily reached from main roads, and the journey is through dry downland.

Not much in the way of lakes here, but of course massive Stourhead Lake was dammed from a stream and feeder springs. It was an enormous undertaking and all the greater because its banks were also graded and shelved with stones to create the desired curves, while features such as the spring-fed grotto had to be built before the basin was flooded.

But back to the beginning. Although the lake and temples can be glimpsed from the public road skirting it for a short way, it is really necessary to park and walk the planned paths.

There is a choice. The full route is the original eighteenth-century circuit, two miles in all, beginning and ending at Stourhead House, where of course the house guests started. This gives a fine curtain raiser – a laurel-fringed viewpoint with a vista towards the Temple of Apollo. But there is also a low level walk around the lake, starting at the village and continuing about 1¼ miles. However, for the important stretches circling the lake, both are one.

So, following in the steps of many before us, we pass, stop, enter and move on. Temples built in classical style await us, and a rustic cottage covered with creeper.

The grotto is a must. Its clear springs gush ceaselessly from the earth. In one recess, a river god, in another a most delicious nymph sleeps.

While nearly back at the village we pass a High Cross, not quite fallen off the back of a lorry, but a medieval monument that did once stand in Bristol. It blocked the traffic.

16

'A ruinous and superstitious relic, a public nuisance' was how the citizens described it. So it arrived at Stourhead in six wagons in October 1764.

Stourhead Garden is clearly in debt to the classical past of ancient Greece and Rome. More of that anon, overleaf and on page 64.

While here, it is worth visiting Stourhead House, if only to see the paintings – one a copy of a view of Delphi in ancient times by Claude Lorrain. In pictures like this we can find the original inspiration for much of what we see at Stourhead.

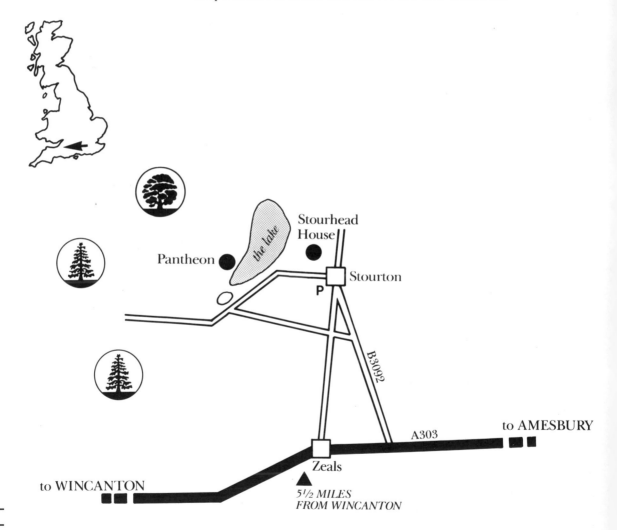

View across the lake in Stourhead Garden

That Age of Reason and Elegance, the eighteenth century, was also the great age of landscaping. Not many were involved, but a handful of men of varied backgrounds sowed a new kind of view.

Their names – Bridgeman, Kent and later Brown and Repton, for example – are as well known today as then, not only for the number of estates they designed but for the sheer scale of their enterprises.

Trees were of key importance. Vast numbers were planted; existing woods were not simply felled, but sometimes moved to better positions. Whole villages were moved if they interfered with the view.

Stourhead, created over a period of 50 years from around the 1750s was unusual in that the owners, the Hoares, a banking family, did not call in a name but did the job themselves – damming the lake, commissioning the buildings, planting the slopes, laying out the circuits for admiring guests and visitors.

It was designed to evoke not only admiration but other responses as well.

For example, above the door to the Temple of Flora is inscribed in Latin: *Procul, O procul este profani* – Begone you who are uninitiated, begone! These are words spoken by a Sybil in Virgil's *Aeneid*; also from that epic tale comes the inscription over the grotto: *Intus aquae dulces, vivoque sedilia saxo, Nympharum domus* – Within, fresh water and seats in the living rock, the home of the nymphs.

Cut into the cold bath by that delicious sleeping nymph are the lines, also classical in origin:

> *Nymph of the Grot these sacred springs I keep*
> *And to the murmur of these waters sleep;*
> *Ah! spare my slumbers, gently tread the cave,*
> *And drink in silence or in silence lave.*

All calculated to evoke in the minds of visitors (those, at least, who could read Latin!) the glories of the classic past. Not a story as such, but a series of hints.

The classic past of ancient Greece and Rome was immensely popular amongst the wealthy of that century. On their Grand Tour they saw its remains at first hand, while artists such as Claude Lorrain captured it in paint.

It is interesting that one of Claude's most famous pictures, *Aeneas at Delos*, contains Pantheon, bridge and temple portico very

THE ANATOMY OF THIS BEST VIEW

● *Trees in stately masses, carefully planted. This is the view in early autumn. Originally, views such as this were structured with native trees (and increasingly with exotic specimens) and sometimes with quick-growing laurel. Here at Stourhead rhododendron was later planted; its flowers colour the scene in May.*

● *A lake. Water in the view was both visually and symbolically important. The springs are celebrated in the Grotto, with its statues and quotations.*

● *The lake shore is carefully embanked to create a flowing line.*

● *Eyecatchers. The Pantheon is in view in this scene. Finished in 1754, in imitation of the building of ancient Rome dedicated to the gods, it is as interesting inside as out, and houses a marble statue of Hercules.*

● *Note also the elegant bridge.*

185

similar to those we see here at Stourhead. Such paintings were a kind of blueprint.

To recreate the lost world in this way was not a simple nostalgia for ruins, for it is likely that amongst the well-to-do, ancient Greece and Rome were felt to be times of bedrock – artistocratic worlds where all men had their place. Their memory extended an invitation to a kind of security, very welcome in an age when many old certitudes were in question and even seemed threatened.

And so perhaps these evocations were doubly meaningful to a newly rich banking family.

THERE IS MORE about the background to the wonderful world of English landscape design on page 62.

GAZETTEER SIXTEEN

GRAND DESIGNS ON THE VIEW

These designs are mainly in the classic mode – often with temples prominent! This list should be read together with those for VIEWS 15 and 17.

During the years 1750–1850, visits to five great estates were considered essential for people of culture. They were Stourhead, Castle Howard, Stowe, Blenheim and Mount Edgecumbe.

1) Castle Howard, *near Malton, North Yorkshire. One of the prizes of the estate is the Temple of the Four Winds, possibly the finest such building in Britain. A village was demolished to create this, one of the earliest of the expansive landscapes in the novel English style.*

2) Stowe, *Buckinghamshire. Now a public school, but the grounds can be visited. Here great names amongst the landscape architects left their mark – Vanbrugh, Bridgeman, Kent, Brown. Temples and other splendid edifices evoke emotions.*

3) Blenheim, *Woodstock, near Oxford. Vanbrugh built an elegant Palladian bridge across the new lake. Brown raised the level of the lake, half-drowning the bridge, and swept away the parterres to bring grass right up to the walls of the mansion.*

4) Mount Edgecumbe, *near Plymouth, Cornwall. A vast park, but also formal gardens in European styles.*

5) Chiswick House, *London. Here William Kent tried to recreate the classic idyll.*

6) Hagley Hall, *near Stourbridge, West Midlands. A 'gothick' ruined castle, built in 1740, is part of the attraction of these grounds.*

7) West Wycombe Park, *Buckinghamshire. Another classic, with various temples (including a newly reconstructed Temple of Venus) around the lake. Also noted for its caves, used for the orgiastic meetings of the Hell Fire Club.*

8) Farnborough Hall, *Banbury, Oxon. Temples, obelisk on ¾ mile terrace walk with fine vistas over the countryside round about.*

9) Claremont, *near Esher, Surrey. Early Bridgeman, with grassed amphitheatre, Vanbrugh Bridge, pavilion, grotto; later 'naturalized' by William Kent. Capability Brown too was here, but this is the earliest surviving English landscape garden.*

10) Shugborough, *Staffordshire. Neoclassical buildings and follies, including a temple, adorn the grounds.*

THE NATURAL LOOK

PETWORTH PARK

Here we have an incomparable view, where nature joins with art, creating something without equal in the entire world. At Petworth Park we have a style of landscaping which was peculiarly English. Although it suffered in the Great Storm of October 1987, when many trees were lost, we can still see it much as it was designed to be seen, and it remains a classic example of Brown's style.

Petworth House and Park are in the care of the National Trust. The Park is open all year round from 9 am to 9 pm, or dusk if earlier, and parking is free in the two car parks shown.

Petworth itself is a charming but crowded place, its huddled streets always busy. This bustle presses close against the high walls which surround Petworth House and its justly famous Park.

Parking is an easily solved problem. There is a free car park in the town. There is also an alternative further out, on the road south from Chiddingfold. Here you find yourself already within the Park wall.

A recommended approach is from the east along the road from Billingshurst. You travel through a delightful countryside of rolling green fields spaciously set with trees which dance stately measures as you pass (these hedgerow trees suffered much less damage than woodlands in the Great Storm of 1987 maybe they are more used to buffeting). And then in front of you rears the boundary of the Park, seeming much the same as this countryside, but somehow majestically different. There can be no better foretaste of the grandeur of Petworth Park.

A recommended route to the Park begins at the town car park. Take the quaint cobbled street which leads towards the church, and then continue to the right past it, reaching a yard with outbuildings on your left. Walk across the yard and through a tunnel. A wrought-iron gate welcomes you into the Park itself. You face a slight rise. When you have breasted this you begin to see why Petworth is so famous. The view opens out before you, dignified and spacious.

Sadly, there are now obvious signs of storm damage: gaps in the trees, uncleared fallen giants. However, already the scars are beginning to heal.

See how the house lawns to the left are surrounded by a haha, a sunken wall within a ditch which keeps grazing animals out without blocking the view. A witty device, hence its name.

17

The animals in question are deer. They are rather shy. If not seen, the turf is in some places generously dotted with mementoes of their presence.

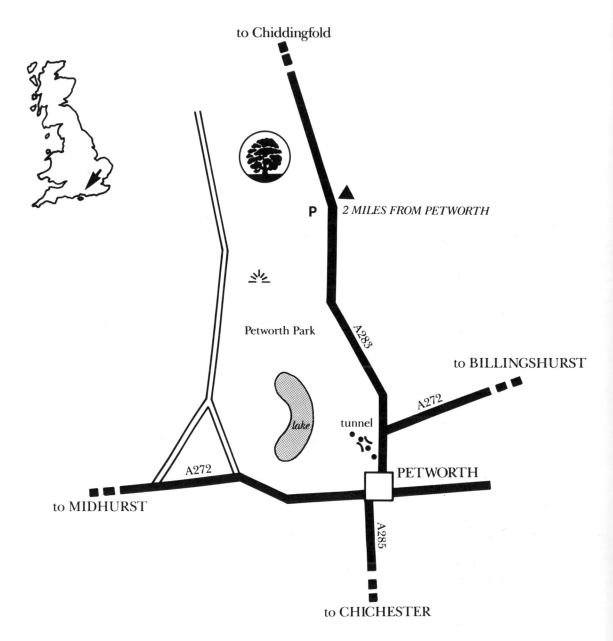

to Chiddingfold

P

▲ *2 MILES FROM PETWORTH*

A283

Petworth Park

lake

tunnel

to BILLINGSHURST

A272

A272

to MIDHURST

PETWORTH

A285

to CHICHESTER

OS grid reference of viewpoint SU 970225

Climb the rise to the urn, there is a rather fine prospect from it. There is also a small temple to be found but far fewer eyecatchers of this kind here than we found at Stourhead.

The statuesque hound on the lake shore directly in front of the house is also worth a close look.

View across Petworth Park

Here we see a created landscape, but very different from Stourhead in VIEW 16.

Lancelot 'Capability' Brown, who died in 1783, was its original author and it retains many of the features which typified his style. He was a man of immense energy, in his time changing the face of well over 100 estates such as Petworth.

Basically, Brown enhanced the natural character that the site already possessed in the way of contours and loose scatters of trees. (Brown gained his nickname 'Capability' from his habit of extolling these possibilities, 'capabilities', to potential clients.) Buildings he held to be less important as eyecatchers, 'nature' was the view itself.

This did not mean that he left what he found, quite the opposite. To create the lake, a standard feature, he was capable of carrying out massive damming works; he also altered slopes. The idea was to create a lake with a delightfully serpentine shore-line.

Although he planted many trees in belts and clumps, he could casually fell those that did not fit his plan, and some old formal avenues have been lost as a result.

He was equally ruthless in sweeping away the gardens around the house, bringing the grass right up so that the windows looked out across a breathtaking spread of green stretching to the far distance, broken only by clumps of trees. It is something seen especially well here at Petworth.

Although there are now one or two gaudy-flowered rhododendrons (planted in Victorian times) and in spring the horse chestnuts add their flowers to the scene, a view of this kind was really meant to make its summer effect with green alone – the green of grass, the foliage of the massed trees balanced by the armadas of clouds in the sky overhead. This effect is ruined if conifers (sometimes planted to add texture) grow tall and peak up above the canopies of the other trees.

Like Stourhead, this Brown landscape was meant to be walked in. These clumps of trees have been planted to create changing

THE ANATOMY OF THIS BEST VIEW

● *Clumps and skeins of trees, carefully grouped on open ground. Here we see them largely bare-boughed as they are for half the year. It is in winter that the storm damage is least apparent.*
● *Sweeping turf. Here browsed by deer.*
● *A distinct browse line on the trees. By snatching the lower foliage, the deer impart a dramatic browse line; on sloping ground this line follows the slants, adding another kind of sculpting to the view.*
● *A snatch of lake. The Park was designed to invite walks through it, and this photograph is taken on one. The lake is a standard feature of a Brown view, enlivening the middle distance of the view from the house itself. From our vantage point we gain only a glimpse of it.*
● *The view is entire: the countryside beyond is barely seen. Brown's parks were usually circled by a belt of trees, screening the outside world.*

picturesque vistas to greet guests and visitors as they stroll through the park. It is a quite sophisticated notion – and had to be planned in three dimensions.

This complex landscape is misleadingly simple. When Brown died, Horace Walpole said that his genius was 'happiest when he will be least remembered, so closely did he copy nature that his works will be mistaken'.

Was it 'nature' he was imitating? The grazed deer park was hardly a natural place. Without management of the herds, the park's turf would quickly revert to scrub.

Nature, like the view itself, is very much in the eye of the beholder. THERE IS MORE about this, and the peculiar puzzle as to why this appealed to the eyes of estate owners in the past on page 62.

GAZETTEER SEVENTEEN

THE NATURAL LOOK

> Improvement too, the idol of the age,
> Is fed with many victims. Lo! he comes,
> The omnipotent magician, Brown appears,
> Woods vanish, hills subside, and valleys rise,
> And streams, as if created for his use,
> Pursue the track of his directing hand.

from The Task, *by William Cowper, 1784*

As gardens and grounds have had more than one hand, this list should be read with those of VIEWS 15 and 16.

1) Harewood House, *near Leeds. Many consider this to be Capability Brown's masterpiece. We prefer Petworth.*

2) Warwick Castle. *Brown was faced with a difficult problem here, with the grounds so tightly closed by the river – he looped the approach drive amongst other things.*

3) Burghley House, *Stamford, Northamptonshire. Another Brown masterpiece.*

4) Luton Hoo, *Bedfordshire. And yet again!.*

5) Woburn Abbey, *Bedfordshire. A vast deer park, 3000 acres, land-scaped by Humphrey Repton.*

6) Rousham House, *near Oxford. The effect of Capability Brown was so blanketing, that it is easy to forget that other approaches to a 'natural' view could be made. Here at Rousham is a jewel – an intact landscape by William Kent, with temples and a memorial to a beloved otter hound, a stream following Hogarth's line of beauty and much besides.*

7) Bowood House, *near Calne, Wiltshire. The park landscaped by Brown between 1763 and 1766.*

8) Longleat House, *Warminster, Wiltshire. Lions roar (this was the first safari park) in parts of this Brown park.*

9) Sheffield Park, *near Uckfield, East Sussex. A Repton red-book landscape, sadly mauled by the great storm of October 1987.*

10) Corsham Court, *Chippenham, Wiltshire. A monument to both Brown and Repton.*

THE WELCOMING WILDWOOD

his kind of woodland is as historic as anything to be found in a dusty museum. Native, natural pine woods remain only in patches in a few places in Scotland. Many lie within easy reach of Aviemore. They have the atmosphere of an ancient time.

A visit here has other benefits – rare birds, a trip to Arctic tundra, reindeer. Patches of old Scots pine forest (such as that around Loch an Eilein) can often be visited without formality.

It is worth starting with a trip to the tops of the Cairngorms. Not as hard as it sounds, a ski chairlift runs all summer.

Up on top, it is clear that these mountains are in effect a rolling high plateau, deeply cut by valleys which were deepened and widened by glaciers in the Ice Age. The cauldron-like corries on the high slopes were the birthplaces of these enormous tongues of ice.

On the tops, the climate is sub-arctic, below freezing for much of the year, with the highest snowfall in Britain. But on the loose gravelly soil, mosses and lichens grow and even flowers in some places. These plant communities were widespread everywhere in Britain when the Ice Age was ending, but are now common only high in the Alps and in the Arctic tundra.

The ptarmigan lives up here. Golden eagles and peregrine falcons are frequently seen ranging over the tops.

Down on the lower slopes, trees begin. Many of these are in modern plantations, but here and there relic patches of the old Caledonian Scots pine forest can be found. How they can be recognized is described overleaf.

Indeed it is interesting to compare plantation and natural pine forest on one walk.

These lower woods are full of birds. Apart from those such as blue tits and chaffinches which are common in other kinds of woodland, these pine forests carry crested tits, and crossbills, which look like small parrots. The rare osprey now nests on Loch Garten, a magnet for birdwatchers of every age.

The undergrowth of the pine forest shelters roe deer, and perhaps red deer too in the winter. However, these animals prefer to spend their summer high up, away from flies (and people). Fox, wild cat and red squirrel also range through these woods.

There are reindeer to be seen in the area. After being absent from the Highlands for 800 years, a small herd has been established on the hills above Loch Morlich. The sight of reindeer would have been very

18

familiar to the first men to settle in the ancient Caledonian forest, and who, by their activities, spelled the forest's doom.

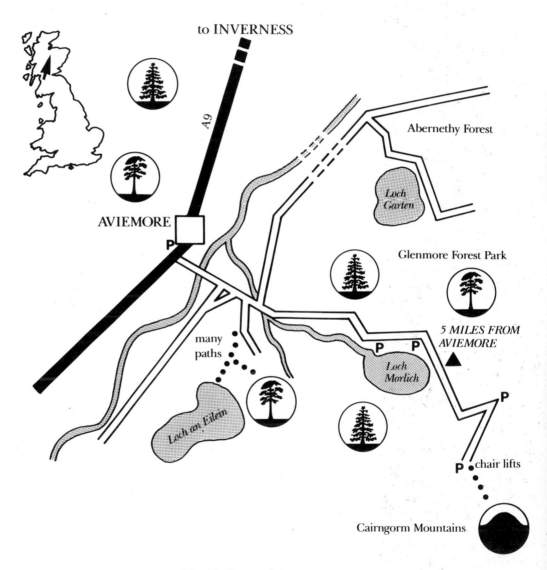

to INVERNESS

A9

AVIEMORE

P

Abernethy Forest

Loch Garten

Glenmore Forest Park

5 MILES FROM AVIEMORE

P   P

Loch Morlich

P

many paths

Loch an Eilein

P   chair lifts

Cairngorm Mountains

OS grid reference of viewpoint NH 900085

196

View of relic Scottish pine forest

We take up the story of these woods 12,000 or so years ago when the Ice Age was virtually over as far as Britain was concerned and the ground was beginning to warm up. From the south, colonizing plants spread over the now exposed bare ground.

In the van were the tundra and alpine plants still to be seen on the tops of the Cairngorms nearby. But close behind were quick-seeding birch and Scots pine. At one time or another they created over much of Britain an open forest of the kind we see here.

The trees have not sprung from some seed bank, or been planted close-set, and so there is great variety in age and in shape and branching.

We say 'at one time or another' because hard on their heels came oak, elm, ash, and other trees which on suitable soil grow to overtop even the pine, and shade it out. These hardwood trees created a dense wildwood over most of Britain. In the wetland wildernesses beside the rivers alder, willows and others of that kind ruled. But in Scotland the Scots pine still held land.

Although there were oak forests in some parts of Scotland, the poor soil of the glens was usually occupied by the great Caledonian pine forest which once covered three million acres in the Highlands. In its depths roamed lynx, elk, brown bears and wolves.

In time people settled here: Picts and Scots. They felled trees for settlements and grazings, and the destruction of the forests began. Trees were fired in clan skirmishes. Forest was also burnt to clear out wolves (the last wolf was not killed until around 1750 – around the time of the last Jacobite rebellion).

THERE IS MORE about clan life and warfare and the later imposition of lowland and English authority in VIEW 5.

The pine forest, which at that time was decidedly patchy, was also affected. Its calculated destruction began. The cowed clans sold off or were robbed wholesale of their trees, the stripped trunks floated down the fast Highland rivers to fuel iron foundries and other southern-funded Lowland industries. It was all rather similar to what is happening to the Brazilian rain forest today.

Only in the last 30 years have attempts been made to regenerate this historic forest. It is a difficult job. It cannot be planted back, for its interest, both visual and wildlife, lies in its natural origins and the accidents of growth and shape. And once the cover of the older trees has gone, young Scots pines find life difficult in exposed Highland soil.

THE ANATOMY OF THIS BEST VIEW

● *Pine trees of many ages and shapes. This is natural woodland, scarce disturbed by man. Scots pines are not the only tree here, there are birches, and rowan (mountain ash), with some alder trees in the wetter places.*
● *Open appearance. Compared with a pine plantation this has, for woodland, a generous, open feel to it. However some areas can be more closely-set on a mossy carpet.*
● *Interesting underwood. In the open light, the vegetation below the trees grows thickly – to create an exotic matted terrain more akin to that of Mediterranean hillsides (albeit with different species). Heather thrives here, strong and woody, and juniper and bilberry are also seen.*

197

Of pine woodland with this feel of ancient time, perhaps less than 20,000 acres (8000 hectares) remain today.

GAZETTEER EIGHTEEN

THE PINEWOOD

Apart from around the skirts of the Cairngorms, relics of the ancient Caledonian pine forest remain scattered in the Scottish Highlands. Where it is seen in the south, the Scots pine has been planted, sometimes extensively – it even forms hedges in some places in East Anglia, for example (but there are plantings of Corsican pine here too). However, some conifer plantations in the New Forest and other places in the south are now quite old. We also give one or two modern plantations of interest.
Only 1–5 are ancient pine forests:

1) The Black Wood of Rannoch. *Open pine woodland. The trees are individually as much as 250 years old.*

2) At Glen Tanar. *An easterly remnant.*

3) At Beinn Eighe. *The shores of Loch Maree – one of the classic relics in one of Scotland's last great wilderness areas. This is a nature reserve of international significance.*

4) Glen Affric. *One of the most picturesque areas in Scotland.*

5) Strathfarrar, *not far away from (4). The largest surviving remnant of the Caledonian pine forest in this part of Scotland.*

6) Kielder Forest, *Northumberland. Extensive modern plantations make this the largest man-made forest in Europe, with some of the feel of the (natural) Jura forests of France.*

7) Grizedale Forest, *Cumbria. Dense plantations, but along the woodland trails are wood sculptures, various and unexpected. Some seem like bridges over non-existent streams, others look like toy dinosaurs. They are all artistic statements and sit well in their setting.*

8) New Forest, *Hampshire. Here there are old stands of conifers, some with the feel of the primeval forest. In some places pines have seeded themselves out onto the heathland.*

9) Thetford Forest, *Norfolk. Again this seems to be blanket planting, but age breaks up the various blocks and some parts have a good atmosphere. As with the New Forest there are some parts of these East Anglian forests which have old trees with natural seedlings growing up underneath – in parts of Brandon Forest, Suffolk, for example.*

10) Mawddach Estuary, *Gwynedd. Some old stands can be found hereabouts.*

THE MIGHTY OAK

MAJOR OAK, SHERWOOD FOREST

Sherwood Forest Country Park encloses some of the finest remaining ancient oak forest in western Europe – which still retains its charm and mystery in spite of large numbers of visitors. Indeed so extensive is it, that it is very easy to slip the path and move back in time and in imagination meet Robin Hood. It is the very essence of the old Greenwood.

Sherwood Forest Country Park and its Visitor Centre are managed by Nottinghamshire County Council. Parking is free, as is entry to the Forest.

Spread between busy modern roads, Sherwood Forest Country Park embraces a unique relic – 450 acres of the once extensive Sherwood Forest.

The walks into it all spring from the Visitor Centre alongside the car-parking areas. This Centre itself is worth visiting first. However you might react to the notion of Automatic Outlaws (you puts in your 10p, you gets your sticker), the sheer buzz of the place is catching. It is busy – not only with people but with things to do. You can snack in Robin Hood's Larder. You can view the 'Legend of Robin Hode and Mery Scherewode'. You can watch videos about the forest and its wildlife or listen to the Ranger's first-hand stories.

And yet – all it needs is a short walk away to enter another world – a unique fragment of a past landscape (whether or not Robin Hood ever existed or even had any basis in reality in the tales told over the centuries). For the old oak forest miraculously remains in its ancient state.

There are waymarked walks of varying length – the shortest from the Visitor Centre to Major Oak and back about a mile long, taking half an hour or so. The longest (which crosses the thicker wooded parts and passes through a Britain of 1000 years ago) takes two hours. However, you can take your own route on numerous small paths winding between the giant old trees to discover your own hidden glades.

Sooner or later, the paths bring you to the conifer plantations which surround the Park on three sides. The difference could not be more acute. On the one side, history and a wildlife-rich habitat. On the other nothing much except trees, and dense at that.

As for the Major Oak itself, it is a mighty tree. It is between 400 and 500 years old, its hollow trunk (12 people can fit inside its hollowed bark) now so weak that branches have to be propped up if they are not to

19

snap off. Here, it is said, Robin Hood's band of outlaws regularly met. Except that, if Robin Hood ever existed at all, he was alive several centuries before this oak was a sapling.

There is no proof that Robin Hood was a historical figure. But myths are usually spawned by fact, at least in a general way. (The first mention of his name is in *'Piers Plowman'*, see page 14.)

What is certain is that the forest laws that once laid the lash on Sherwood brought great hardship even to the normally downtrodden local populace. In the forests even the basic and vital commons rights to pasture were suspended. Poaching the deer led

OS grid reference of viewpoint SK 621680

to mutilation or hanging from one of those handy oak boughs. But the forest was free – deep in the Greenwood outlaws could perhaps survive, and by defying tyrannical evil and greed gain wondrous approbation, which echoes still today.

View of Major Oak, and the ancient forest behind

Apart from the (necessary) branch props, a view of this kind would have been familiar to Robin Hood, and a good many other Greenwood outlaws down the ages.

It is not quite a natural view, but it is not unnatural either.

Normally, in muddy medieval times, lowland villagers cropped their local woods, a long-held right. The underwood shrubs were regularly coppiced, cut to a stump to grow again, while interspersed were numbers of 'standard' trees, left to grow up tall and straight, without rivalry, for timber.

Pigs or cattle (and deer) could not be allowed in the young coppice; they would destroy it. Hence in woodlands where villagers had grazing rights, the trees were pollarded, that is cropped at head height. The short trunk grew a crown of branches which (if custom changed) grew into a crown of heavy boughs. In its shape, Major Oak resembles an old pollard. Pollarding destroyed the timber value; not worth felling, pollards were left to grow old.

But the Country Park is a relic 'forest' – land set aside for the hunt by Norman and Plantagenet kings. Here the interests of the deer overrode all the customary rights of the local peasantry.

A 'forest' might be wooded in part, but it was usually not entirely wooded. The New Forest is partly heathland.

The herds of deer, by their grazing, opened up the wood; nibbling the young saplings, they created glades set with mighty trees, the few that had got away long before.

Of course, that was many centuries ago, long before Major Oak was an acorn. But we can deduce that this fragment of Sherwood Forest captures the feel of those ancient hunting forests.

This fragment of Sherwood is interesting for the natural diversity within it, something not found in hard-managed woodlands. You discover glades of ancient yew trees, self-seeded a long time ago. Elsewhere, there are young groves of birches. These quickly seed – they are often the first colonizing trees of open ground; here they often mark areas disturbed when part of this Forest was used as wartime army storage in 1940–45.

Dead-headed oaks apart, dead trunks lie around like a school of beached whales. A rare sight indeed in today's countryside and a

THE ANATOMY OF THIS BEST VIEW

● *A surprisingly open feel for a 'forest'. This fragment of ancient Sherwood Forest was at one time a kind of 'parkland' with grazed glades between the trees. Today paths through the forest bring you unexpectedly to these open 'plains'; here we gain a real feel for the past.*

● *Ancient trees. Not only Major Oak itself; the whole of this remaining fragment of forest encloses old trees. Many of them are stag-headed, their upper limbs dead from disease or age, a new green crown growing from below the dead antler-like branches.*

rather splendid one; a natural gallery of Henry Moore sculptures.

Why so many dead trunks? A semi-natural wood – that is, a woodland more or less untouched by man, such as this – would contain a number of dead boughs and trunks. But the total points to either an outbreak of disease in the recent past, or (intriguingly) to a change in forest use many centuries ago, allowing many trees to get away at the same time. They grew, matured and when aged, died within years of each other. Only exceptions such as Major Oak live on like human centenarians.

This dead timber is a boon for beetles, whose grubs burrow into rotting wood. They help classify the area as a Site of Special Scientific Interest – the highest accolade. With the beetles come innumerable birds. It is a nature reserve as well as a forest.

And if you don't much like the crowds, then visit it at night by moonlight – owls, bats and a sure chance of believing in Robin Hood's ghost.

GAZETTEER NINETEEN

OAKWOOD

Oakwood once covered much of the lowlands, except in the wetter areas, and lapped up the hills. It still remains in many places.

There are two species of oak tree (although they can cross-seed). The English or pedunculate oak is the tree of the clay vales. Although it will also grow well on good soils, the sessile or durmast oak can grow well on thin, poor hillside soils. This creates a different natural distribution, with the sessile oak being found more in our western and northern hills and the pedunculate oak in the lowlands. There is also a difference in the look of these woodlands. Sessile oak woodlands growing on poor, acid, hillside soils are rather bare between the trees. Lowland oakwoods are thickly tangled.

Many ancient oak woodlands have been largely felled during this century and replanted with conifers. However, fragments of the old woodland may have been left as a belt around the new forest.

1) Dinnet Oakwood, *Grampian. One of the (few) remaining scraps of oak woodland in the Highlands.*

2) Delamere Forest, *Cheshire. One of the famous forest names, and although it has largely been replaced with conifers, the old oakwood lingers in certain areas, with badgers below the trees.*

3) Hatfield Forest, *Essex. Typical ancient forest with a variety of terrains and management, including coppice enclosures.*

4) Pengelli Forest, *Dyfed. The largest remaining fragment of old oak woodland in this part of Wales. It was coppiced in the First World War, but has never been anything but woodland.*

5) The Forest of Dean *sits between the Severn and the Wye, and although partly coniferized, it stills retains a splendid forest feel.*

6) Epping Forest, *Essex. Belonging to London (Londoners had a kind of common right to its firewood) this playground of today is noted for its old pollards.*

7) Wychwood Forest, *Oxfordshire. A romantic enough name. This romantic fragment of forest is opened up but once a year.*

8) Savernake Forest, *Wiltshire, is still widespread enough to keep its forest feel, although it is being rigorously managed (try to find a dead tree, even after the gales!).*

9) New Forest. *This is so vast an area that it contains woodlands of many kinds. Here everybody's expectations of woodlands will be satisfied – old oak woodland, old pine plantation, modern spruce plantation, coppice, self-seeded young forest.*

10) Wistman's Wood, *Dartmoor, Cornwall. This is possibly the only untouched, unmanaged wood in Britain. Its stunted oaks grow amongst boulders.*

THE NATURAL CATHEDRAL

CHILTERN BEECHWOOD

'The beech is the most lovely of all forest trees, whether we consider its smooth bark, its glossy foliage or graceful pendulous boughs . . .' so wrote Gilbert White, the eighteenth-century naturalist-cleric, the father of British natural history. He is right. This tree forms woods quite unlike any other; here we see them at their best *and* most interesting.

Many Chiltern beechwoods are on National Trust land with open access: others can be explored by public footpaths.

The name Burnham Beeches is so well known, and all the world over, that it comes as a surprise to discover that these woodlands are not so very ancient, but perhaps less than 300 years old. More of that anon.

Walking in Burnham Beeches, we realize just how varied the shapes of trees can be. The woodlands are of course famed for wonderfully gnarled giants, but in the Chilterns we see other forms too.

Some of this variety is natural. Beech grows well on chalky soil. Shallow-rooted, it is the only tree that can cope with the shallow steep soils of the chalk slopes hereabouts. But it also grows on acid, sandy soils. It is the sharp drainage of both that it likes, although acid soil tends to stunt and warp its growth.

However, many of the odd forms we see in Burnham Beeches result from pollarding at some time in the past. The trees were topped about 8–10 feet from the ground, and afterwards grew a new head of branches which in time became twisted heavy boughs.

Beech trees grow tallest on goodish, deeper soil of the kind found in some areas atop the Chilterns. At Great Hampden they can be 100 feet tall, the tallest anywhere in Britain. Our map shows another good location.

The beech tree is selfish. Its leaves take a lot of the light, and it is gloomy in a beech wood in summer. Often holly is the only woody shrub growing beneath it; being evergreen, it is able to catch some of its sunlight in winter when the beeches above are bare.

But this also means that on goodish soil, beech woods develop elegantly, with soaring straight grey trunks like the aisles of a natural cathedral. In fact, some claim that cathedral architecture gained its inspiration from such woods.

Few woods are completely dense, however, and in a beech wood other trees may grow in lighter glades – wild cherry is often seen.

Apart from this, beech

20

woods contain some unusual (and rare) wild orchids, flowering amongst the dead leaves.

The smooth bark is ideal for initials. The bark expands as it grows, so that you can tell old inscriptions by their now wide cuts!

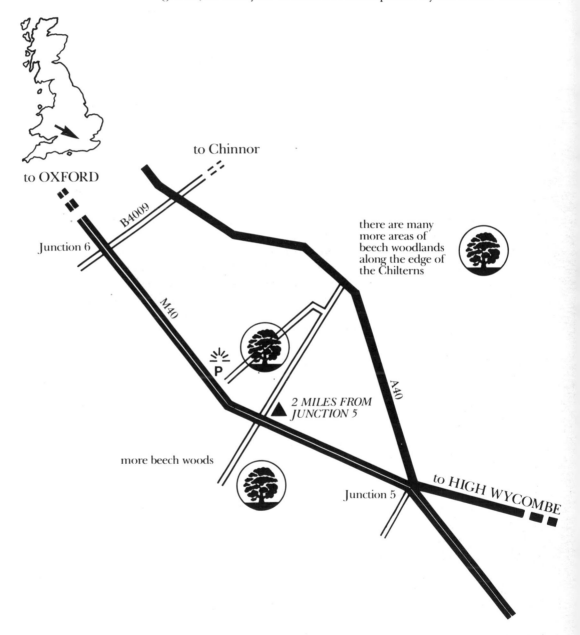

to Chinnor

to OXFORD

B4009

Junction 6

M40

there are many more areas of beech woodlands along the edge of the Chilterns

P

2 MILES FROM JUNCTION 5

A40

more beech woods

Junction 5

to HIGH WYCOMBE

Chiltern Beechwood

The melting of the ice sheets at the end of the Ice Age had the effect of raising the sea level. In time the English Channel was flooded and Britain became an island. Pollen grains found in ancient soil levels show that the last of our native trees to reach Britain before the divide was the beech. Oak, ash, elm, holly, hazel, beech . . . we have in all around 50 certain native trees and shrubs which reached here unaided.

(Vice versa, the chestnut, horse chestnut and sycamore have all been brought by man.)

Given the right soil, beech can compete with oak, and so in some places in the south of England and Wales, beech trees *may* have formed their own woodlands. But no sooner was the Channel cut than it was being crossed by the inhabitants of our first farming communities. Man's attack on the forests began.

There is no written history of what happened then, although the view can be read in one manner of speaking. The Old English name of the beech tree is *bece*, perhaps easily becoming 'buc', to give its name to Buckinghamshire if the tree was common enough here olden times.

What is certain is that because it cannot set good seed further north, all beech trees past the Midlands have been planted. The beech was a popular tree in Georgian times, favoured for ornamental planting – and many a burial mound is topped by a bonnet of beeches. Many shelter belts of beech were also planted. (Very often these had Scots pine as 'nurse'. Some pines may still be growing. So here we see one of our favourite trees, adorning woodland far to the south of its home.)

Here in the Chilterns, there are other surprises, however. Old documents suggest that some of these woods occupy what 300 years ago was open common grazing land.

There were good reasons for encouraging or even planting beech here. There was a thriving furniture industry producing, amongst other things, traditional Windsor chairs. But the close-grained beech wood had many other uses – for everything from clothes pegs to piano frames.

In these woodlands worked the 'bodgers'. They set up camp in primitive shelters of brushwood, but they were certainly not slapdash craftsmen in the meaning of the word today. They bought the stands of timber, felled the trees, cut the planks and roughed out the round legs of the chairs using a simple lathe that men of the Iron Age would have recognized.

Beech woods today tend to be quiet places. Lacking undergrowth, they attract far fewer song birds than oakwoods.

THE ANATOMY OF THIS BEST VIEW

● *Magnificent trunks. The race for light means that beech trees in a wood on good soil such as this develop tall, slim, pillar-like trunks with little branching below the canopy.*

● *Cathedral-like vistas. When in leaf, the beech canopy lets little light leak down. Hence the wood is bare, with little of the undergrowth of an oakwood; evergreen holly (and sometimes yew) may be the only shrub*

● *Magnificent coloured foliage at all times of year. Spring, summer, autumn are all beautiful. Beeches retain dead leaves longer than other trees. In fact, up to about 10 feet from the ground, they tend to keep them all winter. This may be a defence against frost – and is the reason why beech hedges keep their dead leaves.*

209

GAZETTEER TWENTY

BEECHWOODS

In recent centuries, many stands of beech have been planted into other woods, so that what seems to be oak wood may contain small areas of beech, but fine woodland these beech stands make, nonetheless. In the north, although fine specimens of beech trees are seen in the Lake District, beech woodland is less common. Similarly in Scotland: stands can be seen at places such as the Argyll Forest Park, Brodrick Country Park, Strathclyde, and Dunkeld House, Atholl.

Our larger beech trees may be around 250 years old.

1) Alkrington Woods, *Middleton, in the Manchester suburbs belonging to Rochdale.*

2) Sutton Park. *Only a few miles from the centre of Birmingham, this has been preserved as a green lung. There is some beech woodland.*

3) Felbrigg Estate *near Cromer, Norfolk. A fine example of a planted, East Anglian estate beechwood.*

4) Buckholt Wood, *near Gloucester. A superb example of a Cotswold beechwood.*

5) Coed y Bwynydd, *Gwent. A National Trust wood – with oak, but also beech, here growing at its natural western limit.*

6) Windsor Great Park, *Berkshire, has some fine beech stands.*

7) Selborne Hanger, *Selborne, Hampshire. A famous hillside beech 'hanger' this, on the territory of Gilbert White, the father of British natural history.*

8) New Forest, *Hampshire, has some fine beech areas, in Mark Ash Wood for example.*

ANCIENT AND ORNAMENTAL COUNTRYSIDE

Ancient and ornamental countryside is hand-made countryside, hacked field by field from waste and wildwood. Although these labours took place long ago, it still has a frontier feel. There is nothing much ruled straight here.

Coney Castle is National Trust land and it (and parking) is freely open.

On the way, the narrow lanes give only snatched glimpses of the fields beyond, for hedgerows close the view. Many of these hedges grow on earth banks which have at their core surface stones cleared long ago (it is interesting that in Cornwall such banks are themselves known as 'hedges').

But some hedges originated with relic strips of woodland left between the fields on each side, cut and trimmed down to shape in the course of centuries.

The variety of hedgerow shrubs tells us that these are old hedgerows. Indeed a typical length may contain holly, oak, goat willow (its catkins the 'palm' used on Palm Sunday), maple, hazel, wild rose, ash, sloe, beech and elder, with here and there an old wild cherry.

Hawthorn too grows in these hedges, but singly amongst the rest of the shrubs – unlike the hedges of the countryside seen in VIEW 22.

In spring, bluebells flower at the hedgefoot, and bright red campion and white ramsons, smelling of garlic. These hedgerow bluebells also tell us

the hedges are old; they are slow to break new ground.

Farmsteads nestle in elbows in the lanes on sites that are ancient, though their walls may have been renewed many times.

Often they have a patch of small, hoary orchard with wizened trees, sometimes with ancient breeds of apple, and perhaps still grazed by geese or sheep in the traditional way that dates back untold centuries, as you may see on the way here. However, the silage wrapped in black polythene tells you that you are firmly in today.

Coney's Castle itself is a hillfort built by a local Celtic tribe just before the Roman invasion of Britain 2000 years ago. Only the earthen ramparts remain; they were once capped with wooden palisades. Within, the fort was dotted with huts and in times of trouble filled with a jostling bedlam of people, cattle, sheep, pigs and dogs. These forts were probably as much refuges as for day-to-day living. Dorset alone has more than 30 of their kind.

Yes, there be rabbits. Coney is an old name for them. They

21

were in medieval times commonly bred in specially dug earthen warrens, and why not use a long deserted hillfort?

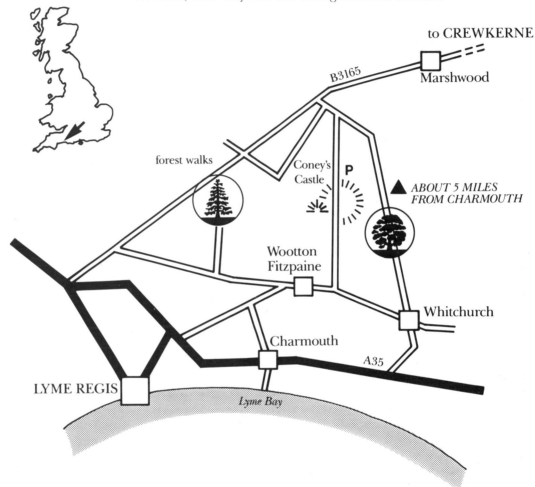

OS grid reference of viewpoint   SY 371975

View from Coney's Castle

This is historically an outback landscape, created by individuals. Its fields were carved one at a time from unfarmed waste land which was probably well wooded. In some places, in Devon for example, this piecemeal attack on the old wilderness took place in the distant past, in Bronze Age times. But here in West Dorset, today's view was fashioned from the old Marshwood Forest only seven or eight centuries ago.

Although at that time plagues and pestilences cast a sombre

shadow, the population was rising. There was a hunger for land hereabouts. Unkempt land was seized but not so much legally, by the then version of the nearby village council, but illegally, by squatters.

Their memory lives on in the names of the farms we passed on the way to our viewpoint. Champernhayes, Bluntshay, Denhay, Sminhay, Manshay just beyond it. In these a medieval personal name is linked with 'hay', a clearing.

In other counties, 'leigh' or 'ley' as part of a farm or village name can be the clue to similar kinds of settlement hacked out of wildwood. The words also mean a woodland clearing, although later farming may have created a very different landscape for our modern eyes to see. Here from Coney's Castle we can still imagine the old forest, for gawky patches of woodland remain.

Traditionally a countryside of mixed farming, the fields remain mainly pasture, with a scatter of meadow for hay, and few acres in crops – after all, it was because it was poor ploughland that it remained forest for so long. (Even on today's high-tech arable farms, the best fields are usually the oldest.)

This intimate landscape (the wood on the near horizon can be reached in less than half an hour's walk) delighted William and Dorothy Wordsworth, for they lived for a while near Bettiscombe, below Pilsdon Hill, not far away. For Dorothy in fact this ancient and ornamental countryside was 'dearest to her recollection upon the whole surface of the island'. For William, this stay was vital – having been in London, here he recaptured his belief in himself as poet, with nature his 'first love'.

Yes, they quickly become a countryside of the heart; yet curiously these ancient and ornamental landscapes have escaped Grand Literature. Even Hardy's Wessex fell short of this view.

Perhaps they were ignored because of the absence of stark grandeur or because the tensions created by villages, towns, and highways are lacking. But that is in part the secret of their charm.

THERE IS MORE about landscapes of the heart on page 74.

THE ANATOMY OF THIS BEST VIEW

- *A gently sculpted landscape. The ridges are low, rising from deeply hidden streams.*
- *Ancient field patterns. Some fields are all elbows and knees, many no more than an acre in size. Many are divided by banks which sport glorious hedges.*
- *Many fields have never been ploughed. These reveal ancient surface patterns highlighted when the sun glances across them from behind the clouds.*
- *Ancient lanes. They twist and turn, their seemingly inexplicable doglegs skirting once uncleared parcels of forest, whose ragged relics still fill odd corners in this landscape.*
- *Old farmsteads. This is a detailed and productive landscape, but here there are no villages, only isolated farms, often modern buildings occupying ancient sites.*

215

GAZETTEER TWENTY-ONE

ANCIENT AND ORNAMENTAL COUNTRYSIDE

Pockets of such countryside can be found in many places throughout England. Here are some main areas:

1) Cheshire and Staffordshire, *or at least, parts of them. Cheshire is a county of black and white – Friesian cattle and timbered houses. The timbering implies much local woodland. Both these counties have much enclosure landscape too.*

2) Shropshire.

3) The old county of Herefordshire. *Now part of Hereford and Worcestershire. Herefordshire is quite an oasis in time, encircled as it is by thousand-foot high ranges of hills.*

4) Essex. *Many 'forest' names recall extensive woodlands – place names including 'end' for example.*

5) The Sussex Weald. *This once impenetrably wooded countryside is still notable for great oaks – even after the great storm of October 1987.*

6) Devon. *An interesting county, this. Dr W. G. Hoskins carried out many of his early investigations here, to lay the foundations of modern research into landscape history. He showed for example that in some parts of Devon the sites of the farmsteads date back to Bronze Age times.*

THE SHIRE VIEW

VALE OF BELVOIR

This again is a classic British scene. It seems to have simpler elements than others with its rather formal grid and straight hedges. However, it holds surprises enough.

The heart of England consists of gently rolling landscapes, and here on the borders of Nottinghamshire and Leicestershire we have an excellent example. The view is neatly lined by the hedges around square-cornered fields.

Tidy this view seems, but it hides as long a past as any.

When travelling, you will see that many pasture fields here are crossed by regular lines of low ridges. Very often these can be seen to run *under* a hedge and continue into the field alongside. Clearly they are older than the hedges themselves. In fact they are the relic of the vast open ploughlands of the medieval manor. Today's hedges were imposed on them at the time of the Georgian 'enclosures', two centuries ago.

Notice too that even minor roads are usually straight and wide between the hedges they too are part of the 'enclosure' map, their width and ditching spelled out.

But this formal countryside also invites us to make our own discoveries. A jumble of slight banks and shallow ditches in a grass field may be all that remains of a medieval village, lost but maybe not quite forgotten, for its name may linger on in the farm nearby; and its church

may also still stand – a church standing alone amongst the fields may be the best clue to its former presence.

It may be possible to make out the worn depression of the village high street, on each side of which are squarish ditched areas.

A hut occupied each of these platforms, sometimes with a small vegetable garden behind. In some lost villages a deeper moat marks the site of the manor house, and fish ponds (now perhaps dry) were important.

Made of wood and thatch, the huts have long since gone – only the stone church survives.

These interesting remains are very vulnerable. Today only part of a village, or of the 'ridge and furrow' of its old ploughfields may survive, on one side of a hedge only. Elsewhere modern ploughing has wiped the slate clean.

These new hedges are crossed by other history in the shape of the local hunt. This is the heart of hunting Britain; our view is in fact in the territory of the Belvoir.

When travelling, look out for bosky spinneys, deliberately planted in this neat view for cover for the fox. And notice the

22

219

curious lack of barbed wire around the fields. Hedges add sauce to the hunt: jumping them adds half the thrill. So this is another clue – barbed wire would tear horses (and riders).

For centuries, foxes had been trapped and killed (as they still are where hunting is not so strong). The time when fox hunting on horseback was first becoming fashionable – in the mid-eighteenth century – was also the time when this neat, low-hedged enclosure landscape, prime hunting country, was being created.

So we have here yet another example of the curious way man combines with nature to create the view we see today!

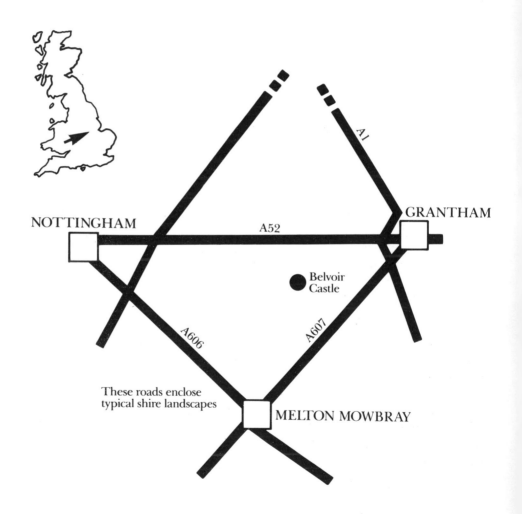

These roads enclose typical shire landscapes

The shire view

In medieval times throughout these lowlands there may have been a few hedged or walled paddocks around the village. However the farmed countryside around (except for the village woodlands and the 'waste') was largely open.

The ploughland was usually divided into three enormous fields, of which one was allowed to lie fallow at a time. Another important open area was the meadowland alongside a stream or river. Here grew the hay, the only fodder then available to keep the breeding livestock alive in winter.

Each peasant worked land allocated to him in strips scattered amongst the open fields – a way of ensuring a fair share of soils, good and bad. The up and down ploughing of the narrow strips threw the soil into the 'ridge and furrow' we still see – where it has not been deep ploughed by modern machinery.

When the Black Death struck in the fourteenth century, half the population of Britain was wiped out. Villages were emptied. In some areas unused land was taken in by the abbeys and hedged or walled for pastures or for sheepwalks – so that by 1500, there were three English sheep alive for every Englishman. Tudor England did sit on a woolsack!

The cross-hatching of the lowland landscape with hedges and stone walls was completed in Georgian times. Innumerable private, local Acts of Parliament allowed the richer and more go-ahead to annex the open village lands, and divide them into a patchwork of neat fields.

The prompt behind these 'enclosures' was the profit to be made from new ways of farming. New breeds of livestock and new kinds of grass and crops such as turnips grew in the new fields. Farming was fast becoming scientific.

In time, even the harsh lines of these imposed fields softened as the hedges grew, breaking with blossom each spring. Elms and other timber trees planted along them grew tall. Such countryside could become idyllically pastoral, the stately trees grouping and regrouping as the lanes were travelled.

Sadly those lowland elms have died; oak and ash remain, but this mild landscape is little able to cope with modern eyesores.

The enclosures spawned bitter regrets. Those dispossessed could only hire themselves out as farm labourers or move on to become serfs in the new workshops and factories of the towns. Gone was the freedom of the open countryside, and the poet John Clare amongst others particularly mourned this loss.

THERE IS MORE about these reactions to enclosure on page 74.

THE ANATOMY OF THIS BEST VIEW

● *A neat grid of hedges. These usually date from the period of the Parliamentary Enclosures of Georgian times.*

● *Many are trimmed; on other farms they have been let go. Nevertheless, they are all of recent date. They are young hedges consisting of few shrubs other than the hawthorn that they were originally planted with two centuries ago. A few trees may stand along them, now grown tall.*

● *Hedges trimmed low often mark the territory of a famous hunt – the hedges are kept neatly trimmed to give good jumps, the gates are kept in repair. Spinneys were often planted as fox coverts.*

● *Brick buildings in the fields. The 'new' enclosure farms were built when brick was coming into day-to-day use – the sheds out in the fields were also of brick, as we see here.*

221

GAZETTEER TWENTY-TWO

THE SHIRES

Prime shire landscape is seen in the countryside of Leicestershire, North-amptonshire and what was Rutland, now absorbed into them and neighbouring Cambridgeshire.

But as typical 'enclosure' landscapes are seen everywhere, in every county, it might be more interesting here to list some pre-enclosure open-field landscapes and a few lost villages.

It is interesting that a rather similar kind of countryside is common in Northern France and other places in Europe – giant open fields, no hedges, and with all trees in the extensive village woodlands.

1) Forrabury, *North Cornwall. There is still an ancient, open-field landscape to be seen here, with curving strips, although many are now amalgamated. The strips or furlongs were separated by balks, marked by bond stones.*

2) Braunton, *North Devon. Here Braunton Great Field is still being farmed in strips. It gives us an idea of what most of lowland England looked like in the Middle Ages.*

3) Laxton, *Nottinghamshire. A relic open-field landscape in the midst of prime shireland.*

Many hundreds of villages throughout the country were deserted in medieval and later times, overwhelmed by history in the shape of famine, plague, or even an eighteenth-century landowner wishing to remove clutter from his view. Here are some, revealed by a church standing solitary amongst the fields, or by ditches and banks in a grassy field. WARNING – by the time you get there, it might have gone. Sadly such sites are being wiped away by deep ploughing, at a rate of dozens a year.

4) Clopton, *Cambridgeshire.*

5) Padbury, *Berkshire.*

6) Castle Camps, *Cambridgeshire. A medieval church stands alone inside Norman earthen ramparts; the villagers left 500 years ago.*

7) Wharram Percy, *North Yorkshire. The roofless Norman church stands alone. This village is being systematically excavated and is revealing many secrets about medieval peasant life.*

8) Heath Chapel, *on the Clee Hills, Shropshire. An early church amidst humps and heavings of ground denoting the hut sites and old lanes.*

9) Ingarsby, *east Leicestershire. Mounds and holloways.*

10) Egmere, *near Walsingham, North Norfolk. A fragment of church ruin left.*

THE STONE-WALLED DALES

WHITE PEAK, DERBYSHIRE

The area known as the White Peak contains classic stone-walled countryside. The rivers deeply carve the limestone to create steep craggy valleys and gorges, but the stone walls make a better show here on the rolling tops. The flower-coloured fields are also a clue to further interest.

Stone usually replaces hedges where it is easily won from the ground. Although it may cost more to lay, a stone wall does not need as much regular maintenance.

The White Peak is a platform of limestone bounded in the south by Ashbourne and by Buxton, Castleton, Matlock and Bakewell to the north. It is mountain limestone of the kind also seen at Gordale Scar (see page 129). Here it can be seen in numerous small crags, especially in the valleys of the Wye, Derwent, Manifold and Dove rivers.

There are numerous small outcrops up here above the valleys. Some are natural, others must have been quarries for the stone for the walls. Some have been mined, the limestone being fired for quicklime for mortar. An occasional limekiln can still be seen built into the hillside nearby.

This is delightful scenery in summer, alight with flowers, the walls set with stately ash trees. In winter, snow can drive across it, and even the lines of the fields can become quickly blanketed.

Despite this winter rigour, there are signs of very early settlement (and at periods the climate was milder in the past). Neolithic or New Stone Age tribes, our first farmers, have left eight chambered tombs in the White Peak. One of them, at Five Wells on Taddington Moor nearby, is the highest megalithic tomb in Britain, 1400 feet above sea level. It is more than 4000 years old.

A few miles to the south lies Arbor Low, a stone circle dating from these times, with a heady view. It is all the more enigmatic in that its stones lie flat atop the ground, and there seems doubt as to whether they were ever raised. Tree pollen (trees are flowering plants too!) found preserved below these large stones show that the area was thickly wooded when they were hauled into position. In other words, the open view we enjoy today was not open at that time.

Those Neolithic people used stone. They also relied on it for tools. They may have worshipped it. It is still easy to be impressed by stone in countryside such as this.

23

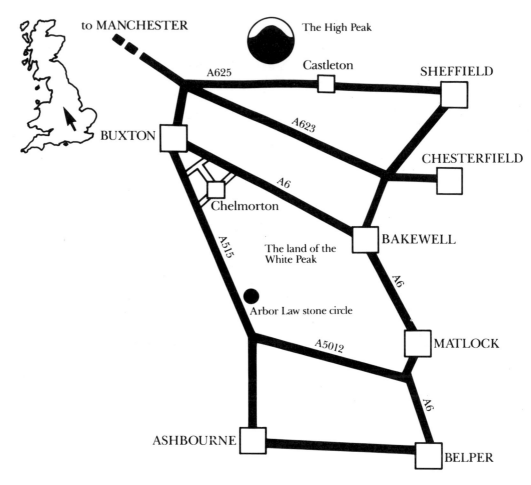

View of the countryside near Taddington, Derbyshire

It was always more satisfactory to build field boundaries in stone where it was ready to hand: they lasted longer without fuss. So a good many of the village paddocks of early times were walled with stone. Stone was also used, as we see here, around the later enclosure fields.

The honey-coloured fields are a delight. Some of them will be cut for hay – and this was once the colour of good hay land all over the lowlands and in the hills as well. Growing good grass, it never felt the bite of the plough. Furthermore, as the hay was not cut until June, a good many early wild flowers could set seed before the cut.

The result was that hay fields, whether alongside streams in the lowlands or in the hills, had a marvellous tawny mane imparted by many different wild grasses set with wild flowers. They were also busy with bees and many different butterflies.

Today, such old hay fields are a rarity. They are prize finds. In the lowlands many have been ploughed for grain, or fertilized and resown with modern hybrid, high-yield grasses of a virulent colour of green. And spreading with fertilizer is often enough to eliminate the flowers without ploughing. The flowers do not flourish as one would expect, the nutrients encourage the ranker grasses to smother the more delicate wild blooms.

This modern grass is not often cut for hay, but is cut earlier for silage. It is cut when green and stored wet. It ferments. Cattle are happy to eat this pickle in winter, but not sheep – nor horses.

Here in the White Peak, horizons containing those marvellous old fields of yore can still be seen; but things change, so catch them while you can.

It is worth a detour to Chelmorton nearby.

Here the walls preserve an antique pattern. Long narrow fields come down on each side of the village. These walls were built across the old open fields when this countryside underwent enclosure. But it is obvious that no square grid was imposed here – instead the walls follow the ancient pattern of strips that were once allocated amongst the villagers.

'They know the trick of keeping the lost sunlight of centuries' – is what J. B. Priestley said of stone walls such as these. They do seem delightful today, but did they always? 'Anything so ugly I have never seen before,' said William Cobbett of stone-walled countryside near Cirencester.

THERE IS MORE about the views of earlier travellers in BOX 4.

GAZETTEER TWENTY-THREE

THE STONE-WALL COUNTRYSIDE

Granite – on Skiddaw in the Lake District; Dartmoor

Ash and other ancient volcanic rocks – central Lake District; North Wales

Millstone grit – much of the Pennines

Limestones – The Peak District; the Cotswolds; the Mendips

Flint – a few walls of flint are to be seen in chalk downland

THE ANATOMY OF THIS BEST VIEW

- *The walls. They are drystone walls, made without mortar; however tumbledown they look they are made with skill to withstand the winds and frosts of this high countryside.*
- *Trees grow along them. These are elegant ash trees. Ash is linked with limestone: it forms its own distinctive woods only in limestone areas. Here it is barely in leaf – it is nearly the last of our native trees to come into leaf (and is sometimes the earliest to drop them in autumn).*
- *Coloured fields. At some times of year these fields are yellow with buttercups. Usually they have a glorious tawny hue, the colour of ancient flowery grassland.*

SWEEPS OF DOWN

WIN GREEN HILL, DORSET

ere we have magnificent chalk downland. Not only smooth slopes, but also scallopings, devil's scoops (if large, they are often known by such names as Devil's Punchbowls). On these swooping slopes are paths, tracks, slips – ancient ditches, ancient mounds.

As a bonus, the view from here, the highest point in Cranborne Chase, stretches for miles.

Win Green Hill is National Trust land. There is parking with an honesty box.

There are plenty of places to view on the way here. Shaftesbury itself – well known – its steep Gold Hill must surely be the most photographed street in Britain?

Less well known, but worth as much if not more of a visit is Ashmore, further south on the B3081. It is a pretty village. At its heart is a round duck pond – with Muscovy ducks – overlooked by an elegant Georgian house with half a cedar (the rest went in a gale).

An archetypal English scene, but in more than one way. There is evidence of a settlement at Ashmore since Roman times; so here we may well have the oldest duck pond in Britain.

Up here atop the chalk there are no springs or streams. In the old days, water for drinking and cooking (washing could wait) was got by building a 'dew pond', which is what Ashmore pond basically was. These saucer-shaped ponds were lined with puddled (trodden) clay. By siting them carefully, run-off from rainstorms

and condensing dew kept them topped up.

Dew ponds do seem miraculous. Maybe the name originates from *Dieu* (Norman French for God) ponds.

Other echoes of the past – although they do not immediately seem so – lie on the route from Salisbury, the A30. A chalk crest accompanies this road, running alongside to the south like a brother. At Fovant, there are regimental badges incised into the chalk slopes, and a handy lay-by to view them from. There is another, elaborate one further on at Swallowcliffe, even nearer Win Hill – 'Royal Warwickshire' – and the pub opposite is The Lancers.

It is an old tradition to cut your tribal emblem into the chalk in this way. Perhaps the oldest is the club-wielding giant at Cerne Abbas north of Dorchester. Perhaps the best known is the White Horse near Wantage, Oxfordshire, which *seems* to be of Celtic, pre-Roman design. Another old one is the Long Man of Wilmington in

24

Sussex. They are all many, many centuries older than these modern military crests.

Look out for flint-built cottages. Chalk isn't all that good as a building stone (although some layers are tougher than others) but flint is virtually indestructible. Lines of flint nodules are found running through the chalk, not too difficult to quarry out. And the flint is sometimes built into a wall with the chalk, in a chequer-board pattern.

Any cottage *with* chalk in its walls is also likely to have overhanging thatch in deep eaves. There's a good reason for this – they prevent the rain dripping down the wall itself. Very often the details of what you see in the countryside reflect just plain good sense!

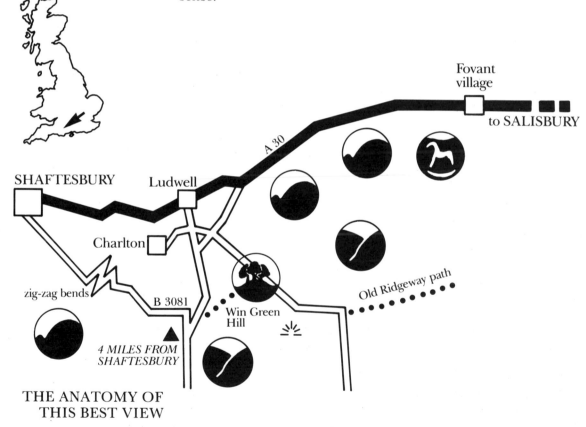

THE ANATOMY OF THIS BEST VIEW

● *Sharp slopes. Although chalk, being a soft rock quick to slump, usually gives gentle curves, it can offer steep gradients. We see some here.*

OS grid reference of viewpoint ST 925206

View of chalk combes at Win Hill

There really is a tremendous view from the top of Win Green Hill. Amongst other places, the viewing table refers to the Needles on the Isle of Wight, 32 miles away, and to Bristol, 40 miles away. But we are really here to see the ground under our feet.

Land-use history has bequeathed us some very special habitats, chalk downland among them.

Up until this century, much of our old chalk downland had never been ploughed, or had last been ploughed when the Romans arrived. It had been kept open by sheep grazing. For centuries these hungry animals moved across it under the vigilant eye of the shepherd, nibbling here and there.

The sheep created a dense turf filled with many wild flowers: yellow vetches, red clover, blue milkwort, while in places swarms of wild orchids stood proud in early summer.

This botanic richness was not due to the rich soil, but rather the reverse. Downland soils are thin, dry and poor in nutrients. This means that ranker grasses and other plants cannot grow strong enough to smother the others: moreover these grasses are also kept down by the grazing sheep. If grazing stops, however, then in time they do grow – the colourful flowers are lost and scrub invades.

Much of our old downland turf has disappeared this century, ploughed up for grain or for sowing hybrid grasses for grazing or for cutting for silage. What remains is in scattered patches, usually on slopes too steep to plough. These too may be scrubbing up as the modern farmer does not find it worthwhile keeping the handful of sheep they would support.

Remaining expanses of downland have usually, as here at Win Hill, been bought up for protection. They are nature reserves in their own right. Apart from the wild flowers they are notable for their colonies of blue butterflies. Skylarks sing overhead.

Meadowland is another habitat which, although farmed, had a regime which encouraged diverse wildlife.

Certain wild flowers and butterflies can be used as badges – indicators – of these irreplaceable old habitats: wild orchids and perhaps cowslips and blue butterflies here on downland; large numbers of brown butterflies and flowers such as ox-eye daisy, pepper saxifrage and adder's-tongue fern in old damp meadowland.

These scoops are largely dry. The soft chalk soaks up the rain which only emerges as springs when the rock is sodden. These valleys were created in much wetter climes at the end of the Ice Age. No streams flow now, but along their bottoms the greener grass shows that the lower layers of chalk are wetter.

● *Lines of soil slip.* The combed lines across the slopes are not sheep paths (although sheep may use them) but natural lines from slight slumping over the centuries.

● *Ancient bumps.* True downland also remains unploughed – or, at least, last ploughed perhaps in Roman times. As a result ancient paths and mounds, banks and ditches can make a history book of it. Bonnets of trees (as seen on top of Win Green Hill) are often rooted in a barrow – a prehistoric burial mound. Ant hills are also found.

● *Tawny grassland.* Again a result of centuries without ploughing. On close inspection it is found to result from the intimate mix of wild grasses and other plants which make up the turf. At some times of the year it can be bright with wild flowers.

● *A scatter of scrub.* Real downland was always speckled with bushes, but many downland slopes are now scrubbing up, a sign that grazing has ceased.

GAZETTEER TWENTY-FOUR

CHALK DOWNS AND WOLDS

The chalk surfaces like an ungainly spider holding the south of Britain in its grasp. Chalk outcrops on Salisbury Plain and Dorset, the North and South Downs. An extension of the chalk runs through East Anglia and it emerges also to form the Wolds.

Some classic chalk landscapes are to be seen at:

1) Ivinghoe Beacon, *Buckinghamshire, with a marvellous coomb below.*

2) Inkpen Gibbet. *On a high downland bluff a few miles southwest of Newbury, a wooden post marks the spot where the hanged dangled in the breeze. Excellent chalk coombs and slopes around here – this is the focus.*

3) Watership Down *is part of the Berkshire Downland.*

4) Martin Down, *southwest of Salisbury, lying in Hampshire. An extraordinary place, with much of the look of the African veldt. It gives us a true idea of how downland looked in past centuries – unploughed, with sweeps of grass and scrub taking hold where grazing was less intense.*

5) Edington Down, *near Westbury, Wiltshire. Famous for more than scenery. Down the coomb in 878 AD swept the forces of King Alfred the Great, to rout the Danes for once and for all. England as we know it today had its birth here.*

6) Eggardon Hill, *Dorset. One of Hardy's favourite locations.*

7) Wye Downs, *Kent. Slopes and coombs.*

8) White Horse Hill, *Oxfordshire. Here is cut the famous White Horse, perhaps of Iron Age date.*

Other chalk-cut figures which may well be prehistoric are:

9) The Cerne Abbas Giant, *a few miles north of Dorchester, Dorset.*

10) The Long Man of Wilmington, *near Eastbourne, East Sussex.*

THE CRUMPLED MOORS

HAWORTH MOORS

Visitors from the opposite ends of the earth make the pilgrimage to Haworth – there is no family in the history of literature quite like the Brontës, and here are the landscapes they knew and loved. The old parsonage, their home, is now a museum. The village is quaintly stone-walled, a bustling place; but a short walk away from it lie the moors, stretching emptily and gloriously away for miles into the blue distance. On them you can be as solitary and remote as when the Brontës were alive.

The moor paths are open at all times of day, all days of the year. Although the heather is in flower in July and August, these moors also make a good winter visit.

To set the scene start with a visit to the Parsonage, now the Brontë Museum. Scattered through these neat, rather prim rooms lie bits and bobs, from writing desks to hats used by this unusual family. It is as if they have, not 130 or so years but just a moment ago, gone to the moors.

Equipped with maps and whatever from the shop alongside, we can join them.

One of the Brontës' favourite walks was to a waterfall and a simple slab stone bridge on Sladen Beck. From here ruined High Withens can be seen ahead; this was possibly the original of *Wuthering Heights*.

For a different approach, park in Penistone Hill Country Park (with its useful information boards) and follow the waymarked footpaths.

Have a look at the waste from the disused quarries. The rock is hard, its grains shining in the sun. It is often mistaken for granite. This Pennine rock is gritty enough for carving into mill stones – hence its name, Millstone Grit.

On the way past Penistone Hill have a look at the valley farms. Some have red doors and window frames, others blue. The former are beef farms, the latter dairy. And green? Most probably newcomers who don't know better!

The stone walls round about are also worth inspecting.

Some are jumbles of rounded boulders collected up from where they lay on the ground round about, precariously balanced, but firmer than they look. They could be quite old, although rebuilt many times.

Others are neatly made with squared pieces of quarried stone. These field walls usually date from the enclosures of about 200 years ago; these enclosure walls also cross parts of the top moor. Even bleak weathery areas such as these were taken in. Today the moorland walls are often

25

tumbledown, being expensive to repair. The sheep roam for miles within barbed wire.

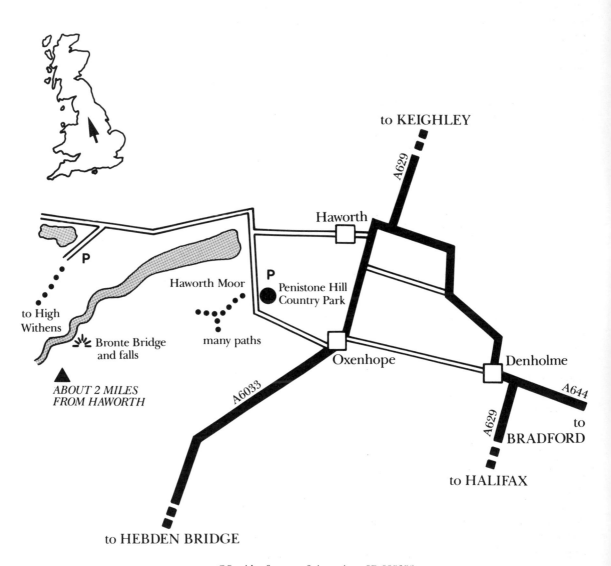

to KEIGHLEY

A629

Haworth

P

to High
Withens

Haworth Moor

P

Penistone Hill
Country Park

Bronte Bridge
and falls

many paths

▲
*ABOUT 2 MILES
FROM HAWORTH*

Oxenhope

Denholme

A644

A6033

A629

to
BRADFORD

to HALIFAX

to HEBDEN BRIDGE

OS grid reference of viewpoint   SD 995358

The Haworth Moors

What a wonderful wilderness moorland does seem. Like many other kinds of countryside it first became really popular – or rather *popularized* – in the course of the last century. Before that all travellers detested it, for it spelled a hard day's ride, subject to mists and drenching rain and other hazards. For those forced to make a living from it, life was as dour and gritty as the fabric of the moor itself.

The change can be measured by the Brontës, who walked and loved these moors. It was amongst these remote, creased land-scapes that their imagination flourished. A snatch of a poem by Emily Brontë:

> *Awaken, O'er all my dear moorland*
> *West-wind, in thy glory and pride,*
> *Oh, call me from the valley and lowland*
> *To walk by the hill-torrent's side.*
> *Few hearts to mortals given,*
> *On earth so wildly pine;*
> *Yet few would ask a heaven*
> *More like this earth than thine*

Yet moorland wilderness is in many ways a deceit. It was created by man, and grazing has kept it open.

Clearance may have begun in Bronze Age times. In some places burial cairns and stone hut circles can be found. Grazing has kept the land open ever since. Without tree cover, it is heather rather than grass which makes better growth on this bleak soil, but grass moors do exist where sheep grazing is very heavy.

The Haworth Moors, like many other moorlands, are net-worked in places by the lines of stone walls. Straight and neat, they date from enclosure times when village commons rights were usurped even here, and land taken into private ownership.

In their heyday, these enclosed fields would have been mark-edly different from the rough grazing around. *Without*, heather; *within*, the green of grass. That such apparent 'wilderness' can be changed by the whim of a farmer is clear from our VIEW opposite; to the left is heather moor, to the right, grassy fields. It is interesting that on the way from Oxenhope to Hebden Bridge, there are some fields let go, which are fast being reclaimed by the moor.

Elsewhere in northern England and Scotland, moors are famous for their grouse, which graze on the heather. To encourage these

THE ANATOMY OF THIS BEST VIEW

● *Unlike downland, exposures of bare rock are here easy to find. Our moorland is in areas of hard rock and although these have in many places in the northern hills been smoothed by ice, outcrops and frost shattered crags abound.*

● *Chattering streams. The moors are in areas of heavy rainfall, which quickly runs off the hard rock into turbulent streams. Patches of boggy land are often found alongside them*

● *Heather. But not only heather grows. Bilberry and other plants are found.*

● *A scatter of trees. These underline the point that were it not for continual grazing by sheep, this moor would naturally be tree-covered.*

● *Ruins of some kind are often seen, a sign of land recently let go.*

● *The bridge is interesting.*

237

game birds, the moorland is usually regularly burnt in patches. The burnt heather grows again from root or seed, to yield fresh green shoots for the birds, while the older heather provides dense cover for their nests. Here birds rather than sheep create the scenery we see today! (And beware if walking the grouse moors in August, the season opens on the 'Glorious Twelfth'.)

THERE IS MORE about the intense feelings the Brontës held for this moorland on page 76. It is interesting to make the comparison with a heath, VIEW 26.

GAZETTEER TWENTY-FIVE

BRITAIN'S MOORLANDS

1) Moorland coats many of Scotland's *mountains. Boggy areas or 'flows' are common, and in some areas, such as Caithness and Sutherland, (Highland regions) these peat bogs can stretch for miles.*

On the famous Scottish grouse moors, the heather is regularly burnt in small patches, creating a patchwork in the view. The burnt heather grows again, from root or seed, yielding fresh green shoots to feed the grouse, while the birds rely on the dense, unburnt growth for cover.

2) The Pennine Moors, *of which the Haworth Moors are part, clothe the backbone of England. There are patches of bog, which were once more extensive. Industrial cities surround these moors on every side, and the smoke from these may well have killed the bog moss and let cotton grass in to take its place, marked by its dancing white heads,*

3) The Lake District *contains some heather moorland and grass moorland.*

4) The North York Moors.

5) Welsh moorland *lies scattered in patches on the high ground. The area of the Brecon Beacons to the south, for example, is open moor cut by ice-smoothed valleys and deep river gorges.*

6) Exmoor *has hardy half-wild ponies, and herds of wild red deer. The area is broken up by roads, woods and farms, the bigger stretches of moorland lying to the west. In recent times, much surviving moorland here has been 'reclaimed' – that is ploughed and fertilized and sown with grass.*

7) Bodmin Moor *is wide and open, unwalled and unfenced. Here and there*

cattle and ponies graze below the rocky outcrops – these animals belong to farms with 'commons' grazing rights to the moor.

8) Dartmoor *is vast, a 200 square mile expanse of moor, capped with the famous tors, granite outcrops weathered into odd shapes. Cattle and ponies graze. There are many hut circles and other prehistoric remains, showing that today's bleak moorland was once quite densely settled.*

THE LOWERING HEATH

DORSET HEATHLAND

ere we see another prehistoric landscape. At first glance it seems very like moorland; but heather is not all. There are subtle differences. One major difference is that this is an endangered view. We have lost more heathland in recent times than any other kind of countryside, and an expanse of heathland such as this is something of a treasure.

The once extensive heathlands of Dorset, like heathlands elsewhere, are sadly at a premium today. Some relic patches are listed in the gazetteer.

Even so, most of us could recognize a heath without prompting. Thickets of tall gorse can grow as well as heather on a heath. They double the scent, smelling rich and glorious when in full flower in late spring. Gorse can be in flower in every month of the year, so that the kissing need never stop.

It is worth looking out for a much pricklier ground-hugging gorse (which only flowers in summer) – it is either western or dwarf gorse, both varieties of limited range.

Trees too may be adeptly seeding themselves out onto the open ground. Scots pine and birch can be colonizers here and may form a wood amongst the heather and gorse. Many heaths have now been planted with conifers, vast silent plantations of young trees, but sometimes the wild Scots pines seed themselves from an older plantation nearby. A long time has passed since the Scots pine was 'native' to the south (see VIEW 18).

The ground is often soft, sandy and dry, though there may be boggy spots to look out for. Colourful dragonflies like these damp areas. Unlike moorlands, streams are not very often found on heathlands.

Heather has very small, thin, overlapping green leaves arranged in four rows up the stem, but on wetter ground it may be ousted by cross-leaved heath, whose sets of four leaves spring from the stem in a cross. Bell heather is also common on heathland. It has leaves in sets of *three* (small shoots can also sometimes look like leaves).

In this way 'heather' can be sharing out the seemingly featureless heath.

On some heaths the path can be sharply flinty. This rock is not true flint however, but chert, a white, flint-like stone.

In places, the tracks can cut deep, deeper than usual on moor, where hard rock often lies below the layer of peaty soil. There are plenty of seemingly inexplicable banks and heaps on a heath; pits too. Maybe they are old diggings for

26

supplies of sand or cherty gravel. The novelist Thomas Hardy, a dab hand at description, likened these to the eye sockets of a skull.

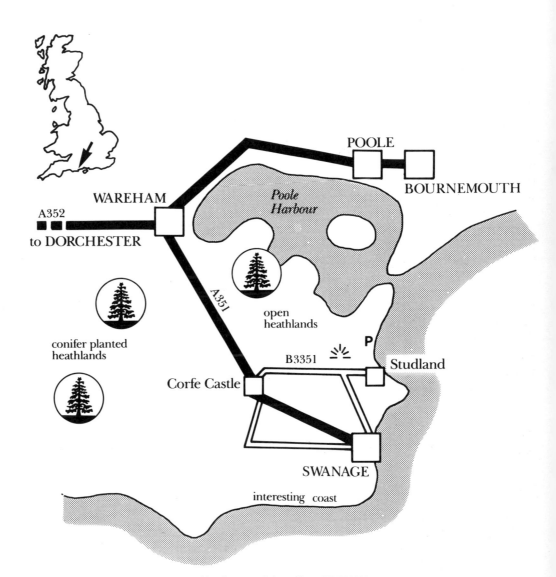

POOLE

BOURNEMOUTH

WAREHAM

A352

to DORCHESTER

Poole Harbour

A351

open heathlands

conifer planted heathlands

P

B3351

Studland

Corfe Castle

SWANAGE

interesting coast

OS grid reference of viewpoint   SY 021824

Dorset Heathland

Heaths have a rather similar ecological history to moors.

Although found in the lowlands, they lie on poor (usually sandy) soil, rather acid in chemistry.

The trees which grew were stripped long ago – Bronze Age barrows and other remains indicate settlement early in pre-history. The land may have been farmed in some places, but was certainly grazed in more recent centuries.

Heather is quite nutritious when young. And so to remove the old wooden tangles and also clear any trees which may have seeded themselves, these grazing heaths were regularly burnt.

Grouse moors in the hills are still fired, in swathes, to provide these birds with areas of young heather. But so fragmentary are our remaining patches of heathland that firing is the last thing they need. Fire easily wipes out the heathland butterflies, snakes, birds and other wildlife; recolonization from other remaining pockets is difficult.

Heathland is nowadays an endangered habitat in Britain. In recent years heaths have been built on, planted with conifers, dug for sand – and used as tank training grounds.

The heath we see here is close to Hardy country.

More than most, Thomas Hardy was a novelist linked to a home patch, Dorset. He decided that his series of local novels needed 'a territorial definition of some sort to lend unity to their scene' and adopted the already historic name of Wessex, which had been the ancient Anglo-Saxon kingdom of King Alfred the Great.

Thomas Hardy did not tamper with geography, he only re-named places: Dorchester became Casterbridge; West Lulworth became Lulstead, and the scatter of Dorset barrens became Egdon Heath – an 'untamed and untameable wild' – which dominated his novel *The Return of the Native*. In this work he uses the heath to portray nature neither as something cruel nor as something kind, but as something simply indifferent to man. It was a reading of nature which was very different from that favoured by the romantics earlier.

Enthusiasts have great fun tracking this Hardy countryside, visiting such places as the churchyard in Puddletown where Troy (*Far from the Madding Crowd*) spent one of his nights, or the roof in Wool under which Tess and Angel Clare spent their wedding night. (This is now the Woolbridge Manor Hotel.)

The Dorset heathland that captured Hardy's imagination does remain for us to see, but there is far less of it. There were around

THE ANATOMY OF THIS BEST VIEW

- *An open ambience like a moor. But although they have this (and heather of course) in common, a heath is rather different from a moor. It is lowland rather than upland, and has:*
- *Dry peaty soil – unlike the wet peat of moorland.*
- *Invasions of other tall vegetation. Clumps of gorse are frequently seen on heathland, and sometimes self-sown pine and silver birch trees also.*
- *Little if any bare rock, unlike the moor, where outcrops are expected. Here we see a fragment left by erosion – the 'Agglestone'.*
- *Little surface water. Rarely a pond or stream.*

243

70,000 acres when he was born in 1840, 50,000 when he died in 1928. Less than 10,000 acres remain today.

GAZETTEER TWENTY-SIX

HEATHLAND

Where heather grows on poor, quick draining, sandy or other acid soils, it creates heathland.

1) Lowland heath is rare in Scotland. But it can form behind sand dunes (the Scottish links, birthplace of golf!) and here we find it at Forvie Sands, Grampian *and* Torrs Warren, *Dumfries and Galloway.*

2) Patches of heathery barrens can be found in some places in the Midlands, at Sutton Park, *Birmingham for example.*

3) Unusual heaths are found in East Anglia. The Breckland *is in fact like nowhere else – heather heaths such as those at* Berber's Heath, *and* Cavenham *and* Thetford Heath *lie alongside areas of very different, chalky soil.*

4) Surrey heaths are found on the gravel and sandy soils here. The Surrey heaths are now fragmented, but Thursley Heath *is still a wild and mysterious place.*

5) Heathlands in Sussex are found on the sandy ridge of Ashdown Forest.

6) The New Forest *contains many heathland areas.*

7) Dorset *heaths are now fragmented.*

8) The Lizard *peninsula, Cornwall, has an incredibly complicated geology which provides superb heathland scenery – with tall heath in the wet areas and low heath strewn with boulders in the dry.*

THE PERFECT PASTORAL

DEDHAM VALE

Here is a countryside hung on many a sitting-room wall, and not only in Britain. This is Constable country – reproductions of his landscape paintings are still as popular today as they ever were.

Many holidaymakers drive around Dedham Vale, identifying the settings of John Constable's more famous pictures. There is parking at some sites, and footpaths make it easy to lose any crowds.

'Constable Country' is a very small pocket of English countryside. Only two miles across and six miles long, it is flanked on both sides by the modest slopes of this river valley.

Across this charming countryside sound the bells of Dedham Church. Its 500-year-old tower must be one of the best known in the whole of Britain, so often has it been painted and by John Constable himself.

Dedham itself is a quaint little town with Georgian houses and many timber-framed cottages. The young John attended the grammar school here.

East Bergholt is also worth a visit. Oddly, its church bells are rung (upside down) by hand, in a timber bellhouse in the churchyard. The church tower was abandoned before it was finished.

It was in East Bergholt that John Constable was born, in East Bergholt House, in 1776. All that remains of that home today is a wing converted into cottages.

Similarly, his father's mill at Dedham which he often painted has been replaced by modern mill-buildings.

All this adds extra interest to what does remain. Flatford Mill, also once owned by John's father, is probably the best-known site of all. This mill is an ancient spot – the mill-house is as old as Dedham Church, built in the fifteenth century.

The picture *Flatford Mill* is painted as if from a position up river on the Essex bank, from the slope up to the footbridge (a modern replacement).

The perhaps even more famous painting *The Haywain* is a view down river from the mill and of course includes Willy Lott's cottage, the home of a local farmer of the time, built early in the seventeenth century. Both the mill and Willy Lott's cottage are protected by the National Trust – the latter is leased out as a field and study centre.

Bridge Cottage, just upstream from the mill, is also National Trust. A restored thatched cottage, it houses a display about John Constable. It also has such things as boats for hire!

27

Perhaps the best way to explore the area is to park and use the footpaths. Many of these were regularly used by John Constable. One, from East Bergholt to Dedham, which he used on his way to and from school, features in his famous painting *The Cornfield*.

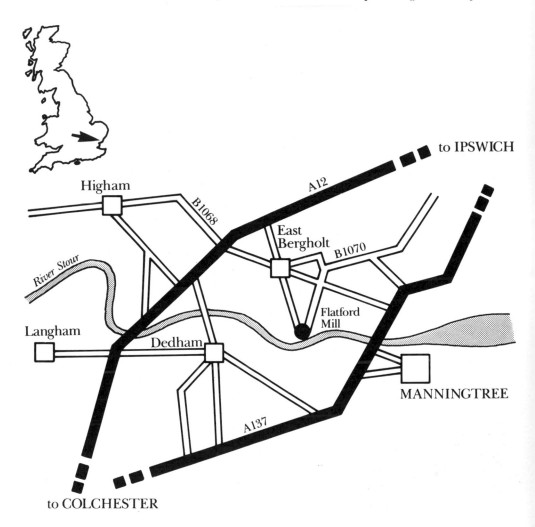

The Stour Valley

All in all, this is on the face of it a muted landscape where negatives rule. There is nothing bold – no wild gorges, no jagged lines, no emphatic contrasts. Not even soil paled by chalk or tinted red by the local rock.

Moreover it is a landscape in which the hand of man is

everywhere. The fields are grazed or ploughed brown, sown green or harvested gold – man colours the seasons in this way. Trees are lopped (and hedges trimmed). Even in Constable's own day, the River Stour had itself been fitted with locks and weirs, to become second cousin to a canal.

Only the sky is capricious.

Within such limits, Constable created a view of countryside which is familiar today. His pictures show nature as most of us understand it; the most familiar nature of all.

Constable was not the first to paint in this part of the world. Thomas Gainsborough, for example, had lived at Sudbury, not far away. Although by reputation a portrait painter, he loved and even preferred landscape.

John Constable was aware of Gainsborough 'in every hedge and tree' as he put it. However, he owed little to others. So strong was his own visual imagination that (as he later recalled) he had shaped many of his own ideas from the familiar countryside of his boyhood before he had even learnt to paint.

If he did have teachers, they were locals. He was a great pal of one John Duncombe, a plumber and glazier, an enthusiastic amateur painter. Sir George Beaumont, another amateur painter and collector, showed him paintings by Claude. Constable admired them, but said he: 'I was born to paint a happier land, my own dear old England; and when I cease to love her, may I, as Wordsworth says "never more hear her green leaves rustle, her torrents roar."'

Later, in London, working from memory and from sketches done previously in the field, Constable could build up his large 'six footers' – *The Haywain, The Cornfield* and the other famous pictures.

Obviously such things as the haywain – a hay cart – are now obsolete, but the countryside shown in these paintings still seems overwhelmingly familiar today.

The churches, mills, lanes, rivers and fields often remain to be seen. Meeting them face to face can be a strange experience.

They are real, and this reality reinforces the image of the countryside that the pictures present. This artist used nothing but paint, memory and imagination to create wonderful atmospheres of sky and view. He gave us English countryside as we truly choose to remember it in our mind's eye. In that lies Constable's greatness.

THERE IS MORE about John Constable's view of nature on page 80.

THE ANATOMY OF THIS BEST VIEW

● *An informal texture. There are no bold strokes here, just a quiet arrangement of simple elements – fields, a lush waterside, a scatter of trees and bushes.*

● *Water in the stream. The River Stour is very near the sea here, and winding.*

● *Pellucid but weathery sky.*

● *A short range of view. The flattish ground supports a great bowl of sky. But the horizon is close, maybe no more than a couple of miles away.*

● *A church tower, Dedham Church, which Constable included in many of his paintings.*

GAZETTEER TWENTY-SEVEN

CONSTABLE'S COUNTRY

Approximate locations of some famous Constable paintings

①   Stratford Mill
(now demolished)
1820

②   Dedham Vale (from
Gun Hill, Langham
1828

③   The Cornfield
1826

④   The Haywain
1821

⑤   The Leaping Horse
1825

⑥   Dedham Mill
1820

⑦   Dedham Vale
1802

to COLCHESTER

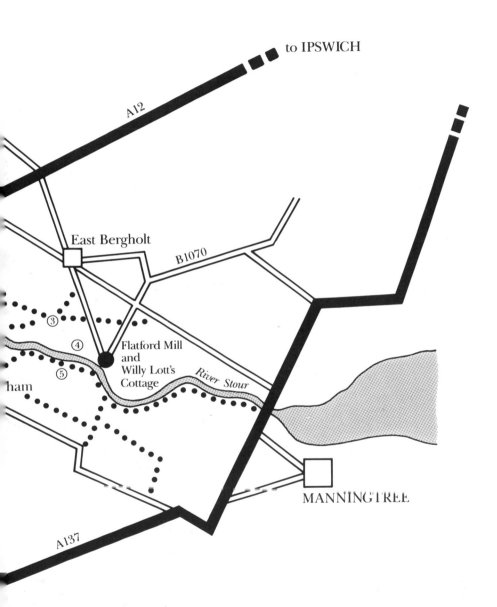

to IPSWICH

A12

East Bergholt

B1070

③

④ Flatford Mill
and
Willy Lott's
Cottage

⑤

River Stour

ham

MANNINGTREE

A137

THE DAWN OF YESTERYEAR

DENGIE AND ST PETER'S CHAPEL

The flatter the land, the less is taken into view, or to put it another way, the vaster becomes the sky. This is seen in fenland areas, but nowhere better than by the sea on an open coast such as this.

This flat countryside and coast at first so seemingly desolate and featureless is on inspection quite detailed and intricate. It is also highly historic.

Its taste can only be discovered by travelling across it.

There is one obvious eye-catcher: the bulk of the modern nuclear power station near the mouth of the River Blackwater. Not far away is a monument of a very different and distant age – St Peter's Chapel.

This tiny place sits defiantly on a bank watching the dawn suns, mild or angry according to the season, climb out of the sea. And it has seen quite a few of these – approaching half a million, for it was built in 654 AD. It is in fact one of the oldest churches in Britain.

It was for a long time used as a barn, but restored in the 1920s.

It is also known as St Peter's-on-the-wall, and a clue to an even longer history lies in this. It was built astride the remains of the Roman shore fort of Othona, and brick and stone from this Saxon Shore stronghold was used in its own walls.

There are fine salt marshes up and down this Essex coast. They are a rather detailed environment, the scene of a bargain between sea and land.

They are usually linked with a river mouth, but here in Essex they are also found on the open coast. The crucial factor is the lack of fierce tides and currents.

Where the river's flow slackens, and where the tides are not too powerful, mud – the scourings of the land brought down by the rivers – is deposited. It is scalloped by currents of course, but in places sturdy plants can take root, and they stabilize it and trap more. In places banks are formed which are only covered by the month's higher tides, and on these flowers can grow – sea aster, thrift and sea lavender. Eventually a flowery meadow is created.

These mud flats and salt marshes are also a haven for shore birds. In fact the Essex County Naturalists' Trust has an observatory near St Peter's. Brent geese are seen as well as many different waders; and hen harriers and short-eared owls also hunt the marshes.

The attraction for the waders is the swarming mass of small shellfish and worms to be found in the mud. They flourish because it contains the nutrients drained by entire river systems.

Indeed, in winter, keep an eye out for giant flocks of birds feeding down this coast – in

28

sheer numbers they are the nearest thing we have to the profusion of animals in the famous African game parks.

Until the 1930s, this creeky coast used to be haunted by numbers of stately Thames barges. Their handsome brown sails can still be seen in July when they meet on the Blackwater river to race.

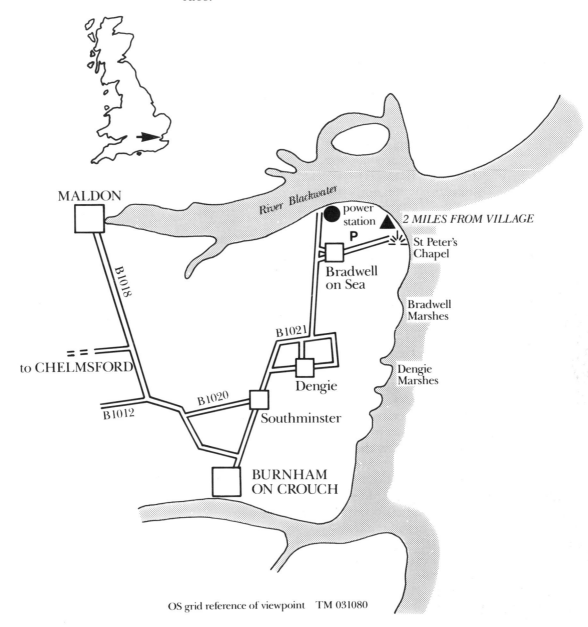

OS grid reference of viewpoint   TM 031080

An ancient chapel on the Essex coast

The English would be hard put *not* to find some kind of ghostly echo in this dawn scene. It was on such eastern coasts in the fifth and sixth centuries that bloodthirsty warbands of our Saxon and then later of our Danish ancestors first set foot on British soil. They often chose to run their ships in under the first light of day. The name Essex itself denotes the land of the East Saxons.

Foreseeing the threat, Roman Britain built a chain of strongholds – the forts of the Saxon Shore – which stretched from Norfolk right round to Portchester in Hampshire. Othona was one of them. It was one of the last imperial gestures before Rome withdrew her army.

In fact Arthurian ghosts may roam here, where the wild geese wing in. Perhaps King Arthur was not some western-fairy Celtic king but of local nobility – of Roman or Romanized family living during these troubled years. A certain Ambrosius, Count of the Saxon Shore, tantalizingly shadows texts of this period; some think that he was Arthur's uncle.

With these skirmishes barely over (and maybe still continuing) sea coasts such as this, remote, facing back to Europe, saw another kind of fight – for men's souls. For it was along such places that Christianity first took root, as tenaciously as those plants of the salt marsh on the muddy flats.

St Cedd who converted Essex starting at this high tide mark, and very probably built St Peter's Chapel. St Cedd's own teacher, Aidan, chose to live on Lindisfarne, Northumberland, Holy Island as it is now called. Here in 635 AD he established the first English see, university and artistic centre. It became so famous that he was forced to retire to the remoter Farne Islands for peace and quiet.

His successor St Cuthbert regularly prayed standing in the foam with otters in attendance (they still hunt fish in the sea in Scotland). It was St Cuthbert by the way who found the easy way to keep the crows from his barley. He spoke to them about it.

In few countries can we pluck such detailed history from such empty looking places (and there is nothing so empty as a salt marsh on a wet Sunday, as you may have the pleasure of finding out). But this emptiness positively attracted many of the first religious groups. At least such coasts offered little in the way of sophisticated temptation.

THERE IS MORE about such matters on pages 14 and 85.

THE ANATOMY OF THIS BEST VIEW

- *A low horizon . . .*
- *. . . Above which rises an angry dawn, firing the mudflats beyond the chapel. The tides retreat 2 miles across these flats – and come racing back.*
- *A site reeking with historic memories. St Peter's Chapel, one of the oldest in Britain, stands on the site of Othona, a Roman shore fort.*
- *In winter, vast numbers of birds – duck, waders, wild geese, even rare harriers – seek food in this seemingly desolate landscape.*

255

GAZETTEER TWENTY-EIGHT

THE DESOLATE FLATS

Britain is fortunate in its coast in more ways than one. Among its outstanding features are the large estuary salt-marsh areas which attract thousands of wildfowl and other birds in winter.

1) Culbin Sands, *South Highland. A remote stretch of coastline this.*

2) Morecambe Bay, *Lancashire. This holds the record for the number of waders, birds such as oystercatcher, knot and dunlin overwintering – well over 200,000 in all.*

3) The Ribble Estuary.

4) The Dee Estuary.

5) Gibraltar Point, *Lincolnshire. This, on the edge of the Wash, has dunes and saltmarshes.*

6) The coast of North Norfolk. *Almost the whole stretch from Holme-next-the-sea to Salthouse consists of a mosaic of nature reserves, protecting the saltmarshes.*

7) Elmley Marshes, *Kent. These are now subject of a bargain between conservation groups and the landowner – they are safe from ploughing.*

8) Bridgwater Bay, *Somerset. A huge shallow bay.*

9) Southampton Water *has interesting saltmarshes alongside it, at Calshot, for example, at the end of the Lepe and Calshot Country Park.*

10) The Exe Estuary, *Devon. This great estuary is the most important in the whole of the southwest for birdlife.*

THE EDGE OF THE SEA

HARTLAND QUAY, DEVON

ur age is a lucky one, for it can love the sea. For those even of recent centuries, the sea spelt only peril. A sea crossing was almost enough to kill the romance of travel abroad; even seaside houses were built facing inland more often than not.

Here we can, romantically, admire the sea in full power at some of the most storm-stressed cliffs in Europe.

Car parking is available both at Hartland Point (National Trust) and Hartland Quay.

This coast around Hartland Point is among the most savage to be found. Awesome seas mount when storms add fury to the offshore tide rips. And here open ocean swells from Labrador break full face. For those with a head for figures, a winter storm wave can hit the rock here with a force of about a ton a square foot.

The rock is tough, but this pressure 'implodes' the air in cracks and crevices. The rock face is blasted into a contorted shape.

Here the rock layers already sway and bunch enough. The layering exposed at Hartland Quay is fantastic, but the waves torture them further.

There are two ports of call here. The first is Hartland Point itself. This headland was called the 'Cape of Hercules' by Ptolemy in one of the first geographies.

It is a short walk down from the car park to the lighthouse, and the cliff face alongside the path can be colourful with wild flowers such as pink thrift and yellow pea-flowered vetch in Spring.

A notice tells you that the lighthouse is open to visitors in the afternoons – at the lighthouse keeper's discretion – and to beware of the vast bray of the fog horn at any time without warning. (Sea mists roll in quickly.) Relish the experience – it is quite likely that lighthouses of this kind will become redundant – shipping today relies on electronic navigation aids, and the lighthouse bray is really a thing of the past.

This coast was a sailor's grave day and night: leaflets on sale at Hartland Quay pinpoint the wrecks, but a recent one lies here below the lighthouse, a coaster (rather, by now half a coaster).

The second visit is to Hartland Quay. There is a coast path, which gives the chance to view the coastal waterfalls for which the Hartland cliffs are also famous.

The road runs inland, however; although the sea may sound even here – it can be heard 10 miles away in stormy weather.

29

Hartland Quay is an odd settlement. The quay itself became so battered that it fell out of use last century. There is a hotel created out of coastguard housing – with its back firmly to the sea!

It is at Hartland Quay that both the incredible geology of the cliffs and the storms that thunder at them can best be seen.

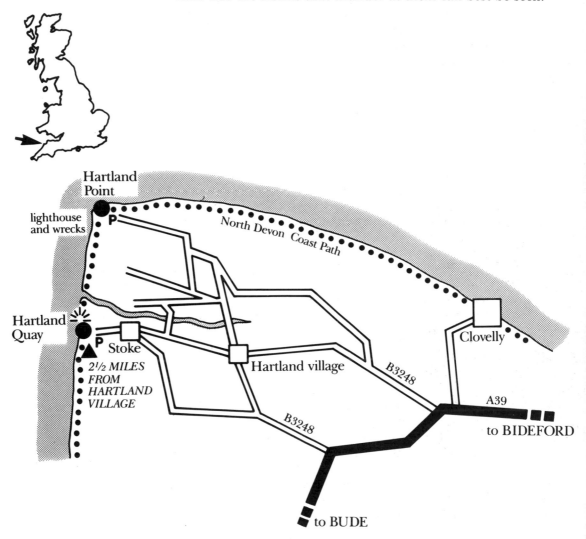

Hartland Point

lighthouse and wrecks

North Devon Coast Path

Hartland Quay

Stoke

2½ MILES FROM HARTLAND VILLAGE

Hartland village

Clovelly

B3248

B3248

A39

to BIDEFORD

to BUDE

OS grid reference of viewpoint   SS 223248

The view from Hartland Quay

Such views are breathtakingly magnificent. Quite apart from appearance, the evil *reputation* of such a coast magnifies awe. We don't have to create drama.

It was 'a sailor's grave day and night'. The times are now gone when coastal wrecks were a common fact of life (or death). They increased in number as traffic grew – in the 1870s British fishing boats and other vessels were being lost at the rate of about 2000 a year.

The popularity of such views as this, in storm as well as in fine weather, is a legacy we inherit from the flourishing of the romantic imagination which reached its height last century. Until then for most people the sea meant only peril.

But once started, the stormy coast could satisfy those who had been brought up on a diet of sublime gorges, ruined abbeys, picturesque waterfalls and the like. It was a dramatic new discovery – on a par with the discovery of a brand new continent.

Romantic poets began to pay tribute to the sea. Here is Lord Byron:

> *Roll on, thou deep and dark blue Ocean – roll!*
> *Ten thousand fleets sweep over thee in vain;*
> *Man marks the earth with ruin – his control*
> *Stops with the shore.*

Thomas Hardy relished such a coast as much as his Wessex. He in fact met his wife-to-be not so far from here. She, Emma, 'found an edge of the world atmosphere' on this wild coast, and the sweeping lighthouse eyes (on Hartland Point and Trevose Head) seemed like the eyes of a demon in the mist.

Hardy was reckoned as much poet as novelist. Head over heels in love, careering along the cliff tops – she on her pretty mare Fanny – above the abyss of the seal caves:

> *O the opal and the sapphire of that wandering western sea,*
> *And the woman riding high above with bright hair flapping free –*
> *The woman whom I so loved, and who loyally loved me*

In time *Romantic Imagination* became the romantic imagination as we understand it today. About love, not views!

All in all, these cliffs are a place for fantasizing, while the gulls look on with cold clear eyes.

THERE IS MORE about the birth of the romantic mind on page 58.

THE ANATOMY OF THIS BEST VIEW

- *Storm-lashed cliffs. There are several visual elements here which add together to create such an impressive scene. They are:*
- *The scale of the view. The cliffs here can reach 200 feet in height.*
- *The repetition of capes one beyond the other.*
- *The sculpting of the rock. The tusks and scalloped lines result from the erosion of the contorted layering of shales and sandstones. The folds in the rock are well seen in Warren Cliff, backing the beach here. The harder rock forms ribs and capes which project; the shape of these reflects the dip of the layers.*
- *All in all, we have here a view as bold as an abstract painting.*

GAZETTEER TWENTY-NINE

SEA CLIFFS

The energy of the ocean waves can erode even the hardest rock, taking advantage of weaknesses in the contorted layers to sculpt out fantastic forms.

1) Duncansby Head, Highlands. Just east of John o' Groats, the lines of the sheer cliffs are continued as 300-foot tall pillars rising from the sea. These 'stacks' are what remain when sea caves are gouged out of a headland. In time they meet, the roof collapses, and the solitary stack is left.

2) Cape Wrath, Highlands. The cliffs here fall 900 feet to the sea.

3) Bamburgh, Northumberland. Here, with the Farne Islands out to sea, a vast castle sits on a headland of the Whin Sill (see VIEW 10).

4) St David's Head, Dyfed. The most emotive headland in Wales, remote and craggy.

5) The White Cliffs of Dover, Kent. Their chalk faces are reflected by the white cliffs of France across the Channel; the sea cut through at some time after the Ice Age.

6) The Needles, Isle of White. Stacks of chalk form a line.

7) Lulworth Cove, Dorset. A very popular visit; a circular, natural basin in the cliffs.

8) Golden Cap, Dorset. This is the highest cliff on the South Coast – 617 feet high, topped with golden coloured sandy layers. It does not fall sheer; the bulk of it consists of grey clays which slump and slither into the sea.

9) Rame Head, Cornwall. An atmospheric headland, with a 600 year-old mariner's chapel. Equally historic now are the remains further towards Plymouth of gun emplacements for the defence of Plymouth against air attack in the Second World War.

10) Land's End. Best seen at dawn, without the many visitors.

THE LUNAR LANDSCAPE

ST AUSTELL CLAY TIPS

ornwall, already quite unlike any other limb of Britain both for reasons of history and of geology, here produces a landscape of a new kind – a truly lunar landscape.

Impressive at close hand, the heaps of spoil are also dramatic when seen from afar, looming at dawn like purple pyramids in the new day. At dusk, they tower like extinguished Everests above the countryside around, shedding the last of the light.

You are in authentic Cornwall when you come within sight of these clay workings.

Generally, inland Cornwall offers a rather featureless countryside, with few trees or even green hedges. The fields here are divided by banks studded with dark granite boulders. Interestingly, these banks are locally known as 'hedges'.

The Cornish landscape makes a bleakly lowering impression. On a dull day it is easy to understand why earlier travellers responded so forcibly to scenery which depressed their spirits – read Sydney Smith on the Cotswold plateau, for example, page 20.

This flat Cornish scenery only dissolves into interest when it meets the sea, with the excitement of coves, dark cliffs, pale beaches, and scintillating light.

In the neighbourhood of St Austell, there is some variety, however, in the shape of low, rounded hills, set with great smoothed granite boulders. These boulders are the remains of tors, of the kind seen on Dartmoor, for example.

Another oddity of the local natural geology is Roche Rock – a solitary pinnacle on which a hermit built his chapel, more than 500 years ago.

Cornwall is a county saturated with the past. Prehistoric forts, tombs, and stones can be found everywhere. Legends also linger; not far from here is Golant on the Fowey river – the traditional setting of the Arthurian romance of Tristram and Iseult.

Cornwall is also pockmarked by the past. Mining for tin and later for copper has a long history in the area. Along the north coast especially can be seen many relic engine houses dwarfed by their tall chimney stacks.

So, clay mining is among the old traditions of the area. It began here around 200 years ago when the deposits of the clay, called kaolin, were first discovered.

This discovery, and how the work is done, is explained in the excellent Wheal Martyn Museum, at Carthew, and the processes involved can be followed outside in the shadow

30

of the spoil heaps.

All mining causes pollution: here it is the streams that suffer. They flow turquoise green with clay, and tint the sea in St Austell Bay.

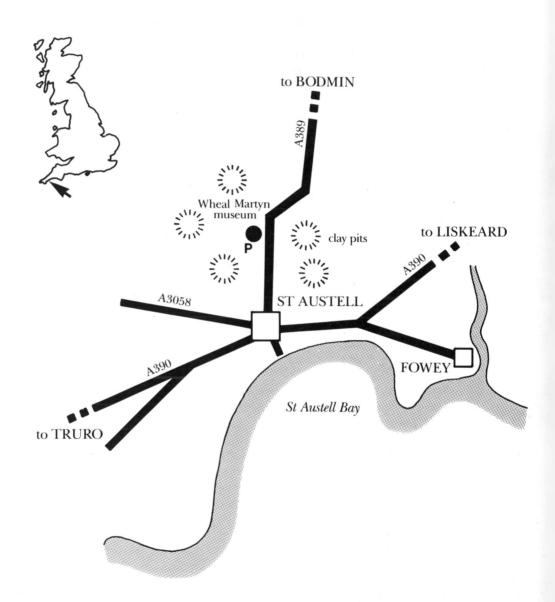

China Clay workings near St Austell

Apart from these clay mines, Cornwall's mining industry is now more or less at an end. The workings lie derelict, grassed over and picturesque in decay.

Mining has an ancient history in Cornwall. Nearly pure tin washed out of its veins in local rocks was being 'panned', gathered direct from the gravel of stream beds, in prehistoric times. By medieval times, the 'streamers' or miners had their own rights and privileges, so important was the metal.

Copper mining has also been important, mined for many uses, including 'copper bottoming' men-of-war to prevent damage by timber-boring shellfish.

Derelict industry has a fascination for modern eyes. The derelict Wheal Coates engine shed overlooking Chapel Porth beach is now conserved as jealously as Tintagel Castle! And of course 'industrial archaeology' is now a popular science. But here with these clay workings we have *active* industry. That it can create its own dramatic and impressive landscape is clear enough.

The spoil heaps are very paintable. They have their own poet too. Jack Clemo was born nearby in 1916. He became blind and then deaf when still a youngster, and his remembered landscapes are as much these clay heaps as the countryside.

> *. . . You never saw*
> *The clay as I have seen it, high*
> *On the bare hills, the little breasts*
> *So white in the sun, all the veins running white*
> *Down to the broad womb with its scars*
> *from 'the two beds'*

We can turn back to the matter of this clay, of the rock which lies below the soil here. It is granite, by origin molten magma exuded from below the earth's crust. But it did not reach the surface, instead it cooled slowly deep down, to yield this coarsely crystalline rock.

The mineral constituents are clear to see on any fresh-broken piece of granite from the fields here (or on shop fronts and gravestones throughout the country; granite is a popular ornamental rock!). The bulk is glassy quartz, in which are mixed crystals of felspar and dark specks of mica.

Eroded into decay, these three separate out. The glassy silica becomes grains of sand found in all soils (shake some earth up in water and let it settle). The felspar breaks down to clay. Here

THE ANATOMY OF THIS BEST VIEW

• *In such things as scale and contrasts, a view such as this can be 'sublime' in the old sense of the word (see page 38).*
• *Note the vivid colour of the pool.*

267

around St Austell, however, the granite has become chemically changed, the crystalline felspar has become kaolin, a white clay mineral.

This is the goal of the workings – the pure kaolin is washed free, the waste dumped. Some kaolin is used for porcelain, but most is now employed on everything from paper-making to paints and drugs.

So in this view we have granite, changed, creating a modern lunar landscape. Granite has been the origin of many other rocks in the long history of the earth. These have created landscapes long gone; and they create the landscapes and the views we enjoy today.

THERE IS MORE about the view of industry on page 86.

GAZETTEER THIRTY

LUNAR LANDSCAPES

These landscapes have been created by man. Two hundred years ago, many would have struck travellers as truly sublime. *Some, with the passage of time and in some lights, appear beautiful – rather like a planned, still-life landscapes.*
Every county has them. We have chosen some of the more dramatic.

1) The Flows *of Caithness and Sutherland. This landscape seems an empty, harsh wilderness, a flat boggy quagmire. In reality it is a fragile place, a European engine for breeding wading birds. But it is being coniferized, and the combed scars of the drainage ditches have a terrible poignancy.*

2) The Alston Moors, *Cumbria. Pitted with the scars of lead mining. Below ground tunnels still stretch from one distant village to another.*

3) Industrial wastelands, *Cleveland. Here where the first steam locomotive ran, the Victorian Industrial Revolution ran completely out of steam.*

4) South Yorkshire. *Coal tips dominate village-like settlements.*

5) Derbyshire quarries. *Scars cut into exquisite scenery for limestone.*

6) Slate quarries, North Wales. *Some of these workings are vast. Dinorwic once employed 3000 men.*

7) South Wales. *Mine tips, much like those of South Yorkshire. But here sheep roam over them, and even along the streets of the tight-packed terraces.*

8) Brick fields, *Bedfordshire. The scale of these workings is awesome.*

9) Portland, *Dorset. Stone from here built much of elegant London. Its extraction has given a strange, stepped, new-horizoned landscape to this rather fascinating, remote feeling edge of Britain.*

10) Delabole, *Cornwall. The slate quarry here, worked for 300 years or more, has left a hole 400 ft deep – the largest man-made hole in the world.*

FURTHER READING · ACKNOWLEDGEMENTS

Part of the pleasure of compiling a book such as this lies in reading a good many other books with pleasure. Here are just a few of them:

Margaret Drabble, *A Writer's Britain, Landscape in Literature*, Thames & Hudson.

Ronald Blythe, *Places*, Oxford University Press; *Divine Landscapes, Viking*.

W. G. Hoskins (Editor), *The Making of the English Landscape* (series), Hodder & Stoughton.

A. E. Trueman, *Geology and Scenery in England and Wales*, Penguin.

The Vision Concerning Piers the Plowman, by William Langland, Translated by J. F. Goodridge, Penguin.

James Turner, *The Countryside of Britain*, Ward Lock.

Edward Thomas, *A Literary Pilgrim*, Webb & Bower.

Adam Nicholson, *Landscape in Britain*, Michael Joseph.

Graham Reynolds, *Constable the Natural Painter*, Granada.

Christopher Morris (Editor), *The Illustrated Journeys of Celia Fiennes*, Webb & Bower.

Peter Bicknell (Editor), *Wordsworth's Guide to the Lakes*, illustrated, Webb & Bower.

Kenneth Clark, *Landscape into Art*, Penguin.

The Phaidon Companion to Art and Artists in the British Isles, Phaidon Press

Our major art galleries and museums also produce excellent books, some linked with exhibitions, for example:

David Solkin, *Richard Wilson*, Tate Gallery 1982

Edward Nygren, *James Ward's Gordale Scar*, Tate Gallery 1982

Landscape in Britain, 1850–1950, Arts Council, 1983

We thank the following for their permission to reproduce illustrations and photographs:

British Tourist Authority: pages 20, 76 and 84

City of Derby Museums and Art Galleries: page 37

Glasgow Museums and Art Galleries: page 33 top and bottom

The National Gallery: pages 65 and 80

National Museums and Galleries on Merseyside: pages 34, 36 and 61

The National Trust: page 68 top and bottom

Science Museum Library: pages 29 and 87

The Tate Gallery: page 40

David Venner: page 19

Victoria and Albert Museum: page 28

Our especial thanks to the following for supplying the magnificent colour photography:

Heather Angel (VIEW 18); Automobile Association Library (VIEWS 3, 11); British Tourist Authority (VIEW 28); Bruce Coleman Ltd (VIEW 27); Bob Croxford (VIEW 29); Robert Eames (VIEW 6); Derek Forss (VIEWS 1, 2, 8, 10, 13, 20); Bob Gibbons (VIEW 9); Julian Lightfoot (VIEWS 21, 24); Sheila & Oliver Mathews (VIEW 15); John Mason (VIEWS 19, 26, 30); National Trust (VIEWS 16, 17); Glyn Satterley (VIEWS 4, 5); Simon Warmer (VIEWS 7, 12, 14, 22, 25); Mike Williams (VIEW 23).

Maps by Sharyn and Michael Troughton.

Extract from *The Two Beds* reprinted by permission of Bloodaxe Books Ltd from *Selected Poems* by Jack Clemo (Bloodaxe Books, 1988)